SCUM A

MAINSTREAM SPORT

# SCUM AIRWAYS

## INSIDE FOOTBALL'S UNDERGROUND ECONOMY

## JOHN SUGDEN

MAINSTREAM
PUBLISHING

EDINBURGH AND LONDON

First published in Great Britain in 2002 by
MAINSTREAM PUBLISHING COMPANY (EDINBURGH) LTD
7 Albany Street
Edinburgh EH1 3UG

ISBN 1 84018 783 2

This edition 2003
Reprinted 2004

A catalogue record for this book is available from the British Library

Typeset in Stone Print and Trixie Text
Printed and bound in Great Britain by
Cox & Wyman Ltd

# Acknowledgements

I WOULD LIKE TO ACKNOWLEDGE THE WORK AND ADVICE OF the following in helping me form and flesh out some of my own ideas: Cathryn Armstrong, Tony Barnes, Ian Bent, Mihir Bose, Adam Brown, Dave Haslam, Jim Hawker, Nick Lowles, Ian Taylor, Eddy Brimson, Martin King, Tony King, Martin Knight, Richard McIlroy, Kevin Mousley, David O'Leary, Mark Perryman, Steve Redhead, Nick Varley, Huw Shakeshaft, Alan Tomlinson, Peter Walsh, and Derek Wynne.

I want to pay a special tribute to Ian Taylor and Derek Wynne, two of the finest urban sociologists that I have ever known – and decent blokes too – who sadly passed away during the course of this project. I would also like to thank all of my close colleagues and students at the University of Brighton and at the University of Sussex who I have bored to death with Big Tommy tales during the last few years, and the University of Brighton in particular for helping to finance my research. My family have likewise had to suffer my many comings and goings and character shifts as I have moved in and out of the world of the grafters and for this I thank them. I would also like to thank Big Tommy himself, and many of the fascinating people who exist in his world for providing the material for this book and not filling me in when they had the chance. Finally, I would like to apologise to those journalists from whom I have raided and lifted the odd snippet without attribution – makes a change, lads, doesn't it?

# Contents

# Preface

'THE LEEDS LADS HATE US BECAUSE WE'RE MAN U. THEY'LL
fly with us but they still call us Scum Airways' – Big Tommy.

Whether you like it or not, some things just have to be done. They are not
planned, not looked for, not part of any preconceived schedule or timetable,
and often they are not even welcome in your already busy life. They happen
along and demand attention anyway. Something tells you that, like the last
bus, there is an important story passing by and that if you do not get on board
now the opportunity will be gone for ever. This book is one of those things.

At the centre of the story is Big Tommy and the company he runs,
International Travel Limited (ITL), or Scum Airways, as the Leeds United Lads
call it (for reasons that will be made apparent later in the story). Lived out in
the shadow of the wealthiest club in the world, Manchester United, in Big
Tommy's realm *Only Fools and Horses* merges with *Miami Vice* around
football. It is a gathering place for ticket touts, counterfeiters, con men, petty
thieves, drug dealers, hooligans, neo-Nazis and a few even more serious
criminals, some of whom are all of the above. 'Grafters' is the collective term
used in this book to describe these characters. Big Tommy is not some latter-
day Fagan who rules this rogues' gallery, but the deals he does, places he goes
to and wheels he sets in motion guarantee that sooner or later he will rub
shoulders with all of them.

I spent two years dipping in and out of Big Tommy's operation and this
book is a record of my experiences. It draws mainly from fieldwork done

9

around the Champions League during seasons 2000–01 and 2001–02, as well as the World Cup of France '98 and Euro 2000 in Holland and Belgium. As I will explain later, it is not the product of a sustained piece of undercover investigative journalism. In the first place, I have a day job and did not have the time to devote to the project to do that kind of fully covert and all-consuming work. Secondly, I do not have the trained reporter's skill, courage and doorstep cheek of Roger Cook, or the death wish of Donal MacIntyre, whose work will be discussed later in this book. There are certain leads that emerged as this story unfolded that may warrant further investigation of the Cook/MacIntyre genre. In these pages, gumshoes interested in that kind of investigation will find the signposts to several buried and serious crime stories, but not the entire dirt that has been dug.

Even though I did not want to be undercover, for reasons that will become obvious as you turn the pages, much of the time that I was in the field I had to disguise the fact that I was researching a book. On occasions this meant that I was mistaken for an undercover policeman – something that I wanted to avoid at all costs, both for the continuity of research and for reasons of personal survival. The style of this research is called 'participant observation', but my level of participation moved from central to marginal depending on the level of legality of what was going down and how much time I had, and what level of access my gatekeepers would allow. Necessarily then, what follows is a limited account of Big Tommy's world as I hung onto his shirt-tails, straining my eyes and ears to pick up as much information as I could during the relatively few windows of opportunity I had to hang out with him and his cronies. I cannot assume that everything that they told me was true, but I like to think that most of it was.

In some ways, then, the unfolding narrative is as much about how I got the story as it is about the story itself. For the first time in my experience as a writer this places me at the centre of the story alongside Big Tommy and his chums. Throughout I have tried to provide readers with a sense of what it is like to do this kind of work while at the same time leading a 'normal' life. I am a sociologist and I have been trained to write mainly in a formal academic style. Re-learning to write in the first person with barely a theory or an '-ology' in sight – let alone footnotes or references to the work of a support crew of a multitude of fellow academics – has been an extremely difficult but nonetheless liberating experience. Because it does not follow the conventions of the academy, I don't suppose this work will be included by my university in its next submission to the national Research Assessment Exercise. Nevertheless, I believe it to be profoundly sociological and I make no apologies for the fact that people outside of the cloisters might be able to read, understand, learn from and, I hope, enjoy this book. With this in mind, what follows is an honest and, as much as possible, non-judgemental account of my experiences in Big Tommy's world. I will let readers judge for themselves whether or not I have achieved the correct balance of fact, observation and my own interpretation.

Using football's independent travel sector as a binding theme, I have structured the book around the key events and places that I have been led to as I followed Big Tommy's progress. Then, within each chapter, I have tried to single out one or more important cross-cutting themes. We begin at the World Cup finals of France '98 where I first encountered Big Tommy in a bar in Marseilles. This chapter allows us an introduction to the world of the grafters and looks closely at the issue of tickets and ticket touts. Then we return to England to track down the Big Man on his home turf and, against the rise and rise of Manchester United PLC, we trace the origins of the black market around football in the backstreets and estates of north Manchester. The first organised away trip I took with ITL was to Germany and the Bavarian city of Munich. And in Chapter Three I explore the origins of football's independent travel sector and raise issues about serious hooliganism and its links with far-right extremism. Next it is off to Holland and Amsterdam – the vice capital of Europe. In this chapter I focus on middle-aged men behaving badly in the Netherlands and the connections between football, drugs and the sex industry. Chapter Five finds us in the Belgian capital, Brussels, where we revisit hooliganism and ticket touting, and reveal the ingenuity and invention of the scams used by the grafters to get people without tickets into games. It is also in this chapter that some key methodological and ethical issues surrounding this kind of research are raised. Chapter Six is set in the Spanish capital, Madrid, and addresses issues surrounding the Bowyer and Woodgate trial and the relationship between this and the aggressive demeanour and racist reputation of Leeds United's travelling fans. In this chapter I also provide more evidence that smuggling, organised crime and serious hooliganism are very comfortable bedfellows. Next we are off halfway around the world to the Far East and Bangkok – the bootleg capital of the world. Thailand is the eastern hub of the counterfeit industry and the global centre for sex tourism. It is here that the complex world of the counterfeiters is unravelled and investigated as we follow English grafters as they stock up on fake replica football kits and other 'snide' gear – as the grafters call counterfeit produce – at the same time having some Rest and Relaxation. Chapter Eight takes us back to Munich to relive England's 5–1 thrashing of Germany. This gives me the chance to investigate more hooligans abroad, the generally bellicose character of the England fanbase, and the growing significance of this market in Big Tommy's kingdom. Beckham's wondrous injury-time free kick against Greece leads us to the final chapter, which fittingly brings us full circle as we follow Big Tommy and the Lads during the 2002 World Cup in Japan and Korea. I have used the word 'Lads', with an uppercase 'L', for serious hooligans and fellow travellers and these are not the same as ordinary 'lads' (see p.49 for a full explanation of this usage).

The book is sequential rather than chronological and although each chapter is set in a different place, there are moments when the reader is whisked through time and space as I pursue a particular theme to its logical conclusion. What follows are a series of character-led stories around which I have tried to wrap the themes mentioned above. Many of these sketches are directly connected to the central concerns of the book. Others are only indirectly concerned with the main story and a few have nothing to do with it at all. They are included because they are interesting, funny, or startling and happened to me as I was gathering material for *Scum Airways*. While the cast of characters who fill the following pages are real, most of the names used are pseudonyms.

In complete violation of my usual academic standards and style, you will find few references in the following narrative, neither is there a bibliography. With regard to my sources, approximately 80 per cent of what follows is raw me. In other words it is based upon my thoughts on what I have seen and heard with my own eyes and ears. The rest – mainly factual stuff – has been culled from a wide variety of sources including newspapers, magazines, web sites and some populist books and academic texts. In the latter case, where I have quoted directly, references are included.

# 1

# Marseilles, June 1998

WE ALL KNOW THAT ENGLISH HOOLIGANS TRAVEL ABROAD.
Ever wondered how they get there? Big Tommy and his ilk take them.

Big Tommy's nickname is without irony. At 6 ft 4 in. and 23 st., Tommy is
a big man. He used to be a lot heavier, weighing in closer to 30 st. Despite
dieting, he's still more bouncy castle than brick out-house, and his ample gut
constantly struggles to escape the confines of his trousers. Tommy's in his
early 40s, but his round, fresh face makes him look closer to 30. This
deception is reinforced by a high-pitched voice that makes his broad
Manchester accent sound as if it belongs to a minor soap-opera star.

I first came across Tommy in Marseilles during France '98. It was the
evening after Holland's 2–1 victory over Argentina in the quarter-final, in
which Denis Bergkamp had snatched victory for the Dutch with that superb
over-the-shoulder take-and-volley in the 89th minute. I was in France
gathering material for a book about FIFA that I was writing with Alan
Tomlinson. The book was about FIFA's pivotal role in the political economy of
world football. The French World Cup was to provide the colour and context
for this Byzantine tale of power, intrigue, and corruption. Before travelling to
France we had settled on chapter headings and divided them between us in an
attempt to direct our fieldwork. One of my tasks was to gather material for a
chapter on the ticketing fiasco that was France '98. By the time I arrived in
Marseilles for the semi-final I had gathered enough factual information to
write this chapter, but I was short of a good angle that would help to bring the
story to life. I was nursing a cold pint of Guinness in O'Mally's Irish Pub on

Quai de Rive Neuve, overlooking the city's Old Port, when I spotted Cockney John flitting among the crowded tables of celebrating Dutch supporters. Suddenly, the fog cleared and I had an angle for my ticket chapter.

Cockney John I had met three weeks earlier during my first visit to Marseilles for England versus Tunisia. I had been in Nantes to see Spain throw away a comfortable 2–0 lead against Nigeria and eventually condemn themselves to an early exit thanks to goalkeeper Zubizarreta's howling own-goal in the dying minutes. The speed of France's fabled TGV express trains is more than balanced by the slowness of the lumbering engines that cover the provincial routes. To get to Marseilles I spent seven hours on a train chugging through the French countryside, seemingly calling at every small town on the way. I shared a small compartment with a prim, bespectacled Frenchwoman, who looked as if she was on her way to work in a small town library, and two kilted and face-painted clansmen of the Tartan Army who had shouted themselves hoarse during Scotland the Brave's 1–2 opening-game defeat at the feet of the mighty Brazil.

Needing some refreshments, I made my way past the mainly French passengers to the buffet car, which was four coaches towards the front of the train. I didn't stay long. A small group of England fans from Sheffield had already occupied the buffet. Flags of Saint George were draped across the windows and three shaven-headed lads were in the middle of a penalty shoot-out competition that kept the harassed bartender for the most part ducked behind his counter. 'Wanna game, mate?' asked one supporter.

At the time I was not particularly interested in the 'England-fans-on-tour' story. It seemed to me that there was already a small army of academics, ex-hooligans and sundry fanzine anoraks roaming around France in search of a bestseller on this rather hackneyed subject. 'Er, no thanks, lads. Too tired, gonna get me head down. Catch you later,' I replied. This encounter was intimidating enough for me and God knows what the travelling French thought of it. Needless to say, other than from the beer-swilling England fans, business was slow. I managed to coax the cowering barman to his hatch, bought a drink and a sandwich and beat a hasty retreat back to my compartment.

Five hours later it was time for another sortie to the buffet. Things had deteriorated. En route the train had picked up several more small bands of roaming England fans and these groups had gathered in the buffet car to make an attempt to drink the train dry. They succeeded and more bottled beer had to be taken on board during an unscheduled stock-up stop at Clermont Ferrand station. Through the miracle of the mobile phone, the Lads knew that there had been a major kick-off in Marseilles and they would shortly be arriving in the middle of a riot. They were getting tanked up so that they could hit the ground running.

Among the shaven heads and England shirts, I noticed one man more casually dressed with short but not shaven hair, a deep five o'clock shadow and piercing, inquiring, blue eyes. Like me, he was people watching and soon he spotted the tell-tale blue cord that hung round my neck supporting the media-accreditation badge concealed in my shirt. 'You press then?' he said, approaching me where I stood with my back against the bar.

'Not quite,' I told him and went on to explain about the book I was researching. He asked to look at my accreditation identification, and from my shirt I produced a laminated passport-sized pass with FIFA and France '98 logos and a photo. It virtually guaranteed the holder a seat at any France '98 game. The stranger's eyes grew wide with envy. Later I would learn that this was more to do with professional interest than personal jealousy.

He introduced himself as John, a Londoner and West Ham fan, and told me he was working his way around France as a painter and decorator while taking in a few games. How enterprising, I thought to myself, not realising at the time that he was lying through his prominent white teeth. We chatted amiably for the last hour or so of the journey before disembarking at Marseilles Saint Charles Station just after 9 p.m. The hubbub of the busy station was soon drowned by the sound of wailing sirens. By then, the battle of Marseilles had been raging for several hours around the nearby Old Port as gangs of local North African French youths took on England's lager-enhanced finest. John disappeared among the gang of lads from the buffet car, hurrying enthusiastically to join the fray.

I headed in the opposite direction and began to pound the streets looking for a room for the night. Not surprisingly, Marseilles was full. I was beginning to think I would have to sleep rough when I found a small hotel on the edge of the city centre that had one room free, but for one night only. I would worry about tomorrow when it dawned and I accepted the room gratefully. Now I had a bolt-hole, tired as I was, I felt the need to check out the action around by the Old Port. Wearily I dumped my bag, stuffed a note pad in my pocket and made for the wailing sirens.

The street fighting the night before England's match with Tunisia has been much written about and (over) analysed. Briefly, this is the way I saw and experienced it. I learned from local gangsters that both the press in the immediate aftermath and the sociologists in their later post-mortems had missed an important feature of the rioting and the police responses. I was there during the later stages of the riot when the many branches of the French security forces – the gendarmerie, the national police, the navy, the foreign legion, and, of course, lined up in full battle gear like Roman legionaries, the notorious CRS riot police – finally moved in to mop up what was left of the English.

Trouble had been brewing all day as the England fans soaked up the sun and cooled themselves with chilled, strong lager in improvised camps set up around the bars and cafés of the Old Port. As dusk fell, local North African youths in twos sped by on motor scooters with knapsacks on their backs. The driver would slow down as the scooter passed one or other English-occupied pavement café and his pillion would produce an empty wine bottle from the sack which he would hurl, grenade-like, to shatter in the midst of the drinkers. This was the catalyst, turning a shimmering showdown into a full-scale running battle in which some of the drunken English fans were only too pleased to engage. For much of the time, it seemed to me that the security forces did little or nothing to stop the fighting. Why not?

As a local spiv – black-market trader – explained it to me, there is tension in France between indigents and first- and second-generation settlers from France's former African colonies. The bitter colonial war in Algeria and its legacy of terror on the French mainland are relatively recent memories and have a particular resonance in the South of France where many of North African descent live and where far-right political groups have a stronghold. This has been exacerbated by what many see as an unstoppable tide of legal and illegal immigration from across the Mediterranean. Marseilles is at the centre of these social and political fault lines. For weeks and weeks leading up to the World Cup there had been simmering discontent among the city's North African youth and regular weekend skirmishes with the police. The bad luck of the draw dropped the England versus Tunisia match into Marseilles's racial tinderbox. For the early part of the riot the police were content to take a back seat as the English did something that the French police had wanted to do for weeks: beat the hell out of the North Africans. Afterwards it was reported in the local press that one French bar owner reopened his premises and gave free drinks to the English as a reward for their chastisement of the local Arabs. Generally, however, there is little love in France for '*les roast beefs*', particularly the shaved-head, tattooed, and beer-bellied variety. Once the local Arab hordes had been seen off, the French police moved in to mop up the exhausted English hooligans, banging a few heads on the way.

The image of the Battle of Marseilles that stands out in my mind, however, was not one that I witnessed first hand, but something that I saw on the television coverage of the skirmish that took place on the beach. It happened near to the big screen that had been erected so that fans without tickets could watch the game and still savour some of the big-match atmosphere. A temporary gallery of bleachers had been occupied mainly by several hundred locals who were supporting Tunisia. A rag-tag army of English crowded together on the sand beneath the big screen. When Alan Shearer headed England's first goal the England fans went delirious. Their joy was short-lived, however, as from the bleachers came a hail of bottles and other missiles. As most others fled, like a scene from Kipling's 'Gunga Din', one Englishman – straight-backed, bare-chested, with a Union Jack draped around his waist – stood defiantly, rhythmically beating the retreat on a snare drum hanging from his neck, while bottles and glasses flew all about his head. Quite a performance, and one which for me epitomised the perverse sense of national chauvinism that characterises England fans abroad and leads to so much trouble.

So, three weeks later, Saturday night, there I was back in Marseilles's Old Port which, apart from a broken window here and there, looked little worse for wear. I expected much resentment towards the English, particularly from the local traders who seemed to have borne the brunt of the damage. On the contrary, it seemed that they would be welcomed back as, according to the barman in O'Mally's, unlike many of the other groups of supporters that visited the town, 'the English drink like fish and spend money like water'. This was worth more to local business, he continued, than a few broken tables and chairs and the odd cracked window. The barman had a point. Whenever I had been in the company of England fans abroad I had noticed that they tended to treat foreign currency in the same way they treated foreign laws and customs – something not to be taken seriously – and proceeded to spend it like Monopoly money, mainly on drink. It was while I was wondering to myself why, unlike the Dutch, the Scots and the Irish, the English had to bring so much aggression to the party when I spotted Cockney John at his real work, which I realised straightaway was not painting and decorating, but ticket touting. Here, at last, was the angle that I had been looking for, for my chapter about the tickets for France '98. Writing the story of the ticket fiasco, at least partially, through the eyes of the touts could really help me embody the story and bring it to life. Now all I had to do was overcome the fieldworker's biggest problem. How was I going to get inside to get the scoop?

I waited for John to pass the bar and tapped him on the shoulder. He turned and looked suspiciously at me before a hint of recognition turned his glare into a smile. 'You're the writer from the train,' he said. 'How's the book going?'

I bought him a pint and gave him the story so far, pausing when I got to the chapter about the tickets. 'I've been watching you for a while,' I told him. 'You're a ticket tout, aren't you?'

He smiled again. 'Thought you'd bought that yarn about decorating,' he laughed. 'Easier work and better money in grafting tickets.' I told him my idea about writing the story through the eyes of the touts. 'You need to talk to Big Tommy,' he said, nodding his head towards the corner of the room where a very large man was holding court. 'I'm working with him and a gang of lads from Manchester. He's the main man round here when it comes to tickets.'

I asked John to give me an introduction, but he was not too keen on this idea as he was unsure how the Big Man would react if he brought a stranger into the camp, particularly one with press credentials. 'Tell you what,' John said after I persisted, 'we've had a good result down here this last week, made a few quid. The Brazil game isn't till Tuesday and things won't hot up on the tickets till Monday. Big Tommy and the boys are having a day off. They're going to take a trip to one of them small islands out in the bay, have a day on the beach, a bit of swimming and a few beers. I'm going too. If you happen to turn up, maybe he'll let you join us.'

Maybe was good enough for me. Sunday morning found me roaming around the quayside looking for signs of Cockney John and the Manchester gang. After a fruitless hour, thinking that I may have missed them, I decided to take a chance and take the small ferry and get off at one of the two or three small islands guarding the entrance of the Bay of Marseilles that I could see in the distance. I chose the largest, the Archipel Du Frioul, which was not much more than a collection of large, rust-coloured rocks interconnected by slender sand and pebble causeways. I disembarked and trudged around the island looking for my prey. Other than the tiny ferry port the island seemed largely uninhabited. On the peaks of most of the rocks stood long-disused naval fortifications and gun emplacements, reminders of a bygone era of gunboat diplomacy and French naval power. Atop of one hill there was a large, derelict hospital-cum-sanatorium that was used almost a century before for the quarantine of Marseilles's plague victims. I was hoping that today another kind of pest would turn up, but after a couple of hours rambling and scrambling the only people I had bumped into that I recognised were the BBC commentator Barry Davies and pundit David Pleat who, like Big Tommy and his chums, were also having a day off before the Brazil versus Holland game the next day.

Eventually I found the island's only usable beach. It was full of French families and parties of young school children taking advantage of the fine early summer weather to sunbathe and splash about in the still chilly Mediterranean. I decided to join them. Unrolling my towel, I stretched out on the beach and took out a book. I was reading a collection of George Orwell's essays in preparation for a seminar on the life and works of the revered English author that I had to participate in soon after the World Cup. As my mind flitted from Orwell to Big Tommy, not for the last time I wondered about how complex life can sometimes be. Orwell's essay on Dickens was heavy going and I was soon half-dozing in the warm sunshine, listening to picnics being unpacked and the excited chatter and shrieks of the French children around me. Just when I had begun to hope that my quarry would not show up, the soothing Gallic melody was disrupted by the sound of heavy determined feet marching through the gritty sand accompanied by gritty Manchester voices. Big Tommy and the Lads had arrived.

Now what? I sat up and watched them wander along the beach to set up camp on the other side of the small bay. Cockney John was with them, which was helpful, but I hardly had an appointment and in the cold light of day the prospect of just ambling up to Big Tommy and introducing myself was no longer so appealing as it had been in O'Mally's the night before. Getting access is the biggest challenge facing investigative researchers, particularly when studying subcultures on the shady side of the tracks. Nevertheless, for social anthropologists, there is a buzz about being in the field and spotting opportunities to enter other people's worlds and this overcame my apprehension. I walked to the water's edge, took a deep breath and plunged into the cool sea, swimming out straight for about 50 metres before turning at right angles and swimming a further 100 metres or so until I was level with Big Tommy and his crew on the beach. I made a final right turn and swam towards the beach, emerging just below the Manchester gang.

Trying to look as casual as possible, I strolled up the beach to Cockney John, who was lying with his arm curled around an anorexic-looking French girl who he'd picked up in Marseilles the night before. 'Hi, John, how are you doing? Bet you didn't expect to see me here,' I said as casually as I could.

Big Tommy, dressed in baggy shorts and a loose T-shirt, was standing up clutching an open can of beer in his right hand and a full one in his left. Before John could acknowledge me, Tommy turned, eyed me up and down and said, 'Who the fucking hell's he?'

For a moment I thought John was going to do a Saint Peter and disown me, but after a little hesitation, he said to the Big Man, 'He's OK, Tom. His name's John, I met him on a train; he's a writer – books and stuff – not a journalist.'

John's introduction was enough for me to take over. I explained to Tommy that I worked at a university and was writing a book on the World Cup that included a chapter about the ticketing chaos. I told him that I wanted to get the touts' perspective on this. Laying it on as thick as I dared, I told him that I thought that the touts' bad press was unfair and that I wanted to put forward the touts' point of view in my book.

Tommy obviously picked up on my Liverpool accent. There has rarely been any love lost between Manchester and Merseyside and there is an intense rivalry between the football clubs of these cities, particularly between United and Liverpool. 'Fucking hell,' replied Tommy, addressing his foot soldiers rather than me, 'your worst nightmare – a smart Scouser! Anyway, we've got nothing to hide, have we, lads? Want a beer?' he asked me.

'Sure, why not?' I replied, feeling both relief and excitement. At least for the time being, I was inside.

Fortunately Tommy likes to talk and as we sat sipping beer on the beach he told me a remarkable series of stories about ticket scams from the World Cup. It was a little bewildering at first as from time to time the group's conversation would drop into tout-speak: an in-house, coded language that mixes back slang, cockney rhyming slang, market-stall tic-tac and the touts' own invented gibberish. For instance, tickets are 'briefs or bits', the latter being the generic grafter's term for any unit of gear up for sale whether it be a ticket, a T-shirt or a 'sleeve' of 200 cigarettes. 'Firms' are hooligan gangs and Lads are the key members. 'Cat' is short for category and is associated with the range and calibre of tickets available, which for the World Cup are A, B, or C, with A being the highest and the most expensive category. Then terms like 'pony', 'monkey', 'wonna', 'carpet', 'chink' and 'rouf' are used to talk about different prices. Making a good profit is often referred to as 'having a good drink' or 'having a good butty'. There is nothing unusual about a distinctive subculture inventing its own in-house language or *argot*. For the touts there is another reason for using such impenetrable slang, particularly when it is to do with sums of money. It means that the touts can negotiate prices with one another in front of punters without the punters having the faintest idea of what the mark-up is likely to be.

As well as the distinctive lingo, everybody in the trade seems to have a nickname. Generically they refer to themselves as grafters, spivs, swag-workers and, of course, touts. On the beach this day with Big Tommy and Cockney John were Rat (Chris) and the Short-Arm Typist (Ricky). Chris was

21

the youngest of the crew, in his mid-20s, and was called the Rat because of his scrawny frame allied to his reputation of being able to disappear into the backstreets of any city and scamper around sniffing out briefs. Ricky was about the same age as Tommy and almost as tall and hefty. His nickname cruelly derived from his arms, which were disproportionately short as they hung well above his ample waist either side of his large torso. The Lads' banter was peppered with references to other characters, some of whom I would meet later, like Jimmy the Mac, Rocket, Fat Vinnie, Tunes, Sailor, Alehouse and my own favourite, Porno Kev. Just as with slang, there is nothing unusual about nicknames in working-class culture, but they have a particular usefulness for gangs who work at the margins of the law as they help to mask real identities.

It is impossible to be precise about the scale of the black market in tickets for France '98, but if the composition of the crowds at England's games is anything to go on, it must have been enormous. The English FA's allocation hovered around 6 per cent, yet stadiums in Marseilles, Lens and St-Étienne were up to two-thirds full with English fans. Astonishingly, this means that for each of these games, somehow up to 20,000 tickets ended up on the black market.

Big Tommy explained that it is easier for touts to get hold of tickets for big international tournaments than for the big domestic games. Largely because of the way that the French organising committee had handled the distribution of tickets, business for the touts had been particularly good in 1998. Official propaganda that names on tickets would be checked against ID before punters would be allowed into games was always nonsense. This would have caused horrendous hold-ups and the security of fans would have been seriously jeopardised. As it turned out, few if any tickets were checked, giving the touts free rein to sell to the highest bidders. Months before the competition had started and long before the draw was made, in order to help to raise money for the development of the infrastructure that was needed to host the world's biggest ever World Cup, tickets had gone on sale to the French public. This was akin to giving the whole country a tax rebate because the French could buy up the tickets knowing full well that they could sell them on to travelling fans at inflated prices nearer the event and once the draws had been made.

While from England to Japan desperate fans could not get tickets for love or money, France was awash with them. This was to be the main source of tickets for the touts as a week or so before the opening game in Paris between Brazil and Scotland, they spread out across France buying up as many tickets as were available. Just like it is for drug dealers, the mobile phone has become the touts' most important accessory. From Paris to Marseilles and from Nantes to St-Étienne, posters went up advertising the buying and selling of tickets and giving a mobile number for interested parties. At the same time they worked with the local spivs, buying in bulk from them tickets they had already got their hands on through their more intimate knowledge of the local black market.

The majority of the touts' tickets for France '98 came this way, but there were other sources. From the point of printing to the moment it is passed over a turnstile counter by the person who is actually going to watch a game there are many hands that touch World Cup match tickets. The scale of French bureaucracy is rivalled perhaps only by large South American countries such as Brazil and Argentina. Where there are long chains of command and communication there are manifold opportunities for corruption. The Comité Français d'Organisation (CFO) for the World Cup was a massive bureaucracy within the intestines of which many tickets went astray. In one case, officials charged with distributing tickets through official channels to bona fide applicants, instead took lists of names from the Paris telephone directory and issued thousands of tickets, which they then sold on to the touts. In another, a telephone engineer rigged the ticket sales hotlines so that only one number worked while the rest registered busy tones; the working number was sold to the touts.

Then of course, there are the legions of FIFA and French FA officials and their media and marketing partners with their wads of complimentary VIP tickets – 120,000 in all – not all of which end up in legitimate, let alone deserving, hands. Before they went bankrupt in 2001, ISL (International Sport and Leisure) were FIFA's favoured marketing partner and they co-ordinated the supply of most of the VIP freebies. It was a huge embarrassment to FIFA and the CFO when the chief executive of ISL France, Marc Loison, and his colleague, Philippe Magraff, were caught selling 2,000 tickets onto the black market. Worldwide many other officials and self-styled VIPs feathered their nest with impunity, according to Big Tommy. The most outrageous case of this, with potentially disastrous security consequences, happened when VIP tickets for England versus Colombia in Lens were sold onto the black market. Panning in on the VIP enclosure, television cameras revealed a bunch of rowdy England fans seated there, right behind Prince Charles and his sons, William and Harry. When I first heard this story from Big Tommy I had my doubts about its veracity, but later experiences would make me think that, unlikely though it may seem, it could have happened.

On top of this there are more than 200 individual football associations who received an allocation of tickets for each game. The largest slices of this cake go to the participating countries for distribution via schemes devised by each national governing body. The English FA, for instance, has the England Supporters Travel Club, whereby, in theory at least, fans with proven and unblemished records of support for the national team are advantaged in the distribution of tickets. The touts can abuse such systems by having multiple memberships in the names of friends and family who have never actually been to an England game. In other countries, with even less rigorous checks and balances than in England, sometimes the fans do not even get a sniff of a ticket.

Take the official allocation to the Cameroon Football Association for instance. All 3,000 tickets were purloined by Vincent Onana, the head of Cameroon's football governing body, and sold on to the black market. He was caught and imprisoned. Also ripe for plucking by the touts is the allocation of tickets for those countries that did not qualify. From the New Hebrides to Armenia, FIFA is required to dish out allocations of World Cup tickets to governing bodies no matter how small they are. The touts have a global reach and are quick to earmark and exploit corruptible officials in such countries, particularly the poorer ones.

Finally, there is a global diplomatic core: ambassadors, cultural and commercial attachés (including minor spies), and sundry embassy flunkies, all of whom seem to be able to get their grubby hands on World Cup match tickets. This is a system which is virtually impossible to police. While there can be no doubt that much of this distribution was handled scrupulously and that many of these tickets did find their way into deserving hands, it is equally certain that a sizeable quantity did not.

Once the touts had soaked up most of the local supply and greased the palms of corruptible officials for most of the rest, it was they who controlled the market and with it the price. All they had to do was wait for the ticketless travelling fans to arrive and it would be open season. And arrive they did – in their hundreds of thousands. One of the best games for touts' business had been the England versus Tunisia game in Marseilles. Tens of thousands of England fans had journeyed to the South of France without tickets. Some came to soak up the atmosphere and watch the match on the giant screens which had been set up on the beaches and in the parks around the city, but many others had come determined to see the game live and that meant dealing with the touts and, albeit reluctantly, paying their prices.

After cleaning up in Marseilles, Big Tommy, Chris and Ricky packed up and made the long drive north-west to Lens for England's game with Colombia. They were just on the outskirts of town when Tommy received a call from a Dutch travel company. The company had sold packages – including match tickets for Holland's game with Mexico – to thousands of Dutch punters. With less than 24 hours to go until kick-off the company were still 500 tickets short and were willing to pay £250 for every ticket that Big Tommy and his team could muster. Tommy turned the car round and pointed it in the direction of St-Étienne.

When the Manchester grafters arrived in St-Étienne the going rate on the local market was £100 a brief. With the car engine still warm, Big Tommy and his crew got straight to work buying up as many tickets as they could at £150 each. They soon began to run out of cash and had to call the Dutch travel company's reps, pleading with them to get to St-Étienne as soon as possible to help them honour their lines of credit with local spivs. With less than two hours to spare before kick-off, Big Tommy and the gang had accumulated 500 tickets and were able to sell them on to the company for the agreed £250 each, pocketing a cool £50,000 in the process. Nice work if you can get it.

One of the main sources of business for the touts in France '98 came from the hundreds of travel companies, that had overstretched themselves by selling packages including tickets well before the actual tickets had been issued or distributed. As usual the fans were conned by greedy businessmen aided and abetted by the incompetence of FIFA and the CFO. They had accredited a limited number of travel companies (Approved Tour Operators or ATOs) to sell official package deals including tickets. Seventeen such companies paid $(US)500,000 for the privilege of legitimately ripping off the fans. For instance, the actual cost of a trip from England to France for one of the preliminary-round matches, including overnight accommodation, flights, transfer and ticket would have been around $(US)350. The average retail price was closer to $(US)1,000.

If there is anything worse than paying way over the odds for a ticket, it is paying through the nose and not getting a ticket at all. Because ATO status was conferred by the French before they allocated tickets, most package deals were advertised and sold out before tour operators or anybody else knew who would get how many tickets. The fans did not know it but they were buying promises. When it turned out that tickets were not so easily available such companies were faced with three choices: cancel the packages and pay back the money to severely disgruntled customers; go into the black market and try to make up the shortfall knowing that this would wipe out any profits and plunge the business into the red; or take the money and run.

Most opted for one of the first two but some closed up shop and disappeared. It is by no means certain that outfits like these had any intention of fulfilling their commitments. Most of the ATOs subcontracted work to other travel agents, making it virtually impossible for fans to discern which of the many companies advertising in the press and, increasingly, on the Internet had a legitimate chance of being allocated tickets. This encouraged fly-by-night opportunists to set up bogus companies, rake in the gullible fans' cash, and run for it. In the UK alone, at least eight such companies declared themselves bankrupt, leaving thousands of fans high and dry.

For the touts, the outcome of the FIFA/CFO ticketing policy became a licence to print money as tens of thousands of fans from all over the world converged on France expecting to be issued with tickets on their arrival; these tickets never materialised. Some of the more reputable package companies got out their diaries and began to ring round well-known touts like Big Tommy, hoping to be able to honour their commitments, knowing that they were going to lose big money, but wanting to protect the good name of their businesses for the future. According to Big Tommy, the company mentioned above, for instance, lost a small fortune honouring its World Cup commitments, a tidy slice of which went into Big Tommy and the Lads' pockets. With so much already invested in travel and accommodation most of the rest of the fans who were let down by less-reputable travel companies stayed on in France, taking to the streets and looking to buy tickets from the locals. This proved a futile exercise because the locals had already bought and sold them on to the touts. With no one else to turn to, the hapless supporters were likewise forced into the inflated arms of Big Tommy and the Lads.

According to the touts, one of the hottest tickets for the touts during France '98 was for Croatia versus Japan. There were two main reasons for this. Firstly, of all the travelling supporters who were hit by the failure of package companies to deliver tickets, the Japanese were hit the worst. Tens of thousands of Japanese supporters paid big money and travelled thousands of miles only to discover on arrival that there were no tickets for them. Just like the Dutch, the Japanese were forced onto the black market. But unlike for the Dutch, the English or the Italians, there is no tradition of barter or haggling in Japanese culture. In Japan, the price is the price and that is it. With demand so inelastic and custom so compliant, the touts could name their own price and in the case of this game it was £1,000 a ticket.

This is how one of Big Tommy's rivals, Jimbo, got really lucky. He flew into St-Étienne and took a tram to the centre of town. A man dressed in a dark suit and carrying a briefcase sat next to him. Jimbo happened to take a brochure out of his bag that had info about the forthcoming match. This caused the stranger to ask Jimbo if he was going to the game. Jimbo said he was but was interested in buying tickets at which point the stranger introduced himself as an embassy official of a certain former Yugoslavian country who might have some tickets for sale.

'How much?' asked Jimbo.

'They're expensive,' replied the diplomat. '£100 pounds each.'

Jimbo had difficulty keeping calm; he sensed a killing. 'How many?' followed up Jimbo.

'One hundred,' whispered the Slav.

Jimbo could hardly believe his ears or his luck. The two men got off at the next tram stop and went into the nearest bar where the diplomat opened his briefcase to reveal the 100 tickets. Jimbo bought the lot for £10,000 and in the next 24 hours sold them for £100,000, trousering £90,000.

This was tout heaven, but it could quickly turn to hell. The touts believe that they perform an effective and essential service to football, particularly during large and complex tournaments like the World Cup. Who else, they argue, can redistribute tickets with the necessary speed and efficiency to ensure that stadia are full and those that want a seat and can pay get one? They see their roles as indispensable, particularly when a tournament like the World Cup reaches the knockout stages and fans that have been waiting at home make last-minute decisions to travel to quarter and semi-final matches. They have a point, but it is not one that gets much sympathy from the fans, particularly those who cannot afford to pay. Touts are generally despised by fans. 'Treated like scum; worse than drug dealers,' as Big Tommy puts it. Occasionally a naïve tout can get isolated, beaten up and robbed of tickets and cash by an angry mob, with the police generally turning a blind eye. This is always a dangerous time for the touts. Even though they are providing the desperately needed tickets, they are universally despised both by officialdom and by the fans because of their profiteering. Things can soon get nasty if the punters feel they are being conned. It is not unusual for a tout to find himself on the end of a good hiding, particularly if he gets isolated from his mates. The police rarely rush to the defence of a tout under pressure from his customers. On the contrary, should they be caught, the police are just as likely to relieve touts of their tickets and ill-gotten cash – contributions to the local police benevolent fund all gratefully received, no doubt.

So Big Tommy and his gang have to be cautious when dealing with mobs of vengeful, ticket-hungry fans who can quickly turn on the touts. In one instance, Tommy told me he had been able to use this fear factor to his advantage. A couple of Canadian touts were working a pitch outside the Sofatel in Marseilles's Old Port prior to the England–Tunisia game. They had 200 briefs with a face value of £75 and were knocking them out for £100 a bit for a quick £5,000 profit. Eager English fans gathered around them before Tommy moved in and offered to buy the lot for £20,000. For some reason the

Canadians refused, preferring to sell to the fans rather than a competitor. But this refusal spooked the punters who began to wonder if the tickets were fakes, a perception that Tommy did his best to encourage. Things soon turned ugly and the North American scalpers found themselves surrounded by an angry mob demanding their money back. The Big Man and his gang moved in to 'rescue' the Canadians, escorting them to the edge of the Old Port area and in the process buying up the remaining tickets, which they proceeded to sell on for £150. 'Yeah, we had a good drink out of that one, didn't we, Lads?' recalled the Big Man, pausing for breath to take a swig from his can of beer.

It is a difficult balance for touts to find places to cut deals. They need a space out of the view of the authorities but public enough to reduce the chances of righteous muggings, heavy losses of blood, tickets and cash. That is why more experienced gangs like Tommy's work in teams, with street runners only handling small numbers of tickets and limited amounts of cash at once, using their mobile phones to place orders to get supplies of briefs and off-load accumulated money to a central and secure location under Tommy's watchful eye.

Sometimes the touts themselves can be conned. Big Tommy recalls a scam in Paris when a couple of English touts were ripped off by a French mob. The English had bought a big supply of black market tickets from local gangsters for £8,000. The next day, much to the astonishment of the English touts, the French returned to the hotel were the deal had been done to return £1,000 that they claimed had been overpaid for the consignment of tickets. The English knew that they had not overpaid, but gratefully and greedily accepted the rebate from their new friends. A few days later, the ringleader of the French outfit phoned the hotel offering a second and much larger cache of tickets for which he needed £20,000 up front. Thinking of the returned £1,000 the English mob believed that this would be a kosher deal and agreed to the transaction. The next day they were picked up outside their hotel and driven to the wooded outskirts of Paris where the touts produced a briefcase full of cash. In return, instead of tickets, the French pulled out pistols taking the money and dumping the touts in the middle of nowhere before speeding off back to Paris, secure in the knowledge that this crime would go unreported.

As the afternoon wears on we sit in a circle on the beach, the Lads trading stories, mobile phones in the middle like handbags on a 1970s dance-floor, piles of empty beer cans accumulating in the sand around us. But it is not all Rest and Relaxation. Every now and again a mobile phone warbles into life and the dealing starts. 'Hello? Yes . . . yes. What's that? Thirty Category A, Dutch end?' asks Tommy in a soft Manchester brogue. 'Hold on please.' He speaks away from the phone. 'Right, Lads,' he barks, his voice drifting back toward north Man-Ches-Ter, 'thirty Cat A. What d'you reckon John, can we do 'em? Let's say carpet chinc? Come on, we'll all get a good drink out of it. Right.' Back to the mobile. 'Hello. Yes, we can fill that order. $350 per ticket. Is that OK? Good, good. You fly in tomorrow? Yes, OK, I'll see you at the station at eleven o'clock. Good, good. See you then, bye.'

Finally, as the sun begins to descend towards Barcelona, Big Tommy raises his giant frame, yawns, stretches and scratches his belly. 'Right, Lads, off your arses, we've got orders to fill. Time to go back to work.' With that we break camp and trudge back towards the tiny port for the short ferry trip back to Marseilles. During the journey, Big Tommy's phone continues to warble. In the middle of taking orders for the Holland versus Brazil game he takes one for a pair of tickets for a Rolling Stones' concert in Vienna coming up next month. 'Nice little earner, that,' Tommy tells me. As soon as the ferry docks, while Big Tommy and Rick take their time, Rat and Cockney John scamper down the gangplank, delighted with the fact they have managed to jib the journey without paying the ten francs. Grafting for these lads is not just a part-time job, it is a way of life.

The gang head into the Old Port, now teeming with yellow- and orange-clad supporters of Brazil and Holland. I arrange to meet up with them later in the day, once they have filled their order books. At around 10 p.m. I discover them sat outside the Irish bar drinking and chatting to two other characters. Jean is a huge 50-something Frenchman, a local spiv who at some point in his past came second in a Mr Universe contest and looks like he would still be in the frame in today's competition. The other is introduced as Jonesy, a man from Nigeria, on the run from Chicago where he is wanted for murder. The Lads are in good form, having filled their orders and then some. As the Guinness flows, Big Tommy wheels and deals with the tide of Brazilians and

Dutch flowing past along the pavement. He does not need to buy or sell any more tickets, but he enjoys the barter and the banter that goes along with it.

At a pause in the conversation Cockney John leans over towards the Nigerian and whispers, "'Ere, Jonesy, can you sort us with some black pussy?'

'Sure man, lend me your phone,' replies Jonesy. Ten minutes later a pretty black girl in a sparkling white trouser-suit materialises at Jonesy's shoulder. 'How about anybody else?' asks Jonesy.

Tommy breaks off from his sidewalk trading to eye our visitor up and down. 'Na,' he says, 'I'd sooner have a kebab.'

'What about the rest of you?' asks Jonesy.

The Short-Arm Typist shakes his head and says he is going with Tommy for a kebab and young Chris, looking sheepish, opts for another beer. That leaves only me. Big Tommy and the Lads laugh at my obvious discomfort.

'No thanks, Jonesy. Busy day tomorrow. Maybe next time,' I reply with false bravado, thinking that it is time to go.

What kind of a world had I fallen into? Without doubt a fascinating one with its own rules and language, one where tickets rule and prostitutes are balanced with beer and kebabs. Unfortunately, with a book on FIFA to write and several other projects awaiting my attention back at my university base, it was a world that I then neither had the time nor space to investigate further. I said my hasty goodbyes, thinking that this was the last time I would see any of them again. I could not have been more wrong.

# 2

# Manchester, April 2000

IT WAS DURING THE BUILD-UP TO EURO 2000 - ALMOST TWO years later – with my desk a bit clearer, that my thoughts were turned once more towards Big Tommy. The catalyst was a phone call from Nick Lord, an old mate in the television documentary business whom I had helped a number of years ago on a programme about Derry City, the Northern Irish team in the Republic's League of Ireland. As ever he was fishing for ideas. The visual media industry's fascination with football has not been limited to live coverage and highlights. The football boom has also yielded manifold editorial programmes, chat shows, dramas and documentaries that cover anything from famous players' lives to not-so-famous players' wives. With Holland and Belgium on the horizon Nick was wondering if I was researching anything that may have potential for a new TV series simply called *Football Stories*.

Nick is based in Leeds and we arranged to meet in York where I was attending the British Sociological Association's annual spring conference. We sat outside a city-centre pub on the banks of the River Ouse drinking warmish bitter in the warmish spring sunshine and bouncing around ideas. At the time my main interest still lay in the politics of world football. I was particularly interested in England's doomed attempt to land the 2006 World Cup. This came as an offshoot of my FIFA interest and I was intending to go to the Low Countries for Euro 2000 to follow the final lobbying and intrigues in the build-up to FIFA's July announcement on where the 2006 tournament would be held. Nick was interested in the story but had trouble seeing any angle that might capture a commissioning editor's imagination. In these days of dumbed-down TV if an idea does not have the potential to make the back page of a tabloid it is usually a non-starter for a prime-time slot. In competition with *At Home with the Beckhams,* racing with Sir Alex Ferguson, sticking it to the Argies, and yet more ex-hooligans telling war stories, in Nick's view a programme about England's 2006 catastrophe stood little chance of being commissioned.

After we had kicked that idea to death, I said, 'Well, I suppose there's always Big Tommy.' It had been in the back of my mind to try and track him down as a kind of insurance policy in case the 2006 World Cup line of enquiry failed to yield enough to justify my being in Holland and Belgium. A more in-depth look at the world of the touts as they worked Euro 2000 would certainly give me enough to write one or two research articles. As I told Nick much of the story outlined in the previous chapter his eyes widened.

Nobody had done a fly-on-the-wall documentary on ticket touts. Nick believed it was a story with considerable TV potential, particularly if we were able to have a camera follow Big Tommy around during Euro 2000. As ever, the main problems with investigations that focus on activities that are somewhere between marginal and criminal are to do with getting access and getting permission to film. Nick asked me if I could track Tommy down and set up a meeting between us. I was not sure I could. When we parted company in Marseilles we had not exactly exchanged business cards. All I knew about him was his nickname and that he hailed from somewhere in Greater Manchester, a conurbation of more than two million souls. Not a lot to go on.

Then I remembered a conversation that I had had with my brother Joe who has lived and worked in and around Manchester ever since he graduated from university there in the early 1970s. I had just arrived back from France '98 and I was telling him of my adventures, including the episode with Big Tommy in Marseilles. Joe thought he recognised the name and the character as a friend of a friend who had contacts in the Manchester underworld. I left York promising Nick that, via my brother, I would do my best to track the Big Man down, still not knowing whether or not the man I had met in Marseilles and the friend of my brother's friend were in fact the same person. Or even if he was, whether or not he would remember me or agree to talk.

Later that week I called Joe in his Manchester office and asked him about Big Tommy. 'I'll have to talk to Freddie,' he said. 'I'm sure he knows him, but he might be a bit cagey about giving you an introduction. You might have to come up and talk to him.' Which is why two weeks later I found myself at 9 a.m. on a Sunday morning surrounded by threadbare sheep, teeing off with Freddie at Lobden, England's highest and bleakest golf course, somewhere in the Pennines between Rochdale and Accrington. I'm not much of a golfer, neither is Freddie, but he managed to scrape a win on the eighteenth, which put him in a good mood. We got ready to head down through Lowry landscapes to Rochdale to meet Nick in a pub ominously called the Cemetery. Freddie had trouble getting his golf kit in the boot of his car, which was overflowing with goods of uncertain provenance – shoes, shirts, designer sportswear and replica football shirts in abundance. As an act of good faith, before we left the golf club car park I paid £20 for a pair of Timberland shoes out of the boot of Freddie's car. They didn't really fit me, but if it got me closer to Big Tommy I considered it a justifiable expense.

Nick was waiting in the Cemetery and for the next hour or more we sat talking with Freddie about his world and his connections with Big Tommy. For the first time I began to realise that this story was much bigger than my narrow focus on buying and selling football match tickets. Listening to Freddie it became obvious that touting was only one part of an underground economy that incorporated football and was a way of life for people like him and Big Tommy. Freddie gave me my first insights into the 'snide' economy, the counterfeiting culture that shadowed the designer fashion industry and had attached itself parasitically to the booming football merchandising business. It was from Freddie that I first heard tell of the ingenuity of the counterfeiters, who had even taken to making things under designer brand names that the branded companies themselves did not even make or sell. To prove his point he produced a Tommy Hilfiger wristwatch that he claimed had sold well, even though the designer clothes company itself did not even make watches at the time! Subsequent to the grafters' intervention, Hilfiger have since moved into watches themselves.

Also from Freddie came the first hints that there was another dimension to this underground football economy, the independent travel business. This, he explained, was something that had grown up in the last ten to fifteen years and had become a good earner for some of the smarter grafters. He told us that Big Tommy had moved into this area and that if we wanted to know more that we should talk to the Big Man himself. It was becoming more obvious to both Nick and myself that Big Tommy was the key to our story and we needed to talk to him as soon as possible.

Freddie claimed no longer to be in close touch with Big Tommy, but said that he had a friend, Alehouse Williams, who was. Freddie promised to call Alehouse and, if Alehouse was agreeable, call me back with his number so I could talk to him directly and through him perhaps get to Tommy. By now I was beginning to think that I had got lost inside a John le Carré spy novel. Good as his word, Freddie called me a few days later with Alehouse's mobile phone number which I duly called.

When I finally got through I introduced myself and explained what I wanted. Alehouse was ready for my call. Freddie had briefed him. He told me that he had called Big Tommy and, much to my relief, said that Tommy remembered me from Marseilles and would be happy to meet up some time. Alehouse then passed on Big Tommy's mobile phone number. It had been a long and arduous journey from the pub in York, but for the first time in this game of cat and mouse I was sure that the friend of my brother's friend was the same man that I had hung out with in Marseilles.

I called Big Tommy and explained very briefly what I was interested in, keeping it as general as possible so as not to spook him. He agreed to meet with Nick and myself in a pub close to Manchester's Piccadilly Station called the Goose. The main research hadn't even started and already my liver was acting up! I walked along London Road to the renovated Edwardian pub-cum-fast-food-place – the brass, mirrors, bare floorboards, steak-and-chips type that could be anywhere in the country. Nick was there on time, but Tommy was late which made me nervous, as I knew there was nothing compelling him to turn up. Just as I was thinking that we were in an appropriately named venue for the end of a wild-goose chase, Big Tommy barrelled his way through the swing doors. If there had been a piano it would have stopped playing.

Tommy had a side-kick with him, a sandy-haired pocket battleship of a lad called Billy. Billy was about half Tommy's size with a deep red scar that went from the bottom of his left ear to his windpipe. I introduced Nick and offered to buy drinks. Tommy went for a Diet Coke – 'trying to lose a few pounds' – while Billy opted for a bottle of Becks. We took a seat in the corner and I began to explain something about the project that we were interested in. Tommy was both interested and affable, but he was obviously unconvinced about the prospect of having cameras follow him around Holland and Belgium. Anyway, during the course of the conversation it became clear that while he was still interested in ticket touting he had also branched out into the independent travel business. Between them Tommy and Billy told a few tales of derring-do surrounding International Travel Limited (ITL)'s football trips. This included the story of Leeds United's ill-fated encounter with Galatasaray in Istanbul when two of Big Tommy's customers were stabbed to death in front of Billy.

Not for the last time the chirping of his mobile phone interrupted Big Tommy's narrative. It was time for him and Freddie to leave, but we could catch up with them later if we wanted to – which we certainly did. Nick and I had been talking with them for more than two hours, but we still had a lot more to learn. The ticket touting remained a strong theme, but other important and interesting issues had begun to emerge that seemed to be gathering together under the umbrella of what Big Tommy refers to as 'the independent travel business'. This is what we needed to find more about, particularly as our gatekeeper seemed to be slightly more receptive to the idea of a documentary about this than one that focused sharply on his touting activities. Before leaving we agreed to meet once more in a couple of weeks time in Big Tommy's office which was then in Moston, North Manchester.

I drove to Moston through the centre of Manchester and northwards along the Oldham Road past Salford, Chetham, Collyhurst and Harpurhey. Unlike the city centre, these neighbourhoods have yet to benefit from urban regeneration and are a mixture of grim terraces and ugly concrete high-rise flats. Irreverent and politically incorrect (read racist and sexist) comedian Bernard Manning's hangar-like Embassy Club marks the boundary between Harpurhey and Moston. It is somehow appropriate because unlike its neighbouring communities, Moston's busy streets betray few non-white faces.

With its terraced streets, rows of shops, and a pub on almost every corner, the area looks more 1960s than 2000s.

At the time I visited, Big Tommy's office was a modest affair just off the main road. A classic front-stage/back-stage set-up, a couple of young receptionists remained in the front dealing with enquiries about standard package holidays – an area Tommy gave up to concentrate on football travel. Meanwhile, Big Tommy and Billy worked in a back room, on phones and PCs, setting up the football trips and related deals. Perhaps appropriately, at the time Tommy decided to focus on football, he also shifted his offices a few miles to a small industrial estate in Newton Heath, the original home and name of Manchester United.

One of the girls made us coffee and the Big Man relaxed back in his padded swivel chair to tell us his life story. Tommy was born in 1962 and grew up in Cheetham Hill, beneath the brooding shadow of Strangeways Prison, in a street of terraced houses squeezed between the city centre's commercial and business districts and the factories, warehouses, and industrial parks to the north. He was born in the 'never-had-it-so-good' 1960s, but grew up in one of the most traumatic periods in the northern capital's rich social and economic history. In his childhood he would have witnessed the beginning of the steady decline of Manchester's industrial infrastructure as one by one the mills and factories closed down around him. By the time he was a teenager the Thatcher years were on the horizon. With 18 years of Tory rule, the deindustrialisation of Britain accelerated so that by the time he left school the factories, mills and engineering works where generations of working-class kids had served their apprenticeships as turners, weavers, mechanics and cabinet-makers had all gone.

The working-class Manchester of Tommy's childhood would have looked like *Coronation Street*: all cobbles and corner shops. By his teenage years the neighbourhood had degenerated and was well on its way to becoming key turf in the city's combat zone. 'Those days,' remembers Tommy, 'all the kids were at it, mainly for fun, messing about, but 15 out of 20 of them would grow up to be villains.' Like most of his mates Tommy left school at 15 at the pre-dawn of the Thatcher years, with no formal qualifications and little or no prospect of getting decent employment.

Tommy was always clever, but in a streetwise rather than scholarly fashion. His employment in a series of low-paid, semi-skilled and unskilled jobs was interspersed with periods on the dole. The unprecedented levels of unemployment in the 1980s, particularly among the young, was a high price to pay for a government's slavish dedication to economic philosophy. In Manchester, however, Tommy's generation of working-class kids refused to lie down and passively accept their roles as Thatcher's sacrifice to monetarism. Not when, only a few miles away in Manchester's regenerating city centre, they could see a parallel generation of Yuppies getting richer and richer on the back of their misery.

Where extravagance and affluence are found shoulder to shoulder with depression and poverty, something has to give. The friction between the rich and the poor in Manchester generated a creative, survivalist energy that sparked its own youth-cultural revolution. This revolution moved in many directions, simultaneously feeding a divergent, entrepreneurial culture. Its clearest and loudest expression came in the music and dance industries. In the 1980s Manchester earned its reputation as 'Madchester', a name that reflected the northern place's image as a boom-bust, happening, frontier city.

Madchester became a national leader in popular culture. It dominated the rock and roll scene and was the home of post-punk, superstar bands like Joy Division, Simply Red, the Smiths, the Happy Mondays and Oasis. The development of its Gay Village meant that Manchester rivalled Brighton as the gay capital of Britain. With the Hacienda at its hub, 1980s Manchester also boasted the best nightlife in the country and became the epicentre of the rave and acid house dance scene. Alongside this, Manchester earned a darker reputation as one of Britain's most vibrant and violent drug cultures and in time challenged London and Liverpool as a centre for armed robbery, gang warfare and murder.

This was a culture of youthful hedonism and consumption towards which a generation of unemployed grafters from north Manchester's run-down council estates were drawn like wasps to an open jam pot. To hell with life on the dole or minimum wage in a biscuit factory – what was an orgy of consumption for many could be a good business opportunity for a few others. There were T-shirts to be knocked up and knocked out at rock concerts; raves and acid house parties to organise and supply with Ecstasy; and there were other, harder drugs to be bought and sold. As Dave Haslam, a former DJ at the Hacienda Club argues, the new-era spivs were drawing on a rich heritage:

> These young creative characters continue to draw strength from their own self-belief and the city's traditions of DIY youth culture. Perhaps there still lingers in them the spirit of the old street hustlers, amateur Houdinis, and hawkers living on in the modern day grafters in Salford, Manchester and beyond, selling a bit of this, pushing stuff, moving in.[1]

However, Madchester's golden period, its so-called 'summer of love', was short-lived. Young men had always fought for turf in northern England's industrial towns and cities, usually over girls and gambling. In the past the main weapons were the fists, feet, knees and heads. Occasionally coshes and cudgels or chains would be used and very occasionally knives and razors. Until the 1980s, guns were virtually unheard of in these circles. Spiralling youth unemployment under Thatcher in the late 1970s and 1980s and the drug scene changed all of that. The old school of Manchester hard men gave way to a new generation of desperate young people brought up in the unforgiving terrace streets and estates of Moss Side, Cheetham Hill, Salford, Broughton and Collyhurst. The infamous and influential Quality Street Gang was replaced by more ruthless gangs such as the Pepper Hill Mob, the Doddington, the Gooch and Moss Side. At the same time, the currency of control changed as the authority of muscle gave way to the power of the machete, Browning and Uzi. Madchester became 'Gunchester'.

During these hard times the only thing that kept Tommy going and the main cement in his life was football and for him football was Manchester United. He had played the game as a youth, but when he was 16 he got a hiding from a bouncer outside a Manchester nightclub and ripped the ligaments in his right knee, ruining what had been a promising amateur career. Instead of playing, like so many other young men in the late 1970s and 1980s, he became a fixture at Old Trafford's Stretford End, where he rubbed shoulders with and eventually joined up with the top hooligans in United's élite fighting crew, the Red Army. Almost as part of the reimaging of Manchester United PLC in the 1990s, the Club's fans' role in the serious hooligan wars of the 1970s and 1980s has been airbrushed out by the PR men. The records clearly show that when it came to hard-core hooliganism the Red Army were up there with the best, or worst, firms (hooligan gangs) depending upon your perspective, and were role models for those that followed in the 1980s, such as Chelsea's Headhunters and West Ham's Inner City firm. Remember, even though the punishment was later watered down to a fine, it was United's fans not Liverpool's who sparked English football's first European ban when they rioted in the streets of St-Étienne after a European Cup game in 1978.

What is less well known today, at a time when hooliganism has become a much more strategic affair, and when serious hooligan incidents have tended to be under-reported in the media, is that Manchester United's firm are still very active. Most of today's top hooligans can trace their pedigree back to hooliganism's self-styled golden era. Some have continuously been involved. Others are born-again hooligans, having come back to it after raising families, building careers, and/or flirting with the drug and club scene. Some not only control and co-ordinate much of the contemporary violence that still permeates through football, but they are also the main movers and shakers in the football black market and other related illegal enterprises. Tommy is one of these 30-to-40-something terrace legends.

It would be a mistake to view the entrepreneurial culture that grew out of the terraces in isolation from the whole Madchester scene. It is not the case that there were football fans, hooligans, touts, ravers, fashion designers, musicians, DJs and drug dealers who were all different people living in discrete, sealed-off worlds. Many of them were the same people and most of them came together in the pubs, clubs and, most significantly, on the terraces and in the stands. In their own ways, Old Trafford and Maine Road were as central as the Hacienda Club to the communication network that underpinned the vibrancy of Madchester. It was in and around football that young people met and shared experiences and ideas. Out of this milieu many things were created, and not just fanzines.

Big Tommy saw football's black economy as an alternative to hooliganism and the highly profitable but exceedingly dangerous and violent Manchester drug scene. Tommy's conversion to full-time grafting did not happen overnight. When he went to games each week he saw people hanging around grounds all around the country buying, selling and swapping match tickets. Even when they were in the football doldrums United maintained a solid supporter base and there was always a market for their tickets. In the 1980s Tommy started doing a few tickets as a sideline to his more focused hooligan activities. He managed to make enough money to fund his devotion to following his club and made a little spending money to boot. Like the legendary tout, Stan Flashman, had done before him at Spurs, Tommy soon realised that rather than being a means to an end, touting could become an end in itself. From that moment, while he would go on being an ardent Manchester United supporter, he now began to view his affiliation with his beloved club more and more as an occupation.

Tommy moved closer to the big time in 1990 when he travelled with the England supporters to Italia '90. Using locally honed touting skills he managed to fund his whole trip, living well, seeing all the England games and keeping his hooligan hand in with the odd ruck with the Ingerland boys. Tommy returned to the UK with £500 in his pocket. Rather than blowing the money as he might have done a few years before, he reinvested it in 20 tickets for United's early season encounter with Arsenal. Tommy made another good profit that once more was ploughed back into his fledgling business. For the rest of that season the balance of his interest began to shift away from hooliganism towards full-time grafting.

At the same time, on and off the pitch, Manchester United's fortunes were caught in an upwardly spiralling thermal. Alex Ferguson arrived in 1986 and within ten years his achievements would be comparable to those of the legendary Matt Busby. At first Ferguson achieved little more than his immediate predecessors, but as the 1990s wore on, under his guidance and with a little help from a prodigiously talented cadre of young home-grown players, United dragged themselves out of mediocrity to become the dominant force in English football. Their crowning achievement came in the season 1998–99 when they won the treble of the Premier League title, the FA Cup and, the jewel in the crown, the Champions League.

It is hard to believe that only ten years earlier, in 1989, Manchester United were in the doldrums, so much so that Martin Edwards, then the club chairman, had to be talked out of selling the privately owned club to Michael Knighton for a mere £20 million. Ten years later, instead of Knighton, the club had a knight, Sir Alex Ferguson, who was honoured by the Queen for his achievements in football and Manchester United PLC had become the world's richest football club with a reported annual turnover of more than £100 million. The unprecedented rise and rise of Manchester United owes itself to a complex interplay of factors, the keys to which were money and timing.

The spreading menace of hooliganism, the post-Heysel European ban, the Bradford fire and the Hillsborough tragedy together conspired to all but kill off football's traditional, post-war persona. Out of the ashes a new and more consumer- and customer-oriented, all-seater version of the game would rise. The repackaged game proved to be more attractive to sponsors, television companies and private investors. United had always been one of the biggest, if not the biggest, English club brand names. Manchester United's board of directors were shrewd enough to see that a rise in their team's fortunes on the field, coinciding as it did with a radical overhaul in the political economy underpinning English football, was a business opportunity that could not be missed. They looked around and pulled together some of the best business practices that other clubs had engaged in. Following the example set by Liverpool and Spurs, they went bullishly looking for multi-million-pound kit sponsor deals; they emulated Glasgow Rangers by dramatically expanding the merchandising side of the club's business; and following the example of Spurs they launched the club as a limited company on the London Stock Exchange.

Also, perhaps more than any other club, Manchester United benefited hugely from the sums of money that came pouring into the game from terrestrial and extra-terrestrial television. In addition to expanding their domestic market reach, they received increasing exposure to television audiences around the globe; this exposure not only gained them more armchair fans, but also more customers for the Manchester United souvenir shops that were springing up everywhere. Neither did the board forget that it was still bums on seats that generated the biggest slice of income pie, so they developed Old Trafford stadium, increasing its capacity from nearly 50,000 to nearly 70,000 and putting up prices at the same time.

Belying a popular myth that Manchester United's supporters are all prawn-sandwich-eating southern softies or foreigners, there remain a hard core of life-long, working-class supporters who are Manchester born and bred. The club also continues to have a long-standing nationwide following, a legacy from the era of the Busby Babes, and the Charlton, Law and Best years. But it is also true that the club's fanbase has undergone quantitative and qualitative changes.

As success followed success in the 1990s, around the country more and more young supporters gave their allegiance to the Reds. I lived in Northern Ireland for a while and my two children were born there. As a life-long Evertonian, I well remember being mortified when one day in 1995 my son, who was then eight years old, came home from school and announced that he didn't want to support Everton anymore, but instead wanted to switch to Manchester United. This was during the rise of the Reds and I suppose it was a reasonable enough request given the level of United's media exposure and the fact that most of the other kids in his class supported them. I imagine that at the time, fathers and sons were involved in similar negotiations the length and breadth of the country. After starvation and a few days in the cupboard under the stairs (only joking), I managed to talk him out of it. Fortunately, at the end of that season against all odds, Everton beat Manchester United 1–0 in the FA Cup final and my boy could hold his head up high in school. Alas, like his dad and tens of thousands of other addicts, Jack is now destined to be a long-suffering Evertonian for the rest of his life.

At the same time, football's reinvention made it attractive as a chic gathering place for the chattering classes and their business clients. Nick Hornby's *Fever Pitch* told the middle classes that it was OK to talk football at dinner parties. It used to be on the golf course where contracts were mooted and cosy business partnerships cemented. Suddenly, the links had a rival in the executive boxes that took the place of prime standing places in grounds throughout the land. Nothing like a five-course lunch in one of United's executive restaurants followed by the match watched from halfway-line seats to oil the wheels of commerce.

Then, aided and abetted by the arrival of cable and satellite TV and the company's own cable TV channel, there was United's growing European and global following. Alongside visits to Stratford and Canterbury, a trip to Old Trafford became an essential part of doing England. In all of these ways Manchester United's traditional support was enhanced by a new and wealthier generation of supporters, many of whom had little or no connection with the city itself and not much in common with each other. Tony King refers to these supporters as New Consumer Fans, while traditional supporters – the lads – see them as anoraks or shirts – in reference to the fact that, unlike them, new consumers buy and wear Manchester United's replica kits. In copying the best of the rest at the moment of the football business boom, on and off the field, Manchester United left the others standing.

As United prospered, so too did big Tommy and the rest of Manchester's football grafters. The new-era fans had more disposable income and didn't mind disposing some of it on tickets priced at double (or more) the face value. Gradually, Tommy built up his contacts and squeezed his way into Old Trafford's touting network. If you moved in the right circles, there were always ways and means to get your hands on tickets. Tommy's tickets came from many sources including players and their agents, corrupt officials and security staff at the clubs, multiple applications to membership schemes, phantom season tickets and sometimes legitimately through getting up early (or paying somebody else to) and standing in the rain at the ticket office on those rare occasions when tickets actually went on public sale.

There is a lot of resentment among fans that so many tickets seep into the hands of the touts – particularly when it is revealed that some of them come from players who are now so highly rewarded. Traditionally, players have been allocated a certain number of tickets per game, ostensibly for friends and relatives. In the past, when player salaries were much lower, there is little doubt that some professionals sold these tickets to touts to supplement their wages. It is less likely today that many players knowingly do this. Complimentary tickets can be traced back to the person to whom they are originally issued. When you are on tens of thousands of pounds per week, getting a couple of hundred for a handful of tickets is not worth the risk. In 1999, for instance, Leicester's Andy Impy and Tony Cottee were fined £20,000 and £12,000 respectively after it was discovered that the tickets that they had been allocated for their team's Worthington Cup final against Tottenham Hotspur had been sold on to the black market. In another incident at Highbury in 2002, Liverpool's Jamie Carragher was sent off for throwing back a pound coin at a spectator who had hit him on the back of the head with it (unusual for a fellow Scouser to give money away like that!). The police investigation discovered that some of the tickets bought from touts for use in that section of the ground had been issued to Arsenal midfielder, Ray Parlour. The problem for players is that once they give their allocated tickets away, they cannot guarantee that the person they give them to will not then pass them on to anybody else.

Working from an office at home, in the early 1990s Tommy set up his own ticketing agency, which prospered until 1994 when buying and selling on tickets (touting) was made illegal in the UK under section 166 of the Criminal Justice and Public Order Act (in 1999 section 166 was amended by section 10 of the Football Offences and Disorder Act, extending the definition to regulated matches played outside of England and Wales). This legislation forced the Big Man to shut down the legitimate side of his business, putting him back on the black market. Hitherto, Tommy and the other Manchester spivs had been able to ply their trade with impunity outside Old Trafford. After the change in the law the police began to harass and arrest the touts, including, occasionally, Big Tommy himself. In 1990 Manchester United hired ex-SAS man Ned Kelly, boss of SPS (Special Projects Security) whose job, amongst other things, was to crack down on the touts.

Of course, there were other ways of making money apart from tickets. When Manchester United opened their chain of replica kit, souvenir and memorabilia stores, Big Tommy and gangs of other Manchester grafters likewise went into business making and selling fake gear. At first the counterfeit merchandise was cheap and its poor quality reflected this. But it was not long before the grafters began to source their materials from the same Far Eastern sweatshops used by the official retailers. Soon their snide replicas were virtually indistinguishable in style and quality from the real thing, and selling at less than half the price. For the impoverished mothers of fanatical kids from Manchester's run-down estates, according to Big Tommy, he and his ilk were viewed as Robin Hoods while the club itself, as it churned out yet another away kit at £40-plus a shirt, were regarded as robbing bastards – a view, it seems, shared by the Office of Fair Trading who in 2002 took kit manufacturer Umbro, the FA and big clubs like Manchester United, to court for unfairly fixing the price of replica shirts. At this point in our conversation Big Tommy failed to point out that, unlike the folk hero, Robin of Loxley, Tommy of Cheetham still managed to make a tidy profit out of the peasantry.

It was about this time that Big Tommy met and fell in love with a probation officer. This caused him to rethink his career options. After all it would not do for him to fall foul of the law now that he had a partner who was virtually one of them. For a while he gave up his black market activities and took a job for a local taxi company, working on 'the switch' – the taxi office desk microphone – taking calls and distributing fares. He hated it, it was boring and the pay was lousy. Big Tommy's flirtation on the sunny side of the tracks did not last long. He stuck it for a year until a friend who ran a travel and hospitality agency called Sports Tours asked him to help out setting up a couple of VIP packages at United and later at the Grand National at Aintree. Tommy made more in a few weeks doing this than he had in a year on the switch and it was much more interesting. It was time for Big Tommy to call a taxi for himself.

When his friend asked him to work full time for Sports Tours Tommy jumped at the opportunity. Part of his job was to act as a courier for parties of Manchester United supporters on away trips. Big Tommy realised that rather than take a relatively low salary for doing all this he could do it all himself and make a lot more money. All he needed was a grubstake. Fortunately for Big Tommy, across the Channel FIFA and the CFO were busy concocting a ticket distribution system that would provide him with all the money he needed to break into the independent travel business.

The concept of independent travel as used in this book should be distinguished from individuals and groups who make their own, independent arrangements to travel around the country and overseas following their clubs. It is also subtly different from the more traditional commercial operations – usually coach companies – which, often with the blessing of the clubs, have long since catered for the needs of travelling supporters. It is best understood in the context of specialist football-related overseas travel, which is necessarily and deliberately distinct from officially sanctioned travel schemes and which most definitely does not have the blessing of either the clubs or the Football Association.

The catalyst for the emergence of independent operators as defined above was the makeover of the European Cup competitions and their rebirth as the Champions League and an extended UEFA Cup. It meant that in any given year, at least six, and potentially more, British clubs would participate in a pre-programmed series of games abroad. The rationale for the expanded format of UEFA's blue ribbon competitions was clearly a business one, designed to milk the most out of the holy trinity of football, sponsorship and television. In fact it is well documented that the Champions League was invented by UEFA's marketing partners TEAM (Television Event and Media Marketing). The increasingly greedy appetites of Europe's biggest clubs, with their threats of breakaway superleagues, was an additional spur to UEFA/TEAM's pan-European strategy. Unintended by them, their new initiatives were heaven-sent for the football black market. For Big Tommy and a few other far-sighted grafters it opened possibilities for generating more regular income around a semi-legitimate enterprise with fewer risks and higher margins.

Grafting tickets and flogging swag is hard work, high risk, unpredictable and, for the most part, illegal. The innovative European competitions gave Big Tommy a new structure within which to deploy all of his hard-come-by streetwise skills, catering for the travel needs of a new generation of migrant fans. Most clubs have official ticket allocation and travel schemes, either run by themselves or as subcontracted commercial ventures. Many fans, however, choose to travel independently because official one- or two-day trips are not long or flexible enough to permit the kind of sightseeing mini-break doubled up around football. There are also tens of thousands of fans who are ardent supporters of their teams but sworn enemies of their clubs as commercial entities. They choose to turn their backs on official schemes of any kind. Some others have no choice but to make alternative arrangements because, for a wide range of legitimate reasons – work

47

commitments at weekends; working away from home, playing Saturday football – they cannot fulfil club requirements for access to allocated tickets and package deals. Then there are those supporters who are barred from taking part in officially approved travel schemes because of their records of hooliganism and related misdemeanours, but have yet to be legally banned under the terms of the Football Offences and Disorder Act. Unintentionally, the FA and the clubs, panicked by the menacing reputation of England fans abroad, have together conspired to help to create a niche market for the likes of Big Tommy. The catalyst for this came in 1993 when Manchester United, in their first competitive overseas foray since the lifting of the European ban, travelled to Turkey to play Galatasaray in Istanbul. United lost 2–1 in a hateful atmosphere, summed up by a huge banner unfurled by the Turkish fans proclaiming 'Welcome to Hell'. (I laughed heartily eight years later when Liverpool played at the same ground and a group of their supporters brandished their own banner that said 'You think this is Hell? You should try the Grafton on a Friday night' in reference to a notorious grab-a-grannie nightclub in Liverpool, that I must confess to having frequented in my youth.) After the 1993 match there were serious disturbances and six United fans were detained. The clubs' response to this was to blame the independent travel operators. They issued a joint statement declaring that in future only those who had bought officially sanctioned travel packages would be supplied with tickets. The FA, concerned that unofficial travel companies would take supporters to areas where they were most likely to get into trouble, backed the clubs; Graham Kelly, then the FA Secretary said, 'Having been made aware of various problems experienced by supporters of clubs playing in European competitions in season 1993–94, the clubs had unanimously decided that tickets should be restricted to supporters on official trips, which, as you know, is a practice we endorse.'

Increasingly, official packages became hit-and-run affairs – home, plane, airport, match, airport, plane, home. What is more, these official whistle-stop trips were usually way overpriced. For a whole range of reasons such arrangements did not suit all supporters and it certainly did not suit the Lads. Enter Big Tommy. His is a remarkable business concept. Getting started, he used his old hooligan and touting connections to corner and cater for a market of regular customers who will always travel abroad with their teams, not simply for the football, but more importantly for thrills and spills of being abroad with like-minded groups of likely lads who want little or nothing to do with official packages.

Big Tommy always refers to these punters as the 'Lads'. In my early conversations with him, he used this term over and over again and I got the feeling that he meant more than the more neutral, common parlance usage of the word 'lads' as a generic descriptor of young, male and macho. When I ask him to clarify this he says, 'Come on, John, you know the Lads – the Lads, the top men, the firms.' The Lads for Tommy then are the hardcore, 30-something, hooligan-hedonists who are the unofficial ringleaders of football's die-hard supporters. Subsequently, he expanded his market reach and by leafleting outside grounds and advertising in local newspapers, ITL now caters for a quite diverse group of clients. But he still views the Lads as the keystone to his whole operation.

Tony King, in his study of the social composition of Manchester United's supporters, likewise refers to the core of traditional fans as the lads. However, his categorisation misses the edge and menace implied by Big Tommy, which I witnessed on numerous occasions. It is for this reason that I have used the emphatic capital 'L' when referring to this type of travelling fan. Another way of thinking about fans is to consider them in relation to the National Criminal Intelligence Service's (NCIS) three-fold categorisation:

- Category A – Peaceful, bona fide supporters.
- Category B – Possible risk of disorder, especially alcohol related.
- Category C – Violent supporters or organisers of violence.

Tommy's target market, particularly during the early stages of his development, were Categories B and C, who together I refer to throughout this book as the Lads.

In the past these groups of fans had to go it alone, getting hold of tickets, finding transport and booking accommodation. This is where Big Tommy and the independent travel business come in. Beyond the reach of UEFA, the

English FA and individual clubs, Big Tommy has put together quite an operation. He block-books flights and, if demand is sufficiently high, charters whole planes. He arranges hotels, and acquires tickets for targeted matches abroad. ITL never gets an allocation of tickets from the clubs who generally disapprove of and despise the independent travel business. Tommy likes to posture the businessman, but he is still an experienced and knowledgeable tout who skilfully works the local underground ticket market in places like Munich, Madrid and Milan to garner enough briefs for his clients. So long as you do not mind whom you're sitting next to, Tommy will get you there and get you in – making nonsense of UEFA's policy on fan segregation.

We had been talking for several hours and, even though we had barely scratched the surface of this fascinating world, it was time to leave. Before going I asked Big Tommy when his next trip was. 'Leeds have got to play a Champions League qualifier in Munich against 1860 at the end of August,' he replied. 'Billy's taking a group of Leeds Lads over for me. D'you wanna go with him?'

What better way to investigate this than to go as an insider on one of the Scum Airways European adventures? Not for the last time I was off to Germany with the Lads.

ENDNOTES

[1] Haslam, Dave, *Manchester England: The Story of the Pop Cult City* (London, Fourth Estate, 1999) p. 261

# 3

## Munich, August 2000

'IT'S A COLD, COLD YORKSHIRE NIGHT TONIGHT,' BARKS BIG Tommy as he strides towards Elland Road. 'It's a bit naughty this,' he says as he stops to tape one of his flyers over the sign for the players' car park. Wearing a black anorak with a baseball cap pulled tight to his head, Big Tommy stands outside the main entrance to the Leeds end calling out, 'International Travel: Anderlecht, Roma, Real Madrid. Get your orders here. International Travel . . .' He stuffs leaflets into the hands of fans as they make their way to the ground. Only yards away stand two pretty young girls dressed in the livery of Leeds United. 'Leeds United official travel,' they take turns to sing while, like Tommy, they give out leaflets. One of the official leaflets blows by Big Tommy's feet. He looks at it contemptuously. 'See plenty of those thrown away tonight,' he sneers, 'but I bet you don't see many International ones in the gutter.'

Most clubs have official ticket allocation and travel schemes, either run by themselves, as is the case with Leeds United, or by favoured commercial partners, like Travel Care or Miss Ellies who sort out Manchester United's travel. As explained in the previous chapter, however, many fans choose to travel independently because official one- or two-day trips are expensive and usually not long or flexible enough to permit the kind of sightseeing mini-breaks, doubled up around football, that many of today's fans prefer. Others travel independently out of protest. There are thousands of fans who are ardent supporters of their teams but sworn enemies of their club as commercial entities.

This is one of the great paradoxes of today's game. Universally, fans want their teams to be the best they can be. They want the best players, the biggest grounds and the best facilities and they expect the clubs to finance this. At the same time many of the same fans are highly critical of their clubs for being over-commercial. They tend to hark back to a mythical golden era when it was football first and business a distant second. When, in their imaginations at least, the club and the community were one and the same thing. Of course, it was never quite like that and, as the game has grown as a global media commodity, it has become even less plausible for the biggest clubs to continue to operate as if they were local co-operative societies. Those who have are no longer in the top flight. Nevertheless, there remain large cadres of supporters who feel alienated and disenfranchised by the increased dominance of those in business suits over those in tracksuits and choose to turn their backs on official schemes of any kind. Big Tommy is sensitive to the Lads' particular requirements and arranges his trips accordingly: plenty of time for binge drinking, local knowledge of the red-light district, and tickets in the home supporters' end.

Big Tommy is by no means the first hooligan to exploit knowledge of the Lads and their needs and appetites in the service of the travel business. In the 1970s and 1980s hooligan wars came to rival *Grandstand* as an institutionalised feature of Saturday afternoons. In its earliest phase modern hooliganism was a relatively spontaneous affair taking place between large groups of youths in and around grounds on a Saturday afternoon. Soon, however, the fighting became more organised. Every club developed its élite hooligan gang or firm that planned and were at the forefront of the fighting. Defending local turf at home games was important, but taking on their lot at away fixtures became the Lads' favourite pastime. At this time potential hooligans were easy to spot with their skinhead looks, DM boots and club colours. They were also easy to follow when they travelled on specially designated trains and buses. More intensive policing and security posed problems for the hooligans and they reacted by changing the way they looked and how they travelled. Getting around the country while avoiding police surveillance became a major feature of hooligan culture.

In the 1980s the top hooligan gangs reimaged themselves as the 'casuals' in reference to their adoption of designer, but club-anonymous leisurewear as a Saturday afternoon dress code. There is much argument among the fans as to who started this trend. Undoubtedly it was anchored in part in London's 1970s and 1980s Mod and Indie dance scene when it became de rigueur to wear Ben Sherman and Fred Perry shirts in both the nightclubs and at the match. This trend was developed by Liverpool's period of European domination when travelling fans returned home wearing designer casual gear and foreign football shirts and hats picked up in Rome, Milan and Madrid. The casual, post-punk style of the Liverpool Scallies was soon picked up by the Manchester scene and not long after the same look began to appear in London's dance clubs and on the terraces. In their new apparel, potential hooligans were now more difficult to identify, although there was, of course, an ironic uniformity among the casuals. The grafters, of course, were not slow to exploit this turn of events. Alongside snide replica football shirts there was now also a market for a wide range of casual-hooligan apparel, favoured labels today being Fred Perry, Adidas, Puma, Nike, Lacoste, Stone Island, Hilfiger and Hacket with hats by Burberry. This casual style became so well established as a new hooligan uniform that in some pubs close to grounds the usual signs barring customers that wore replica football shirts on match days were replaced by ones that refused service to Lads dressed in this sort of designer gear.

In addition to travelling in 'disguise', more inventive ways of travelling were required if the Old Bill were to be avoided. Officially sanctioned travel schemes were too easy for the police to monitor and football special trains had to be avoided at all costs. Newly affluent fans travelled in threes and fours in their own cars while others continued to use public transport, but in unpredictable ways, using regular bus and train services and travelling at odd times. Some firms even used names that referred to their favoured mode of transport. West Ham's Inter City firm adopted their name as a reflection of their preference for travelling to away games in the first-class carriages of inter-city trains. Leeds' firm were the Service Crew, another reference to the railways, and Portsmouth's top Lads called themselves the 6.57 Mob because of the time of the train they would take out of Portsmouth on Saturday mornings.

Other firms used private, unofficial coach companies, some of which were run by top hooligans. In London, Manchester and Liverpool enterprising Lads moved off the terraces and into the travel business. Foremost among these was 'Icky's Luxury Coaches' operated out of Tunbridge Wells by Steve Hickmott, then the self-styled leader of Chelsea's top firm, the Headhunters. Icky was a legend during these hooligan heydays. Two ex-Headhunters, Martin King and Martin Knight, remember that 'Icky's convoy travelled around the land causing havoc and having fun', avoiding the police and turning up out of the blue to confront other firms when they least expected it.[1] Icky's activities were brought to an abrupt end when he was dragged out of bed in a dawn police raid and arrested for hooligan-related offences. Based on evidence gathered during a police undercover operation, Hickmott was tried at the Old Bailey, found guilty and sentenced to ten years in prison, by some distance the longest ever jail sentence given for hooliganism. Icky served two and a half years before he was released after it was revealed that the police had tampered with some parts of the evidence that was used against him. Hickmott now lives in self-imposed exile in Thailand, running a bar called the Dogs Bollocks in Pattaya, the seediest seaside sex-tourist hang-out in South-east Asia. We will come across Icky again later in the book.

Big Tommy followed in Icky's footsteps. He started business with those he knew best: Manchester United's Red Army. There was already a small but significant number of top United Lads of Icky's generation who were into the travel business and who had graduated from laying on a few coaches to chartering planes for the Reds' firm during the first phase of born-again United's European adventures in the late 1980s and early 1990s. Big Tommy found himself working in a crowded market, but, just as he had done with the tickets, he managed to elbow his way in. After a few successful trips his reputation grew and he built up a steady following. The Big Man's timing couldn't have been better. Just as he launched himself as a serious player in the travel business, United had their best ever run in the Champions League, ending in a famous victory over Bayern Munich in Barcelona. United had not performed on such a stage since the era of Charlton, Best and Law. There was a whole generation of supporters that had not been alive to witness the Reds' last European Cup triumph. Every man and his dog wanted to be in Barcelona to experience the culmination of United's attempt at the treble. Estimates vary, but as many as 60,000 Manchester United supporters went to Barcelona and a few thousand went with Big Tommy. Billy remembers being sent out to Germany with £40,000 in a rucksack to buy up tickets for this match on the Munich black market.

This early coup gave the Big Man further scope for investment and development. Given local competition from the officials and other grafters doing unofficial packages, Old Trafford alone was too slender as a base to build a business. Just like the clubs themselves, the unpredictability of qualification for the Champions League makes it difficult for the grafters' forward business plans. 'Heaven forbid, but what if the unthinkable happened and the Reds didn't qualify for Europe?' asks Tommy. 'I'd be back on the streets grafting T-shirts,' he answers himself. Like all good capitalists, Tommy was shrewd enough to know that he would have to expand into other markets to survive. In London the market around Arsenal and Chelsea – the only clubs in the capital with a reasonably predictable European pedigree – was already monopolised by the London spivs, and the Scousers had Liverpool's firms well covered. It was a godsend for Tommy when David O'Leary took over a young Leeds United side and took them into Europe. Leeds' official travel company is actually owned by the club and when they first qualified for Europe there were no established independents challenging their monopoly. Leeds has more than its fair share of dissident fans and a significant number of Lads. Neither constituency were particularly enthusiastic about travelling with the officials. It promised to be a ripe market for the Big Man.

When Leeds qualified for Europe Tommy went to Elland Road to make contact with some of the Leeds Lads that he knew through his Manchester United hooligan days. At first Leeds firms were reluctant to travel with Big Tommy because of his reputation as hard-core Manchester United. It is usual for anybody who does not support Manchester United to profess a hatred for them. Leeds' enmity, however, is in a league of its own. The Leeds fans routinely refer to Manchester United and its supporters as 'Scum' and profane songs and chants about them, including irreverent references to the 1958 Munich air disaster, are regularly aired at Elland Road. Some supporters even go so far as to have 'Munich '58' tattooed on various parts of their bodies. But ITL's prices are hard to beat and a handful of Leeds Lads took a chance and went with Big Tommy to Prague when their team played Sparta. They came back mightily impressed after a cheap and cheerful, hassle-free trip during which they had been put up in the Renaissance, the Czech Republic capital's top five-star hotel, a better hotel than the one that the players were staying in. Since then, whenever Leeds play in Europe, ITL takes hundreds, sometimes thousands, of Leeds Lads. 'Aye,' says Big Tommy with a laugh, 'but because they know we're Man U, even though they travel with us, and enjoy themselves, they still call us Scum Airways.'

The clubs generally take a dim view of the independents and none more so than Leeds. LUT (Leeds United Travel) has anonymous offices directly opposite Elland Road's south stand where a full-time staff of 28 work on not just the team's and fans' travel needs but also a range of other business travel packages. The blue fitted carpets, the uniformed staff and the quiet, efficient and busy atmosphere, contrasts sharply with my memory of ITL's two-person operation in a small room in Manchester's Newton Heath. I spoke with Stuart Priestly, the boss of LUT, and asked him how he felt about Big Tommy's operation. 'It's unfair, really, but there is not much that we can do about it. In the past he has undercut us because he doesn't have the same overheads and doesn't take all of the precautions that we do when we plan a trip. Also, he picks and chooses which trips he does, only picking the ones that he thinks will make a decent profit. We do all Leeds' away games. We want to make money, of course, but we are also obliged to provide a service for the fans.'

Priestly is aware that many of the fans do not travel with LUT because they are enemies of the system. 'They'll never come with us, because they don't like the business side of the club and there is not much we can do about that. They don't seem to realise that we provide them with a good service. OK, it might cost them an extra tenner or so, but unlike the independents, we do a lot of extra work for that. We employ stewards – one for every twenty-five customers – and do a lot of checking before every trip to make sure that we give good value and get the fans there and back safely.' He is also concerned that some of the fans that go with Big Tommy are troublemakers who tarnish the club's image abroad. 'We operate a members system called Strikers. Only fans who have attended so many games are issued with official tickets for European games and there is a sort of vetting system. If they have a record of bad behaviour at Leeds, then they lose their Strikers membership and don't get official tickets and we only take those who have official tickets.' An unintended consequence of this is that many of these miscreants either travel alone or are forced into Big Tommy's welcoming arms. His touting skills mean that he can relatively easily get his hands on tickets, usually procuring them from the host city. This means, of course, that many of Tommy's customers end up in parts of the ground occupied by the home fans. Often, however, local police, realising that these are actually away fans, herd them into the sector reserved for LUT's customers. If they then cause trouble it can be wrongly assumed that this was the fault of LUT's travellers, and by implication Leeds United itself.

Tommy explains how he chartered an aircraft and took a plane-load of Leeds fans to Istanbul for the ill-fated Galatasaray game in 1999. Speight and Loftus, the two Leeds fans who were stabbed to death before the game, were Big Tommy's customers. Billy, Big Tommy's right-hand man at the time, was the courier for the trip. He was in the bar with the victims when the trouble started. 'The Lads weren't causing any trouble,' he recalls. 'Just having a few beers and a bit of a laugh. Then the Turks came. Some of them were tapping on the windows with those long kebab knives, challenging us to come outside.' When they did eventually leave the bar, Galatasaray fans attacked them. According to Billy, the Turkish police did nothing to protect them. On the contrary, they set about the Leeds fans even as two lay bleeding to death on the pavement. Most of the Leeds fans were blissfully unaware of what had happened. Billy had the harrowing task of ringing around the hotels the next morning to let all the people on the ITL package, most of whom were close friends of Kevin and Christopher, know what had happened. Tommy and Billy went to the funerals in Leeds and, some time later, ITL organised and gifted holidays for some of the grieving relatives.

My actual role in Big Tommy's world was a difficult one. He and Billy knew I was researching for a book, as did one or two other grafters, but most of the people I met assumed I was one of Tommy's helpers. I was warned by Tommy not to let on to anybody else what I was doing. Some of his customers were 'straight members', but many others were not so straight and a few were out-

and-out villains. They would not take kindly to strangers nosing around. Leeds' visit to Munich 1860 would provide the first test for my assumed, insider identity.

Big Tommy was taking about 150 for this trip. As soon as the draw had been made he had got on the phone and block-booked flights from Leeds–Bradford, and London Stansted to Munich. Billy was travelling with a group from Leeds–Bradford and I was scheduled to meet him at Munich Airport. I was to collect my ticket from Kenny, who was in charge of a small firm from Leeds that was travelling to Munich via Stansted. I had to call Kenny on his mobile and arrange to meet him in the bar. 'But don't tell him what you're up to,' warned Tommy, 'just let on you're one of Billy's mates.'

The flight left at noon and I got to the airport at 10 a.m., by which time half of the Lads were well into the swing of things, having been drinking on the bus since leaving Leeds at dawn. With some trepidation, I walked into the bar looking around for my contact. Among the bags and beer I spotted a small, wiry man, with thinning sandy hair and an excuse for a moustache who fitted Kenny's description.

'You John?' he asked, walking over, and I nodded. 'Want a drink?' Kenny bought me a pint of lager and invited me to join his mates who were sitting around a table reading tabloids and talking football. He introduced me as one of Billy's mates. Things seemed pretty relaxed and I did my best to join in with the conversation and banter. But after a while one of Kenny's mob, a square-headed hefty bloke in his early 40s, lowered his copy of *The Sun*, and looked at me suspiciously. ''Ere,' he said, 'you're a Scouser, aren't you? What's a fucking Scouser doing going to watch Leeds?'

I was half-ready for this. I explained that I was an Evertonian now exiled on the south coast of England. I bemoaned the fact that of all the clubs that had suffered when English clubs had been banned from playing in Europe, Everton, who had won the League twice and the old European Cup-Winners' Cup, had fared the worse. Howard Kendall's fabulous mid-1980s team had broken up and the club had never recovered, to the extent that in my adult lifetime they had never played in Europe. I told him that I was a 'ground hopper' who liked to travel and watch football at different stadiums. While Everton remained in the doldrums, when I could afford it, I had taken to following other clubs when they played in some of the Continent's nicest towns and cities. I had never been in Munich's Olympic Stadium. Billy, an old mate who I had played football with when I lived in Manchester, told me about the Leeds to Munich trip and suggested that I come along for the fun of it.

Most of them seemed to accept my story, but my original inquisitor was yet to be convinced. He took a sip from his pint, licked his lips and said, 'Right, if you're an Evertonian, who played for Everton and England and is named after a town in Yorkshire?' Ask the audience? Phone a friend? I realised that I was being tested and that getting the answer right would be important if I was to establish my credibility with this crew. Fortunately, I had been a regular terrace dweller at Goodison Park in the late 1960s and early 1970s and, from a time capsule deeply buried in my mind, I was able to conjure a name. 'That would be Fred Pickering,' I told him. 'Great player, had to quit because of cartilage damage,' I added for effect.

'Aye, right then,' he responded. 'What you having?'

For the time being I was one of the Lads.

At Munich Airport there were rigorous checks by nervous police and immigration officers who looked bemused and certainly not amused as a group of tipsy Leeds fans marched defiantly into the airport whistling the theme from *The Great Escape* – not, I am sure, the Germans' favoured Christmas Day viewing. In the wake of the disorder around Euro 2000 Jack Straw, at that time the British Home Secretary, had pushed a Bill though Parliament that increased the use of banning and exclusion orders for fans deemed to be persistently violent and unruly at home and abroad. This legislation made provision for banning not just those actually convicted of public order offences, but also those who the police deemed capable of such actions. On this basis lists were compiled and circulated to police and immigration officers at UK ports and airports and listed fans that were spotted were prevented from travelling. Such lists were also shared with police and officials of countries that were hosting English teams. Leeds' visit to Munich would be the first significant test of the new legislation and the German authorities had agreed not to let listed fans into their country. Several of Big Tommy's customers were stopped in England and a few others were collared and repatriated before they got through German customs. Many others (including me) were given a good grilling by plain-clothed German policemen who pounced on likely looking suspects as they approached the arrivals hall.

Billy was in arrivals with his impromptu International Travel sign, hand-scrawled on a piece of cardboard, out of place among the glossy corporate logos and professional VIP meeting-boards, including the ones from Leeds' Official Travel Club. We boarded an awaiting coach and headed into the city. I laughed as Billy spent most of the half-hour journey trying to stop some of the Leeds Lads from smoking at the back of the bus; he reminded me of a harassed schoolteacher.

As we were checking in at the hotel the police arrived with three Leeds Lads (not Big Tommy's customers) who had come in on the earlier morning flight. They were ordered to their rooms to retrieve their belongings before being taken into custody. They had been part of another group who had made straight for Munich's famous Hofbräuhaus, a lager lout's paradise, which, with its associations with Hitler, is even more attractive for those, like some of the Leeds Lads, with far-right sympathies. The 500-year-old *Bierkeller* is renowned for good beer and conviviality. It is a massive, cavernous place of stone columns and arches, with rows and rows of trestle tables and bench seats. Accompanied by the oom-pah-pah and polka of the resident brass band, buxom, broad-shouldered serving girls in traditional Bavarian costumes, clutching improbable numbers of huge, two-litre steins brimming over with frothy Bavarian beer, glide across the flagstone floor servicing the needs of up to 1,300 drinkers. What the establishment's promotional literature fails to mention is that the Hofbräuhaus also used to be used for political meetings. It was a favourite venue for Hitler – a place where the wannabe Fürher and his henchmen plotted the 1923 Munich Putsch.

Public, Nazi-type displays are constitutionally outlawed in Germany – even in ultra-conservative Bavaria. When the Leeds Lads' advanced guard arrived in the Hofbräuhaus and began giving straight, right-arm, Nazi salutes and chanting Sieg Heil, other tourists looked on, shocked and bewildered, while the local drinkers looked shamefacedly away. This happened at a sensitive moment in Germany's political development. The post-unification honeymoon was over and there were fears that social unrest, particularly in the former East Germany, was stimulating a neo-Nazi revival.

Whether it was done with genuine political purpose or as a very bad-taste joke, the Lads' Nazi-style celebrations could not be tolerated. Eventually the police swooped, making 13 arrests on the spot. Another three culprits, identified from the *Bierkeller*'s security video, were spotted in the crowd at the match the following evening and arrested by a police snatch squad at half-time. They faced a maximum custodial sentence of up to three years in prison or a fine of up to one year's earnings. In the end, after a few weeks languishing in a German prison, they were deported back to England without having to face trial.

Months later, in Spain for the Madrid–Leeds game, I met one of those who had been arrested in the Hofbräuhaus that morning in Munich. Appropriately dressed in a beer-stained Fatty Arbuckle T-shirt, the 30-something computer programmer for Leeds City Council talked easily about his ordeal. He claimed that he just happened to be standing in the *Bierkeller* when the German police swooped. Another innocent bystander. 'Aye, I were in t' Munich jail for two weeks. Put me in t' cell with seven Turks! I've never been in prison before. Weren't too bad. At least now I'll be able to tell people I've been in prison!' He had earned his campaign medals and was proud to show them off.

The far right's connections with English football are well documented. In the 1970s and 1980s the political left ignored football, viewing it as a misguided diversion and opiate of the working classes. As left-wingers peddled the *Socialist Worker* in the high street, up and down the country, neo-Nazi groups like the National Front, Combat 18 (so named because the first and eighth letters of the alphabet correspond with the initials of Adolf Hitler) and the BNP (British National Party) sold *Bulldog* and *Flag* outside football grounds and recruited new members on the terraces. Elland Road was one of the grounds where the far right made its most significant inroads. Nick Varley recalls a game he attended in the mid-1980s.

> Hitler was a Leeds fan. That was the simple, sinister message carried in
> graffiti on a city centre wall. And while it may not have been strictly true

of the Führer himself, it was for a number of his latter-day devotees. Before the club's most important game in five years – the promotion play-off replay against Charlton in 1987 – one of the known ringleaders of the racism at Elland Road was spotted selling copies of *Mein Kampf.* At other games Nazi-style salutes were all part of the intimidation – and not just from those on the terraces. Watford and England's Blisset complained. Normally the abuse is from the terraces, but at one Leeds game whole groups in the stand were doing Nazi salutes and shouting 'Sieg Heil'.[2]

Knowing that some of the Leeds Lads fell into this category ITL had included suggestions of visits to the Hofbräuhaus, and to the notorious SS-run extermination camp, Dachau, on the tour itinerary. A few had also wanted to take in the Aldershorst, Hitler's Bavarian mountain eyrie, in Berchtesgaden, the Valhalla of the Nazi gods. But the eagle's nest was a little too far away to squeeze in before the match. Some of the Leeds Lads went to Dachau and most downed a few litres in the Hofbräuhaus. Some, no doubt, did so out of genuine historical interest, but others, equally without doubt, made the pilgrimage because they are pro-Nazi. It is not as if the displays at the Hofbräuhaus or the trip to Dachau are isolated incidents. Supporters of Leeds and other English clubs have engaged in this sort of morbid tourism before. Combat 18, for instance, has literature giving details of Chelsea fans' pilgrimages to other Nazi death camps such as Auschwitz. One of Tommy's customers had obviously come kitted out for the full tour. He was blue-eyed and shaven-headed. Each day he sported a fresh military-issue drill shirt (black on Tuesday, blue on Wednesday and khaki on Thursday) and combat trousers topped off with a military-style, canvas cap. To their credit, since those days, Leeds United, both the club and its fans, have done a lot to root out and eradicate the racist and fascist following and propagandists. From my experiences in Munich and Madrid, it is clear to me, however, that there still remains much work to be done. I do not believe that most of the Leeds Lads who flirt with Nazi trappings are politically and ideologically informed Fascists – although neither can it be ruled out that some are. It is just that Nazi symbolism and style suits the Lads' menacing irreverence and helps them to intimidate their victims.

Once everybody was billeted in their hotels we headed into the town centre to see what the rest of the Lads were up to. A group of about 20 of them had gathered around tables in the stylish, open-air, courtyard restaurant of the nineteenth-century town hall. This was the team whose two mates, Kevin and Christopher, had been murdered in Istanbul the night before the Galatasaray match. This was their first trip away with Leeds since. One of the murdered men's brothers had been in Istanbul that night and he was on this trip. They had just been on their own pilgrimage to the Hofbräuhaus, led by Benny – the team's main fixer. Fortunately for Billy, none of the ITL group had been arrested. The fact that arrests had already been made earlier in the day made sure Benny kept his Lads on short leashes inside the *Bierkeller*.

Billy has explained to me how the Leeds Lads are really a series of loosely connected gangs or firms. Big Tommy prefers to deal with the various ringleaders, like Kevin and Benny, when he's setting up different packages. The ringleaders then co-ordinate the gangs' arrangements, organising payments and co-ordinating travel plans. This time, because he's brought a big crew out with him, Big Tommy has given Benny a free trip. Benny – in his mid 30s – is casually well dressed and looks out of place with a mop of thick black hair and his olive complexion. I discover that he owns and operates his own business with a turnover in excess of £1 million per year. He has followed and fought for Leeds, home and away, as long as he can remember. Benny's profile is not untypical of many of Big Tommy's regular customers: 30-something, married (or with a steady partner), children, self-employed and not short of money.

As the figurines on the ornate town hall clock dance to the tune of the passing hour the rest of the establishment's respectable, bourgeois clientele look on aghast as the Leeds Lads knock back gallons of lager and become louder and louder. They are not being intentionally objectionable. In their own world they are 'just having a laugh'. But just having a laugh can be deeply offensive to those not sharing the joke, particularly in sensitive cross-cultural settings. Grim-faced waiters, wearing black waistcoats and ankle-length aprons, hover around the Lads' tables. A stein falls to the floor shattering on the ancient cobbles. Sensing the unease of the waiters and the imminence of a call for the police, Billy suggests to Benny that he takes his Lads to an Irish bar in an area called Muchener Freiheit, a less conspicuously bourgeois part of town, where the Lads' kind of behaviour might be more acceptable.

Once they have had a skinful of strong lager, the Lads are in full Saturday-night-out-in-Leeds mode. What happens next? They look for a curry house, of course, and I tag along. That Lads from Leeds, Doncaster and Bradford – the home of the British love affair with Indian food – demand a curry in Munich is a bizarre and complex expression of ethnocentrism. I feel like I have been trapped in a Rowan Atkinson comedy sketch: a dozen drunken white males stumble into an Indian restaurant, abusing the Asian staff, ordering lager and demanding the hottest food on the menu. A large potted plant balanced on a table near the entrance crashed to the floor as the Lads made their entrance. Only Billy's diplomacy and Benny's wallet prevented the proprietor from calling the police.

After a curry, for some it's off to the 'brass house' (brothel). A few of the Lads have sniffed out a seedy Munich nightclub that is also a brothel. One tries to negotiate a deal with a working girl, but once he hands over his money no sexual favours are forthcoming. He gets into a fight with the Madame who holds him in a headlock and tries to wrestle him out of the door. His friends intervene and the Madame punches one of them before being decked herself by one of the Leeds Lads. The Lads flee out of the club and are hotly pursued by a gang of irate Germans in a black Mercedes. They have a narrow escape, but it was a good laugh and they are able to entertain the rest of the gang with tales of their adventures in the bar the next day. All in all, it's a good start to the trip for the Lads. The use of brothels and prostitutes will turn out to be a recurring theme throughout my research.

The next day is match day and the game not due to kick-off until 8 p.m. In the morning Billy has to go to the airport to meet more punters coming in on planes from Stansted and Manchester (via Paris). Both flights are scheduled to arrive at the same time but at different concourses. I volunteer to be Billy's assistant and pick up the group off the Manchester/Paris connection while he waits for the larger party from Stansted. Yesterday, Lads who had come via Paris, unlike the arrivals direct from Stansted, had sailed through immigration without any bother. Today is different. The authorities have spotted this loophole and as anybody who looks remotely like a football fan approaches the sliding-door exit into the arrivals hall, they are intercepted by two undercover police – long hair, blue jeans, casual shirts – and carted off to a side room for searching and interrogation. One member of the ITL group with 'football hooligan' written all over him – shaved head, beer belly, tattoos and shades – never makes it through and is taken away for further questioning, only to be released later as a case of mistaken identity. In defence of the German police, it is hard to tell one shaven-headed, beer-bellied, tattooed English football fan from another or distinguish between the conventional, peaceful supporters and the likely troublemakers.

By about 3 p.m., once everyone is safely checked in, Billy and I head back into town to see what the Lads have been getting up to. He advised them to hang out in the Schiller Bar, a rough-and-ready joint near the station open 24 hours a day and a favoured haunt for taxi drivers, small-time crooks, grafters and hookers. The bar's extensive French doors open onto the street where many of the Lads are gathered around tables with their shirts off allowing the hot Bavarian sun to redden their ample bellies, faces and skinheads. Billy's arrival sparks a chorus of 'Stand Up if You Hate the Scum', sung to the tune of the Village People's 'Go West'. They all get to their feet to ridicule his associations with Manchester United. Billy shrugs and heads into the Schiller's dark interior, where the walls are plastered with fading photographs of boxers, footballers and minor show-business celebrities, mostly in the company of the Schiller's proprietor. More Lads prop up the bar and sit around tables drinking more strong German lager.

A well-made-up woman in her late 30s, who might be a working girl or might not, sits at the bar talking to a lone and very weary-looking black waitress. One of the Lads, determined to find out, approaches her and gallantly asks, "Ere, luv, where can you get a fuck in this town?' She gives him a tired smile but otherwise ignores his oafish overtures. The red-light district in Munich is in a place which in English translates as Arts Park, but which in German is Kunst Park. When Billy explains this to the Lad in question, the Lad roars with laughter and shouts over to his mates, "Ere, lads, if you want to get a jump in this town you've gotta go to Cunts Park!'

As this is one of the main gathering points for the Leeds Lads, it is not long before the police, accompanied by the media pack, turn up at the Schiller. A green and white mini-bus full of riot police sits outside while television camera crews and newsmen patrol around the edges filming for colour and hoping for a bust-up and good copy for the evening news – a depressingly familiar scene wherever English fans gather abroad. But nothing is going to happen today. The Munich 1860 fans have stayed away as have the local Turkish population. With no one else to goad it is time to pick on Billy again with another chorus of 'Stand Up if You Hate the Scum'.

In the middle of the afternoon, the first black man I have seen in the company of the Lads enters the bar with another man with longish hair and a moustache who looks like one of the German undercover cops from the airport. They stroll around the bar, looking at the various groups of Leeds Lads. Once in a while the black man, who is dressed in black jeans and a white polo shirt, with a small rucksack slung over his shoulder, stops for a chat. Billy waves to the visitor. 'Hi, Stan, how's it going?' he calls.

Given what I have already seen and knowing of Leeds' reputation for racism, at least among some of the club's fans, I say to Billy, 'He's a brave lad coming in here among this lot. Who is he?'

'Oh, that's just Black Stan,' Billy replies. 'He's Leeds' undercover Old Bill. A bit of a joke really. I suppose it's part of Leeds' attempt to clean up its image – having a black bloke working with the hoolies. All the Lads know who he is, but he seems to get on all right.'

Most professional clubs in England and Scotland have policemen with special responsibility for co-ordinating anti-hooligan activity. These are known as Football Intelligence Officers (FIOs) or 'spotters'. They have two related functions. They try and get to know the fans by mingling with them and getting a feel for their behaviour patterns. This way they hope to spot trouble coming and, if possible, use this knowledge and a rapport with the fans to prevent it happening. As well as this liaison role they also identify and gather intelligence on the most serious troublemakers, particularly the Category C types who organise and co-ordinate the most serious hooligan incidents. FIOs were introduced in the 1980s when their work was confined to domestic duties. They were first used abroad in 1990 when England played in the World Cup in Italy and have been increasingly involved in policing hooliganism abroad ever since. As we shall see, the pervasive use of these undercover police spotters, particularly abroad, was something that would dog my own investigations.

Billy told me of a scam that the Leeds Lads had pulled on Stan on another away trip. The Lads were drinking in their own hotel bar when Stan wandered in for his usual look and learn. One of the Lads chirped up and said, 'Hey, Stan, see you're in the same hotel as us.' Stan nodded his head. 'No I'm bloody well not,' he said and made the mistake of telling them which hotel he was in. As soon as Stan left, a group of about 20 legged it round to his hotel, got his room number and camped in the bar where they proceeded to drink away the afternoon, running up a £300 bar bill on Stan's account.

Billy has just finished telling me this when a tall, broad-shouldered man, with brushed-back fair hair walks into the Schiller Bar and grabs him by the shoulders. For a second I think Billy's about to be arrested, until he smiles broadly and says, 'Mick! I thought you'd turn up here eventually.' It turns out that Mick is a grafter like Billy and the two have worked a lot together, not so much around football, but mainly on the European rock concert circuit. Mick explains that he is in Germany flogging unlicensed T-shirts outside Foo Fighters gigs. Mick tells me that if anything, the rock concert scene is more lucrative for the swag workers than football. 'Been there, done that, bought the T-shirt' is surely a cliché most suited to the rock and roll industry. If you have been to see the Stones in Paris in 2000 it is expected that you will buy a decorative and dated T-shirt proudly proclaiming your presence there. Of course the concert promoters prefer punters to buy the official gear from their own licensed agencies inside or at the entrance to the venues. This does not stop people like Mick and Billy getting thousands of counterfeit products and flogging them in surrounding roads and car parks. Later Billy confides in me that Mick had trained to be a Catholic priest before he quit for the swag trade. Funny how he turned out to be a man of the cloth after all.

Mick is in Munich working with somebody called Fat Larry who is in a bar around the corner with a couple of other swag workers called Jimmy the Mac and Porno Kev – so named because of his hooded eyes and drooping, Pancho-style moustache, that give him the look of a 1970s porno movie star. We join them for a bite to eat before heading to the game. For an hour or so I sit back and listen as Fat Larry and his gang exchange tales of their adventures, dodging customs and running from security agents in the snide rock and roll and football rag trade.

Billy recalled how before Big Tommy moved into the travel business, the two of them were working the swag around Liverpool FC during one of their pre-season tours in Scandinavia. They had checked into a hotel outside one small town and by chance it turned out to be the one being used by the Liverpool team. They got chatting to some of the players in the hotel bar, but things turned sour when Big Tommy made some less than complimentary comments about the playing career of the then Liverpool captain, Mark Wright. Later that night, when Billy and Big Tommy were settling down to sleep there was a knock at their door. Big Tommy got up to answer it and found Wright and Bruce Grobbelaar at the threshold. More words were exchanged and suddenly punches were thrown. Billy dived out of bed in his boxer shorts and found himself grappling with Liverpool's eccentric Zimbabwean goalkeeper. 'Tommy was boxing with Wright and I was trying to restrain Grobbelaar. I had him in a headlock and even though he couldn't move he kept saying to me, "Watch it, sonny, I'm a bush fighter. I'm a bush fighter!" [referring to the time he spent with the Rhodesian army's special forces]. Eventually we managed to calm them down and we finished up the night back in their room having a drink with them and John Barnes.'

Mick also happens to be a Leeds fan and Billy gives him a ticket for the game. In return for this Mick volunteers to help Billy sell the two dozen or so snide Leeds United shirts that he has brought with him. Wanting to assess the quality of these counterfeit shirts, I buy one from Billy for the £20 asking price. I cannot see any obvious difference between the snide and the real thing, except that it would have cost me closer to £40 in the Leeds United souvenir store. When I got home I gave it to a Leeds fan, a PE teacher mate whom I play football with, and he still wears it proudly. Of course, I neglected to tell him it was a snide and he is none the wiser!

I wait in a beer tent outside of the ground as Billy and Mick work their swag. Inside, the ageing but still mightily impressive Olympic Stadium is about three-quarters full but few, if any, 1860 supporters have come to fight. The match itself is a cagey affair that Leeds manage to shade thanks to a second-half Alan Smith goal. The most exciting moment of the match comes at half-time when German police spotters single out three Lads in the Leeds end who have been captured on the Hofbräuhaus's security cameras giving Nazi salutes. The police send in a snatch squad and instead of watching the second half, the three wannabe members of the Hitler Youth are hauled off to jail. Just before this I notice black Stan on the pitch behind the goal pointing up into the Leeds crowd. 'Stan's obviously not such an easy touch as the Lads think he is,' I say to Billy as we watch the protesting fans being led away.

At the Irish bar after the match, Benny and his Lads arrive back in twos and threes. None of them are wearing any Leeds colours – too easy to be identified by the enemy – but they wear a uniform of sorts. Dark designer leisure shirts and windbreakers and expensively anonymous baseball caps. It turns out that there had been a bit of a skirmish outside a bar near to the ground, the outcome of which caused dissent in the ranks. It seems that the Lads were badly outnumbered and, when the 1860 mob charged them, the more seasoned campaigners, including a brother of one of the men murdered in Istanbul, decided to leg it. At least one newer recruit had stood his ground against the 1860 fans' charge and had a bottle smashed over his head for his trouble. He managed to escape and miraculously, apart from a bad headache and ringing in his ears, found his way back relatively unscathed. He berates the rest of the gang for being chicken and they him for being a 'dickhead' for not knowing when to cut and run when heavily outnumbered. For a moment it looks like they might start fighting among themselves. Benny calms things down and the Lads spend what is left of the night talking about the fight that never was and embellishing their roles in it.

The next day, back at Munich airport, waiting for my passport to be checked, I find myself in line behind Brownie, one of the more loud-mouthed and obnoxious Lads. As he passes his passport over to the German immigration policeman he turns to me and says, 'Hey, you were in that bar last night, weren't you? I got hold of some great charlie there. Did three fucking lines. It were great.' The policeman just looks at him as if he's a piece of dog dirt and hands his passport back, relieved, I'm sure, to see him and the likes of him leaving the country. Once inside the departure lounge there is time for another gallon of lager before the flight takes off. Brownie provides the entertainment by loudly recounting his adventures last night in a 'brass house' with his fat, red-faced, bald mate whom he humiliates for not being able to consummate his liaison. 'I couldn't believe it,' he shouts, 'she were a fucking Paki and he went with her and we're from Bradford!' Brownie certainly had a way with words. 'Cost him £90 for a Paki and couldn't even throw a fucking mix, could he?' I will be glad to be home.

All in all then, a good trip for the Lads. A lot of drinking, plenty of sex for sale, a minor scrap after the game and Leeds through to the first round proper of the Champions League. It has also been a very good trip for ITL. Nobody hurt or arrested and no damage done to any of the hotels. Not a bad trip for Billy either. He has got the Lads there and back safe and sound and with Mick's help sold all of his snide Leeds tops, pocketing more than £300 profit. The best news is for Big Tommy himself: Leeds are through and there will be at least another three Scum Airways trips for the Lads in the next few months; this, of course, is also good news for me as I intend to burrow deeper inside the Lads' and grafters' worlds.

ENDNOTES
1 King, M. & Knight, M., *Hoolifan: 30 Years of Hurt* (Edinburgh, Mainstream, 1992) p. 93
2 Varley, N., *Park Life* (London, Penguin, 1999) p. 140

# 4

## Amsterdam, November 2000

I HAD TO DRIVE THROUGH THE NIGHT TO MANCHESTER TO catch Scum Airways' morning flight to Amsterdam. The airport was busy with its regular business traffic and package-holidaymakers hoping to fly off for a little late-autumn sun before the winter set in. Their ranks were swelled by hundreds of Manchester United supporters making their way to Holland for their club's encounter with PSV Eindhoven in the Champions League.

ITL has a group of about 20 going out on the 11.20 a.m. KLM flight to Schiphol. Big Tommy was hoping for a bigger group, but most of the regular travellers are saving themselves for the later stages of the competition in the early new year. Lower than anticipated demand means that Tommy's wallet has taken a hit. Expecting more travellers, he bought up 100 tickets on the black market, paying £70 a piece. Big Tommy leaves 20 in an envelope at the KLM desk to be picked up by Mikey Williams, one of Manchester United's top ticket touts. He is now stuck with 50 that Tommy's instructed Billy to try and sell in the departure lounge, on the plane itself, or later in Amsterdam and Eindhoven. It will be a tough sell because the tickets are all in the PSV end. Big Tommy recognises that, in the touts' game, the adage 'you have got to speculate to accumulate' is the rule of thumb and that once in a while touts, just like stock market investors, will get stung.

Just as with any other product, successful football match ticket sales are dependent on demand and the buyer's understanding of the elasticity of the market. This market is controlled from London where the biggest touts have their headquarters. Finals notwithstanding, the European ticket market is particularly hard to gauge as the market responds to a number of different factors including location, pedigree of opposition, stage of the competition and the history of European adventure of the fans themselves. When the draws for the European competitions are made, Big Tommy rapidly has to weigh up which of the fixtures are most likely to attract large numbers of away supporters. He has flights and hotels to book and tickets to mop up and the earlier he starts doing all of this the better are the prices that he can get. A big European capital is likely to be more attractive than a provincial town and a high-status, pedigree team will pull in more punters than a little-known, one-season wonder. The big teams in the big cities are bankers. Leeds or Manchester in Madrid or Milan, for instance, is bound to pull in the punters. Big Tommy also has to consider the curiosity factor: on the surface, Kiev in November might not appear to be the most attractive trip, but if fans have never been there before, this is likely to attract a certain kind of ground-hopping/adventure-seeking supporter. In addition, there is the legend dimension. Lisbon or Prague may not be home to the Continent's most high-status clubs, but fans that have been to these cities for past European games have always had a fabulous time. Word rapidly gets round to other fans who are then more likely to want to go there should Porto or Sparta come out of the hat next time round.

Then there is the level of European education of the fanbase to consider. A decade ago for instance, before United were firmly re-established as one of the most formidable clubs in Europe, those fans who could travel tended to do so to every European match their team qualified for because it was still a relatively new experience. Also, a combination of unpredictable play and a tighter competition structure meant that they did not know whether or not there would be a second phase for their team, or a place for them in Europe the following season.

Similarly, this seems to be the current mentality of the Leeds fans as they follow their team's early adventures on the European stage. Every game for them might be Leeds' last in Europe and this is why they have proven to be such good customers for Big Tommy. Manchester United's travelling support have become a little more discerning. They are now used to European success, have been there, done that, and of course bought the replica kits. Also, many understand that the way UEFA have rigged the tournament to suit television, sponsors, and the accountants of the big clubs, it is virtually certain that a team of United's stature and TV-audience potential will go beyond the first phase and qualify for next season's competition. These supporters save their money, anticipating the bigger and better games against some of the champagne clubs later in the tournament.

PSV Eindhoven in the first phase was never going to be a huge draw for Manchester United's away fans. With Amsterdam within easy striking distance it scores quite high on the location factor but pretty low on most other measures, which is why Tommy's left with tickets on his hands. There are some die-hard supporters, though, who go to every overseas away game regardless of its status, and ITL has a few of these on this trip. As we wait for the delayed flight in the bar of the departure lounge these supporters entertain the rest of us with tails of derring-do going back 20 years set against a backcloth of cities like Moscow, Kiev, Barcelona, Istanbul, Rio and Tokyo. While there are some individual differences, the stories all have the same structure and follow a similar narrative, involving heavy drinking, petty theft (usually through 'steaming' the duty free – charging through the shop in a large group, grabbing anything that comes to hand before flooding past the cash registers and disappearing into the crowd), adventures in the red-light district, skirmishes with local fans and thugs, and run-ins with police, customs and immigration officials. Somebody usually gets left behind in a police cell or bordello, but eventually everybody returns home to their loved ones and to work, eager for United's next global adventure. Some in the past may have been Category C Lads, but now with thinning hair and thickening waistlines it's more about escaping, having a laugh and staving off the mid-life crisis than looking for serious aggro.

Lardy Les is the last to arrive, having been delayed in the long-stay car park waiting for a shuttle bus. Les is a big-time swag worker who lost thousands at the 2000 Champions League final in Paris when he had all of his snide gear confiscated by the police and was hit with a hefty fine for the unlicensed selling of shirts with the UEFA logo on them. As if things were not bad

73

enough, Les copped for a triple whammy when he was fined by customs at Calais for taking too much currency out of the country. Les is not really working this trip but he's brought a bag full of pin-badges to cover his expenses. There is good money to be made out of badges. Pins can be sold for a couple of quid but when bought in bulk cost virtually nothing. Also, they take up little space in your luggage and there is a good market for them, particularly among fans who recoil from ostentatious displays of club loyalty but like some discreet reference to their fidelity on their Hacket sweatshirt or Stone Island bomber jacket. It is a bit of a busman's holiday for Les, whose wife is in tow for some sightseeing and shopping in the Dutch capital. A second honeymoon of this kind is the last thing on the minds of most of the rest of the Lads – they are more interested in Amsterdam as a venue for a second stag party.

Though small in number, PSV still promises to be a good trip for this detachment of middle-aged men behaving badly. Eindhoven is only about an hour from Schiphol Airport, so can easily be done in a day or a night. If fans had wanted to stay overnight there, there are quite a few reasonable hotels to choose from, but they are not likely to satisfy most of Big Tommy's clients. The match is important for them but it is also an excuse for a few days of unrestrained self-indulgence in Amsterdam, Europe's capital of hedonism. Listening to their conversations and eavesdropping in on their mobile-phone calls it is clear that several are self-employed, businessmen and professionals. It seems that apart from supporting their team, they use Manchester United's forays into Europe as an excuse to get away from the restrictions of work and home – to overindulge in drinks, drugs and prostitutes. 'This is my eighth trip,' one tells me. 'It's fucking great!'

There are also a few football anoraks on the trip – or 'straight members' as Big Tommy refers to Category A supporters – and in the light of the police crackdown on Bs and Cs this is a market that Tommy is more than happy to cultivate, even though they are not as much fun as the Lads. Frannie is typical of these. He is a placid, easygoing character, whose life revolves around supporting Manchester United and running a Sunday league football team in north Manchester. He's 52, divorced and has two grown-up daughters. For the duration of this trip Frannie will be on the edge of the action: looking, but not touching or buying. Likewise, marginal to the Lads and the middle-aged men behaving badly troop are a few social misfits for whom supporting Manchester United and being part of the Lads scene, if only off-stage, is life's main anchor.

One is Jim, a gangly, shaven-headed 20-something who rolls his head and avoids eye contact at all times. He is a late substitute for his father, a 20 st., small-factory owner who's travelled with Man U home and away since 1969. But his wife's been rushed into hospital and he has reluctantly decided not to travel to Holland. He looks gutted as he leaves his son at the ticket barrier. For a living Jim 'looks after things' at his dad's factory in north Manchester. 'In fact they call me "Jim Who Looks After Things",' he tells me earnestly. On this trip he will end up rooming with Clancy, a small man from Peterborough with a retro 1970s hair-do, an out-of-date Manchester United top and grubby jeans. One of his legs is slightly deformed and he shambles around Amsterdam after Jim in a passable imitation of Dustin Hoffman's Ratso trailing after Jon Voigt's Midnight Cowboy. Throughout the whole trip I never saw Clancy without at least one drink in his hand.

On the outbound journey the ITL mob are all casually and anonymously dressed and there is hardly a replica kit in sight. I ask Billy whether there will be any trouble. 'No, not with this lot,' he tells me. 'There'll be plenty of boozing, and there'll be a few drunks, but there are no real bad Lads on our trip. There are a couple of small firms that'll be showing out in Eindhoven, but I don't think there'll be any bother. There's no real history with the PSV lot.' Billy explains that these firms will either have made their own way there in ones and twos using a variety of routes or travelled in a larger group sorted out by Rocket O'Connor.

I would come across Rocket later in the story. He is a similar character to Chelsea's Icky who used the independent travel business as a way of shifting his gang of Headhunters around the country during the 1980s. Making money for Icky was incidental to being at the centre of the action. In similar ways and for similar reasons, O'Connor facilitated the movement of one of United's top firms of which he remains a key member. Rocket and Big Tommy may have started their journeys at the same point, but were now heading in different directions. It was already becoming clear to me that while Big Tommy still had regard for the hard-core Lads with whom he had started out in the travel business, he was endeavouring to move away from a reliance on them and attract more straight members.

As we shall see, one reason for this is his growing desire to give his image a makeover – to go from grafter to respectable businessman. Another, perhaps more significant factor, is strictly business. Since the introduction of the Football Disorder Act it has become increasingly difficult for the hard-core Lads to travel abroad. The political setting for this draconian piece of legislation involved Euro 2000 and England's ill-fated bid to become hosts for the World Cup in 2006. The British authorities were concerned that with the proximity of the Low Countries it was inevitable that Euro 2000 would be a big draw for Category B and C hooligans, particularly with England scheduled to play Germany in the opening rounds. With the events of Marseilles in 1998 in mind, there was real concern that England's reputation would be severely damaged if there was a repeat performance in Brussels or Amsterdam. This fear was exacerbated because of FIFA's impending decision (made in early July 2000) on whether Germany, South Africa or England would host the World Cup in 2006. The English bid was already struggling and any major hooligan incidents during Euro 2000 would be the final nail in England's 2006 coffin. Hence the impetus for Jack Straw's hastily cobbled together legislation. Unfortunately for him Parliament was too busy to get the Act passed before the start of Euro 2000 and could have had little or no impact upon subsequent events in Belgium. For the record, largely for reasons of arrogance, perfidy and poor diplomacy, England's bid was dead before the first plastic bullet was fired in Brussels or plastic chair thrown in Charleroi. All these hooligan episodes achieved was to give England's inept and morally dubious campaign team a smokescreen under which to slink off.[1] But by then the new anti-hooligan legislation was well on its way to becoming law, which it did in July 2000.

To summarise the key features of the Act, the courts are able to prevent individuals who have been convicted of a football-related offence from attending matches at home and abroad (these are banning orders). In addition they can now ban those who have caused or contributed to any kind of violence or disorder in the UK or elsewhere, where the court believes that such a banning order would help to prevent violence or disorder at football matches. People who get involved in a fracas in their local pub or get done for being drunk and disorderly down town on a Saturday night, in addition to any other punishment, can find themselves banned from attending football matches at home and abroad. Also the police can now stop individuals leaving the country and refer them to court for a banning order hearing if they suspect they have caused or contributed to violence and disorder and might constitute a threat to public order at football matches. Even if the police do not have any hard evidence upon which to build a case for a banning hearing, they can detain someone for up to six hours while they make further enquiries – which is tough luck if you are trying to catch a flight!

This Act extends previous legislation that focused only on those convicted of football-related violence, and empowers the police and through them the courts to stop fans attending matches at home or overseas on the basis of suspicion and belief. Those convicted can be banned for between two and ten years and if they break their banning order can be sent to prison for six months and/or fined up to £5,000. It also has implications for fans who manage to get out of the country to follow their teams abroad. For a wide variety of reasons, some of which are not even remotely connected to actual hooliganism, fans can be stopped and questioned by foreign police who share intelligence with their UK counterparts. Once their names have been taken abroad, fans can end up on the NCIS (National Criminal Intelligence Service) database back home, sometimes for doing nothing more serious than being found without a match ticket or not having their passports on them. Such lists are then circulated around Europe making it very difficult for labelled fans to follow their teams. Despite the furore coming from civil rights groups concerned with the way this Act infringes upon civil liberties, human rights appeals to the High Court against banning orders have been thrown out.

On the plane I finally get to meet 'Alehouse' Williams, one of the go-betweens I used to track down Big Tommy. Alehouse, who has the build and face of a retired middleweight boxer, seems to know most of the people on the plane. He is a leading figure in the North West swag trade and has a bag full of shirts with him to sell in Holland. Alehouse is a bit of a folk hero in grafters' circles. He is legendary, amongst other things, for his opportunism and poor spelling. When, after the 1998 World Cup finals, Manchester United signed the France goalkeeper, Fabien Barthez, Alehouse immediately printed hundreds of snide T-shirts and goalkeepers' tops with 'Bartez' on the back of them.

Alehouse is just a small player in the counterfeit goods business. It is estimated that globally the trade in counterfeit goods generates around £250 billion. As much as £60 billion of this circulates in Europe, of which the UK accounts for approximately £8 billion and is viewed as the counterfeiting centre of Europe. Trading Standards guess that as much as 10 per cent of all clothing worn in Britain is fake and a huge slice of this market is in sporting goods. Alehouse and his mates make a nice earner out of Manchester United. For this trip Alehouse has a large blue football kitbag packed to the gills with fake replica shirts and other snide shirts that reproduce the Manchester United logo and trademark. In 1999 the club's anti-fraud team seized fake replica shirts worth more than £2 million – and they were only the ones that they found. But as fast as they seize them Alehouse and the other grafters source more from illegal workshops in Leicester or from sweatshops in the Far East.

I went to Manchester United to talk to the people who are responsible for policing this trade in counterfeit gear. They work from a small office tucked away in a flat-roofed, red-brick warehouse next to Old Trafford's north stand. Manchester United no longer have a club crest, they have instead a brand mark that cost the club more than a million pounds to register. Before this, people had been able to trade legally in goods that bore Manchester United's crest, claiming that this was a badge of affiliation and loyalty. Now that 'Manchester United' is a trademark such trade is outlawed. Angela is the Club's Trademark Manager and Elaine is her assistant. I was confronted by a photograph of a bare-chested David Beckham adorning the wall above the two women's desks and couldn't help noticing that, pinned to a display board, were what looked to be home and away copies of Manchester United's new team shirts. In 2002 the club abandoned its long-standing relationship with Umbro in favour of a multi-million-pound deal with Nike. One of the unwanted by-products of the marriage of the brand name of the biggest football club in the world with the globally sought-after Nike swoosh was a dramatic boom in the counterfeit market for the latest shirts.

In fact, the shirts that I saw in May were snides. The public launch of the real thing was not scheduled until June. Angela explained how, back in February, they had organised a closed showing of the new kit for the press. No cameras were allowed, but the next day artist's impressions of the new shirts appeared in the tabloids. In less than two weeks the first counterfeit shirts appeared on the streets of Bangkok and not long afterwards they were being worn in and around Old Trafford. 'Those who buy them like to think that they are genuine and have come out of the back of a factory in Taiwan,' explained Angela, 'but look closely and you can tell they're fake. Anyway, the real ones are being made in a factory in Morocco.'

Manchester United have five hit-squads that operate around the ground on match days, closing down counterfeit traders and confiscating their material. They pay particular attention to grafters that they see on a regular basis, but there are not many of these regulars. Just like drug dealers, the main players do not sell the product themselves, they have a series of runners who do the work for them. Rarely do they use the same ones on consecutive weeks. However, Angela and Elaine recognise that most of the snide shirts are sold well away from the ground. 'It is getting more and more difficult to control. It used to be that we could get intelligence of container loads of the stuff coming into the country that we could then grab with Trading Standards and police at the port of entry or some warehouse,' Angela told me. 'Now it tends to come in by the van-load. They just drive up to the back of a factory or club and let it be known that they have some gear to sell which they do out of the back of the van in the car park. It's costing the club millions.' If such trade is hard to control at home it is virtually impossible to do so for Manchester United's away trips. Which is why Alehouse and his fellow grafters are such devoted away supporters.

After an incident-free journey we arrive at Schiphol International Airport. Alehouse collects his swag off the conveyor and is waved through with the rest of us: nobody questioning the fact that he appears to have enough luggage to be staying for a month rather than the two-night stop-over that he is actually on. We board our coach to be bussed into the city to the Eden Hotel on the banks of one of Amsterdam's many canals. Harry, Big Tommy's partner's teenage son, has already arrived with four of his mates. They had come on the overnight ferry from Hull. Claiming to be part of the ITL party (which they were not), they bunked into the room reserved for Billy and me. Billy cleared them out, but would not let them go until they had paid bills that they had already clocked up watching the pay-per-view porno movies. The lanky quartet postured like junior Lads: all testosterone and smouldering animosity, dressed up in dark designer casual wear, expensive trainers and coolly anonymous baseball caps. Three of the group would later be arrested by the police in Eindhoven.

Once everybody's checked in Billy and I trek across town towards the red-light district . Billy has been in Amsterdam many times, sometimes staying for several months. He obviously knows the city very well and makes a good tour guide, particularly when it comes to the seedier side of 'the Dam'. This is my second trip with Billy as a courier and my second time rooming with him. By now I have come to know him pretty well and we seem to be getting along fine. We decide to stop for a cold beer by the side of a canal and watch the world pass by. After Billy has explained a little more about the city, its music scene and its nightlife, I decide to ask him about the pink scar that stretches from beneath his left ear, through the sandy stubble under his chin, to the edge of his windpipe.

Billy's explanation takes me aback. He tells me that it had happened years ago back in Manchester when he must have been about 17 or 18. 'I was living with a brass [prostitute] at the time, but she was also involved with some other bloke who was a bit of a nutter. One night – it must have been about four in the morning – I heard all this shouting down in the street outside the flat we were sharing. I went downstairs to find out what was going on. When I opened the door the bloke rushed at me and swung something at my head. I didn't realise then that it was an axe.' Instinctively Billy turned his head to one side, but his assailant's axe caught him a glancing blow across the side of his neck. 'There was blood pissing everywhere,' Billy continued. 'He ran off and I managed to stagger to me mate's who took me to hospital to be patched up. They wanted to keep me in for observation, but I was having none of it. Instead we went home and got a few of the lads together, got tooled up and went looking for him. We found him in his flat with some of his mates. Honest, it was like a scene from *The Three*

*Musketeers*, with knives, swords, machetes – the lot. Eventually his mates legged it and we grabbed him. I helped to hold him down and one of the lads held his arm across the kitchen table while another chopped off all the fingers of his right hand with a hand-held scythe.'

By then somebody had called the police. Billy was arrested and done for GBH. He was too young for adult prison and did a stretch in Borstal. He came out and was soon arrested again, this time for football violence. After a second term inside Billy decided to do his best to stay out of trouble. He started to play regular Saturday football which gradually took him away from Manchester United's top hooligan gangs where most of his problems started and settled down with a steady girl and had a couple of children. Decent-paying jobs for a young man with little education and without a trade did not exist so Billy moved into the grafters' game. OK, he knew that at best lots of the things he did by himself or with or for Big Tommy were at best marginal, but he felt that they were not the hard-core kind of things that would get him sent down again. In Billy's and Big Tommy's community, given the levels of criminality that were endemic, compared to what else was on offer, becoming a grafter was in its own way a fair attempt at going straight. We drained our glasses and headed for the red-light district.

Amsterdam's combat zone can come as a bit of a surprise to the newcomer. Unlike in Britain, where prostitution is illegal and where areas frequented by prostitutes are usually in the filthiest and most run-down quadrants of cities and towns, the red-light district in Amsterdam is quite tastefully integrated into the centre of the Dutch capital. It is not much more than half a dozen narrow streets that criss-cross the city's network of canals, it's about half a mile from the main railway station and just around the corner from the Anne Frank house. It can be quite startling to be strolling along a street looking in the windows of antique shops, jewellers, boutiques, and galleries to suddenly find oneself staring at one or more full-figured females, naked but for small G-strings, beckoning passers-by to come inside for a sample. Just a tap on the window and it is unlocked. As the punter steps inside a curtain is discreetly pulled across, preventing his performance from being a public one. A short time later the curtain is thrown back once more, the window reopened and our hero steps back onto the street a few guilders lighter.

Eventually, most of the Lads and grafters turn up in one or other of the bars like the Sailor or the Grasshopper at the fringe of the red-light district. Billy introduces me to Dotch (Dogherty), a notoriously unorthodox Manchester City fan who comes along with the Manchester United Lads for the hell of it. Dotch is an ice-cream man who should never be allowed out, let alone near children. His rationale for travelling with Manchester United is a bit like the cover story I gave to the Leeds Lads on the Munich trip. City have not played in Europe for decades so without actually supporting Manchester United, he has hitched his wagon to them so he can travel around Europe having some crack with the Lads. Even so, he is rarely seen in their midst without his Manchester City shirt.

Dotch has been banned from going to Manchester City games because of his persistently bad behaviour and one particular episode stands as Dotch's Andy Warhol moment. In the mid 1990s he was at a City away game at Crystal Palace's Selhurst Park, when City were in free-fall and on the verge of being relegated into the Nationwide League's second division. The Maine Road men had a free kick on the edge of the Palace penalty area. Nigel Clough was in the process of teeing the ball up when Dotch leapt out of the crowd and rushed over to confront the player. Dotch grasped his own replica sky-blue City shirt (no doubt snide) above his heart, a gesture that questioned Clough's and his team-mates' commitment to Dotch's beloved club. He then picked up the ball, turned and smashed it into the back of the net. 'That's how you fucking well do it!' he snarled at Clough junior before disappearing back into the roaring crowd of City fans behind the goal. This incident was captured by the television cameras and although it caused him to be banned it made Dotch a legend among the Manchester City faithful.

Billy also introduces me to Brooksie, a manic, jester-type figure with a high forehead and thick, oily black hair. He rolls a fat joint and passes it round. Like Alehouse, Brooksie's got a sack full of shirts that he is hoping to sell the next day in Eindhoven. He is constantly pestering Billy to use his contacts to sort him out with some 'charlie' (cocaine). Soft drugs are legally obtainable in Holland, but the police take a dim view of the harder variety and crack down hard on those who deal in it.

The relationship between the grafter's culture and the drug dealers' world is hard to figure out. For one thing it looks and sounds the same: lots of wheeling and dealing on mobile phones, conducting the buying, selling and movement of a wide variety of stuff. Big Tommy claims that he moved into grafting around football as an alternative to getting involved in the drug scene, and all of my evidence specific to him suggests that he is telling the truth. But I am less certain that this rule can be applied to all of those who graft around football. It would be astonishing if those who share in this world are solely concerned with making money out of football. In Munich I had already seen how football and the rock-concert scene overlaps for the swag workers. In Amsterdam I was beginning to suspect that drugs may also feature in their world. More than once there had been heavy hints dropped that Liverpool's top firm were involved in drug smuggling around football. Even though Big Tommy had good contacts with those who did the Liverpool Lads independent travel, he warned me off going away with them. 'Problem with the Scousers, John, is that they're in the import and export business, if you know what I mean,' he once told me over the phone. I had been asking him about one of Liverpool's trips to Turkey – incidentally the main European supplier of heroin to a UK market believed to be controlled by gangsters from Liverpool. 'They're all charlie-heads. You start sniffing around them and what with your accent they're bound to take you for Old Bill. They'd do you in as soon as look at you.'

Certainly, the NCIS (National Criminal Intelligence Service) believe that the kind of football culture being described in these pages can be a gathering place and flag of convenience for serious villains of all descriptions. In a press release issued in August 2001, Bryan Drew, Head of Specialist Intelligence at NCIS, said:

> While football hooliganism is rather different from other organised criminal activities where profit is the main motive, it has developed into an increasingly mobile problem bearing many of the characteristics of other more serious areas of organised crime. As well as being violent it is also highly organised and attracts other serious criminal activity such as drugs dealing and counterfeiting. Travelling supporters provide a market for drugs as well as cover, through weight

of numbers, for drug dealers. We think that payment card fraud may
help these organised groups finance travel and other costs. This is the
21st-century face of football hooliganism.

Already it had struck me that there were no neat, cut-and-dried distinctions to
be made between grafters, Lads, and out-and-out villains. It seemed that
many of the Lads used a number of petty and not so petty criminal activities
to fund their trips abroad with their teams. At the same time, football itself
was the target of a variety of fraudulent activities to the extent that such trips
could often be at least self-funding. I put this to Mark Steels, NCIS's Head of
Corporate Communications, and he confirmed my suspicions. 'When we
stopped looking at the crime and started looking at the criminals it was open
sesame. We realised that a lot of the hooligan generals– as the ringleaders like
to call themselves – were involved in organised crime. Mainly low-level stuff,
counterfeiting, drug dealing, amphetamines and stuff like that. They had a
ready-made network for doing this. A Chelsea gang could go up to Newcastle,
for instance, and be tipped off as to which pub they could go to buy cocaine.'

I already had little doubt that these big European away fixtures were
important gathering places and sites for communication among a rich variety
of underworld characters that went beyond the game itself. I had no intention
of burrowing too deeply into this terrain because it was too dangerous.
Nevertheless, I would have good reason to reflect upon the overlap between
Big Tommy's world and the more pernicious and predatory activities of vice-
land later in my journey.

Meanwhile, the middle-aged men behaving badly bunch had been filling
their boots. Three of them spilled into the Sailor, tripping over one another,
roaring and shouting. They spotted Billy and I and tumbled over to recount
their window-shopping exploits. 'Three fucking times, with three different
birds he's done it,' exclaims one, gesturing towards his mate who is grinning
broadly. I suspect much of the boasting is youthful bravado. Judging by the
way our hat-trick hero is having trouble standing up I think that at least one
poor working girl has made easy money tonight.

Strait-laced Frannie is fascinated by the sights and sounds of the red-light
district. He does plenty of window shopping, but doesn't take the plunge. He

claims to be worried about contracting AIDS and won't take the risk even when Billy explains to him about the rigorous checks carried out on the city's working girls. 'Never paid for it in me life,' boasts Frannie.

'What d'you mean, "never paid for it"?' laughs Billy. 'That divorce cost you a fortune and you're still paying for it now. Difference is you're not getting it!'

The next day is match day, kick-off in PSV's stadium at 9 p.m. local time. This leaves a long day of boozing ahead. Billy loads up the coach at 11 a.m. Competing with cars, trams, buses, bikes and barges, we edge our way through Amsterdam's narrow streets and out onto the motorway for the hour-and-a-half journey to Eindhoven. I look out of the window across the miles and miles of reclaimed land noting the tidiness of the tree- and dyke-lined countryside. Across from me on the bus slumbers Clancy, who appears to be sleeping while clutching an open bottle of Carlsberg in each fist. Like the dormouse at the Mad Hatter's tea party, every once in a while Clancy stirs, takes a gulp out of one or other bottle and nods off back to sleep.

Eindhoven is a neat and tidy conurbation of less than half a million souls, symmetrically arranged around a large cathedral that overlooks the town's main square. It took a pounding during the Second World War when it was a key centre of the Nazi occupation. As a main staging post for the German blitzkrieg into neighbouring Belgium and France at the start of the war and a key objective for the advancing allied forces after D-Day, Eindhoven was virtually flattened by both armies. Today it is rebuilt and looks like the prosperous and well-organised town that it is. Eindhoven is a company town and its prosperity is dependent upon the fact that it is the main centre for the manufacture of Philips electrical goods and home to Philips's company headquarters. PSV (Philips Sport Vereniging) are a one-team advertisement for the company, as is the modern Philips stadium that, along with the cathedral, dominates the city's orderly skyline.

Today's occupying army are the Reds. The Scum Airways party spill off the bus and eagerly merge into their massed ranks in the bars and cafés in and around the town's main square. I had been here for England's ill-fated encounter with Portugal during Euro 2000 and was not surprised when Billy made straight for the Crown and Shamrock, one of the town's two Irish bars, to check if any of the Lads were in town. Despite the xenophobia and anti-

Irishness that is often associated with the Lads, they have a tendency to use Irish bars abroad as their temporary headquarters. 'No Surrender to the IRA', may be a favourite chant of the English hooligan firms, but the open-plan layout, non-continental ambience, English-speaking bar staff, English papers and TV coverage and, of course, familiar beer, make the network of ex-pat Irish bars ideal for the Lads' European tour.

The pub is crowded both inside and out. Billy spots a few people he knows and we join them at their table. He has still got most of Tommy's tickets to sell on and he manages to pass a few on to one of his fellow grafters who offers to try and move them for him. 'I'll see what I can get, Billy, but I doubt you'll get more than face for Eindhoven end.' Billy just wants to get rid of them and nods his approval, before passing over an envelope full of tickets.

I remembered being in this pub for one of England's games during Euro 2000. Then I knew very little about the extent of police surveillance into hooliganism. I had a big camera hung around my neck and a press pass. I was taking a few colour shots of beer bellies and tattoos when three lads demanded that I take their photo. I was happy to oblige and they asked me what paper I was with. 'No paper,' I quipped, 'National Criminal Intelligence.' They almost lynched me! I hastily explained that I was only joking, telling them that if I really was an NCIS spotter I would hardly broadcast it. Thankfully they accepted my explanation and sheepishly I beat a hasty retreat.

We take a walk around the square and spot Alehouse, Dotch, Brooksie and a few other grafters having a few beers in the afternoon sunshine. We stop for a bit of banter and Billy manages to shift a couple more tickets. We walk around the corner and immediately I realise that we have stumbled upon one of the Reds' Category C firms. Not a colour in sight, just dark bomber jackets and designer baseball caps. Billy knows this mob but is very reluctant to let me get amongst them. 'Some bad Lads here, John,' he tells me, 'better steer clear.' One of the Lads spots Billy and comes over to talk to him. I step to one side. Ignoring me, he starts talking to Billy. I cannot help but overhear. It seems that there is a bit of a panic on back in Manchester. Some of the Lads have been running a major counterfeiting scam with forged first-class rail tickets between the north of England and London. The serious crime squad along with the railways police had busted the operation and it looked certain that one or more of the Lads would go down for it. Billy starts to look uncomfortable and not wanting to compromise him I walk away. Not for the last time it strikes me that the NCIS's analysis of the cosy relationship between football and organised crime is sound enough.

Billy talks with him for about ten minutes before rejoining me. He doesn't talk about the train ticket scam and I don't ask him. He tells me that this firm are in town looking for trouble, but that they do not think PSV's firm are up for it. Certainly there are very few PSV supporters on the streets before the game. The only significant Dutch presence is that of the police who, like during England's visit during Euro 2000, are plentiful, integrated, and laid back. With an average height of 6 ft. and a fearsome reputation, few doubt, however, that if trouble does start they are more than capable of finishing it. It was not so many years ago when Leeds played here that more than a hundred travelling supporters were arrested and repatriated for being drunk and on suspicion of being a threat to public order. No doubt some of those arrested were trouble-makers. Nevertheless, many innocent fans found themselves handcuffed and herded onto coaches before being deported without their belongings, which were left in hotels in Amsterdam and Eindhoven.

For me, the most memorable thing about the game itself was that United lost. Alex Ferguson thought he would try out some of his fledgling players, leaving the likes of Giggs, Keane and Beckham on the bench. PSV went through the Reds' midfield like it wasn't there and before Ferguson could do anything his team were 2–0 down; they went on to loose 3–1. I sat in the middle of a row of United supporters, themselves in the middle of the Eindhoven end. The United supporters around me – not a scarf or bobble hat in sight – seethed and squirmed but could not express their feelings for fear of being identified. As an Evertonian and a fully paid-up member of the ABMUSC (Anybody But Manchester United Supporters Club), I felt a sense of delight at the English champions' humiliation. Only my self-interest in seeing the research through prevented me from jumping up and down with the PSV lot. The travelling United fans were furious with their team's manager. 'Didn't pay all this money to come and watch the bloody reserves,' fumed Frannie on the bus back to Amsterdam.

It is well after midnight when we get back to the Dam. Unless you are in the know it is difficult to get a drink in Amsterdam after 2 a.m. Billy, of course, is in the know and we head off down backstreets with Frannie in tow. Eventually we arrive at a Thai bar which is full of ladyboys. With lots of Adam's apples on view I pick up straightaway that they are not women but slender oriental men in seductive women's clothes, but Frannie doesn't catch on until he spots a particularly unfeminine one coming out of the ladies. ''Ere, she looks like a bloke,' he says.

'Frannie,' I reply, 'they're all blokes.'

He looks around in disbelief and picks out a tall, slender, high-heeled figure with long black hair, huge silicon-enhanced boobs and a face like Mike Tyson's sparring partner. 'Aye, but she's not a bloke, is she?' All I can do is smile and think that Frannie needs to get out more. I would think of Frannie months later when, after a late-night encounter with a ladyboy in Bangkok, I had cause to reflect that maybe I should stay in a little more.

This was my depth-immersion in to this strange world of touts and louts. I had learned a lot more about the Lads and grafters on this trip, but my abiding memory is of middle-aged men behaving badly. In the past, if you were invited to a stag party it usually meant a night on the local town, a few extra pints, and your mate left tied naked to a lamp-post at 2 a.m. If you were really lucky you took in a strip show or had an overweight strip-a-gram turn up at the Dog and Duck. These days it's not unusual for gangs of lads to jet off for the weekend to wreak havoc in cities like Dublin, Paris, Prague and, of course, Amsterdam. In effect, helped by Big Tommy and his ilk, the Champions League has turned into a rolling series of stag parties for the over 30s. The football provides an excuse and cover for getting away from the constraints of home and work and indulging the senses fully. I was beginning to understand that when this kind of Englishman is abroad the rules do not count. I am certain many of the people, on this trip and other ITL packages, at home would not usually be seen roaring drunk in public at 10 a.m., nor would they be abusive to hotel employees, customs and immigration officials, or single women walking down the street. They would certainly take more notice of the police at home and most would not dream of walking into a pub in Manchester smoking a joint and asking the barman where the nearest brothel was. Take the same people to Munich, Amsterdam, Madrid, Brussels or Istanbul and anything goes and local rules, customs and those that defend them are treated with contempt. Sharing the Lads out-of-structure experiences – as the anthropologists would say – 'ballooning' or 'having a laugh' – as the Lads put it – can be exhilarating and fun. However, quickly and easily, the carnival can turn nasty and become extremely dangerous both for those on the inside and for those at the receiving end of the Lads masquerade.

ENDNOTES
[1] Sugden, J. & Tomlinson, A., 'International Power Struggles in the Governance of World Football: the 2002 and 2006 World Cup Bidding Wars', in *Japan, Korea and the 2002 World Cup*, ed. J. Horne & W. Manzenreites (London, Routledge, 2002)

# 5

## Brussels, February 2001

THE UNEVENTFUL RETURN FLIGHT FROM AMSTERDAM ARRIVED back in Manchester at 10 p.m. I was tired and had intended to check into one of the several hotels that ringed the airport before driving south in the morning. Unfortunately there was no room at any inn, leaving me with little choice but to once more drive home through the night. It was with mixed feelings of exhilaration and relief that I arrived at my house at 3 a.m. in a sleeping village on the edge of the Sussex Downs. I was relieved because I was out of the field and safely back home to a world inhabited by bank managers, city brokers, school-teachers and retired colonels. The exhilaration came from my field worker's instinct that told me that I was now burrowing deep into a world that was in a different solar system to that of my neighbours – the world of Big Tommy.

Driving through the night I kept myself awake by drinking coffee and Red Bull and by wrestling with a problem that had been growing the more intimate I became with Big Tommy's operation. At this point in my research the idea of a television documentary was still on the table. In addition to getting the narrative facts of the matter, part of my task was to advise Nick on possible story lines and plausible and articulate characters who might look good on film. I realised the original idea of a television documentary just about ticket touts would only capture a fragment of the fascinating subculture that I was beginning to uncover and the larger-than-life characters who dwelt in that world. While I was certain there could be a compelling documentary about all this, there was so much going on either directly or indirectly connected to Scum Airways that was, to say the least, marginal to the law, that I could not imagine being able to film it without going completely undercover. Even if I wanted to make my research fully covert I was already 'known' by the inner circle and this ruled out undercover work with this particular gang. There is so much networking in the grafters' trade that it was likely, should I choose to try and infiltrate another mob, say, for instance, in London, that I would, sooner rather than later, have my cover blown.

When I have done research like this in the past my working principle has always been to be up front at the outset and let the key gatekeepers know what I am doing. Then I work hard to help them to forget this by becoming a helpful part of the furniture. This, for me, was the key to good participant observation (as sociologists call this kind of research). As well as being more ethically defendable than fully covert research, it was also useful as an escape route should things get dangerous. If I ever get too close when the Lads decide to steam the duty free or take on Inter's Ultras, I want to be able to remind somebody that I'm a researcher rather than a foot soldier, and fade away without arousing too much suspicion.

Another question that was troubling me was: what was in all this for Big Tommy? At least part of the answer to this was to do with ego. No matter who we are or what we do it is usually flattering to have somebody take an interest in our lives. I think the Big Man was flattered by the idea that a university professor and a television producer wanted to write a book and make a film about him. I was equally sure, however, that there was a particular version of himself that Tommy would like to present for public consumption. If Tommy consented to have cameras and microphones follow him around, he would surely only present a carefully self-edited version of himself and his business: more Del-Boy Trotter than Ronnie Kray. This was confirmed when he allowed us to make a short demo-tape that we wanted to use to help to sell the idea of the programme to a TV commissioning editor. Out came the South Manchester accent and on went the charm. 'Lads? What Lads? Hooligans? No, not me.' Big Tommy came over like the respectable businessman that his front-stage persona was eager to become. The cameras would not be allowed backstage and without this the TV documentary idea was looking shallow.

In honesty, the more I thought about this the more I began to hope that the programme would not be commissioned. The main reason that I had gone along with the documentary idea was that I was hoping to have a TV company pay for my research. Otherwise I was operating on a shoestring budget, much of which came out of my own pocket. I still had a lot of work to do, but already I knew that there was a good and important story to be told and that cameras would only get in the way of my own backstage research. For me there is an important difference between investigative journalism and the kind of investigative social anthropology that I do. Investigative journalists are usually only interested in digging the dirt and showing the bad and the ugly. After all, this makes headlines, sells newspapers and attracts television audiences. Likewise, I am interested in the bad and the ugly, but accounts of the ordinary and the good are also interesting dimensions of the whole canvas. I was increasingly forming the view that with cameras in tow I would be under pressure to distort the picture. On balance, I decided that I would rather pay my own way and get good material for this book, rather than be paid for and miss the plot. What was I going to say to Nick?

As it turned out events were to take this decision out of my hands. In autumn 1999, before my research into Big Tommy's world had seriously begun, as part of the *MacIntyre Undercover* series, the BBC had broadcast a documentary made by their reporter Donal MacIntyre. He had gone undercover to investigate the activities of Chelsea FC's notorious Headhunter hooligan gang. Using concealed cameras and microphones, MacIntyre and several other BBC journalists secretly filmed football violence, the organising of fights, links with the National Front and related ultra-loyalist and neo-Nazi organisations, including the Ku Klux Klan. In order to get close to the central members of the gang, MacIntyre rented a top-of-the-range Mercedes and, interestingly – given what I have already written about football, organised crime, and drugs in the previous chapter – posed as a wealthy drug dealer. Clearly for the Headhunters there was nothing unusual in fraternity between top Category C hooligan generals and drug barons. Indeed, one of the main targets of MacIntyre's investigation already had a long criminal record, including a conviction for importing drugs. To help to convince the gang of his authenticity, MacIntyre even went as far to have a Chelsea FC tattoo on his upper arm.

Most significantly for this story, MacIntyre recorded the boasting and bravado that accompanied the Headhunters' activities. Released at a time when many people had been duped into believing that the menace of hooliganism was a thing of the past, the programme caused a public outcry. There were few regrets several months later when the police swooped and arrested two of MacIntyre's unwitting informants, Andrew 'Nightmare' Frain and Jason Mariner. I was reminded of the neo-Nazi antics of some of the Leeds Lads in Munich when, on a secret recording, Mariner bragged about a trip that he and Frain had taken to the Nazi death camp in Auschwitz while following Chelsea to Copenhagen. 'I quickly took the photo of Frain doing a Nazi salute, and a Polish geezer started crying,' boasted Mariner. 'I think I put the final nail in the coffin when I tried to get into the oven.'

The two men were charged with conspiring to commit violent disorder and sent for trial at London's Blackfriars crown court. Donal MacIntyre was a key witness for the prosecution and his film was used in evidence. On the basis of MacIntyre's testimony both men were found guilty of planning violence at a game between Leicester City and Chelsea and trying to disrupt a march through London in commemoration of Bloody Sunday. Frain and Mariner were sentenced to seven and six years respectively and banned from attending football matches for ten years.

I have no sympathy for either of the convicted men. I have seen too many of their type in action and I believe that they got what they deserved. What I do have a problem with is MacIntyre allowing himself and his research to be used by the authorities to secure Frain and Mariner's convictions. I always thought that it was an unwritten rule of investigative journalism that you do not, except in exceptional circumstances, compromise your sources by delivering them to the police. It is actually a written rule of sorts for the professional body that informs my work, the BSA (British Sociological Association). Clause 40 of its statement of Ethical Practice (published in March 2002) states, 'during their research members should avoid, where they can, actions which may have deleterious consequences for sociologists who come after them'. I may, during the full course of this research, violate many of the BSA's principles, but I was determined that this should not be one of them. By being heavy-handed, judgmental, moralistic and, as in MacIntyre's case, legally censuring, you not only shut down important future avenues of enquiry for yourself, but you also make it difficult, if not impossible, for others to gain access to life and times on the dark side.

As it is, it is hard enough to gain access to deviance-style research. By all means, if there is heinous villainy afoot, tip the police off, but let them carry out their own investigations and gather their own evidence. MacIntyre's programme, I believe, was still a skilled and important piece of journalism that alerted the public to the fact that not only has hooliganism not gone away, but that it has been born again with more sinister dimensions than it displayed in its first life in the 1970s and 1980s. It also made a good general case that would help the police and related authorities frame measures to combat this revived menace. In the grand scheme of things, directly helping to secure a couple of convictions is neither here nor there. What MacIntyre's court appearance did do was make the work that I and others like me were attempting to do exceedingly difficult and much more dangerous than it might have otherwise been.

Ever since the police undercover operations that saw top Chelsea hooligans – including Icky – arrested and imprisoned in the 1980s and the release of *ID*, the movie that parodied this kind of undercover hooligan police work, it has been difficult and perilous for sociologists to do participant observation in this field. The danger used to be about being wrongly identified as a police spotter. This, as we shall see, is still a big problem. Post MacIntyre's undercover operation on Chelsea, the Lads became even more nervous and suspicious of strangers in their midst. Even if you could prove that you were not Old Bill, pulling out the press pass or playing the researcher card would not guarantee immunity from a good hiding or worse. As soon as I read about the trial I knew that the TV programme was a dead duck. Whether I would still be allowed access to Big Tommy's world, and whether I would survive long in there if I was, were now my most vexing questions.

When news of Mariner and Frain's convictions broke, I was scheduled to take a Scum Airways trip with the Leeds Lads for their team's game with Anderlecht in the Belgium capital, Brussels. Nervously I phoned Big Tommy to ask him how we now stood in the light of the MacIntyre affair. 'I'm sorry, John, there'll be no cameras,' he told me. 'The Lads won't have it, they're all a bit nervous and you can understand that, can't you?' I agreed, but was still apprehensive about my position.

'What about me, what about my research for the book, Tommy?'

The Big Man hesitated, but then said, 'No, no, you're sound, John, I've got no probs with you, you'll just have to be a bit careful what you say to people. You still coming to Brussels?'

I was mightily relieved. At one level the MacIntyre trial had made my task easier by getting the cameras off my back, but at another level my fieldwork had become even riskier. It was with these thoughts in mind that I packed my bag and set off for Belgium.

Unlike previous trips, when I had met up and travelled with one of Tommy's parties, this time I decided to make my own way. The Eurotunnel rail terminal at Ashford in Kent is only 40 miles or so from my home and from there you can catch Eurostar directly to Brussels. Big Tommy was chaperoning his main group over on the Wednesday morning of the game. I decided to get there a day earlier, to get to know the lay of the land and try to sniff out some other groups of Leeds Lads. Tommy booked me in the same three-star hotel as his group close to the centre of town. I checked in early evening and set off to see who was about.

I knew the city pretty well as I had been based here for a week or so during Euro 2000. For the most part Brussels looks like what it is – the centre of Europe's Kafkaesque bureaucracy. It is a tidy, low-level city of joined-up Whitehalls linked via wide, tree-lined roads, interrupted by tidy squares and parks. Only the very centre reminds the visitor that Brussels was once one of medieval Europe's finest merchant towns. It is now Brussels' main tourist attraction and it was there that I thought I might find some of the Leeds Lads' expeditionary force. Gran Platz, a large cobbled quadrangle surrounded by a fairytale architecture of turrets, gargoyles, musical clocks, gilded spires and stained-glass and leaded windows, was once home to the old city's most prosperous merchants; most of the buildings have long since been converted to restaurants, cafés and bars. During Euro 2000 this square had been packed with rival bands of football fans who occupied all of the bars and drank and sang beneath colourful canopies of flags and scarves under the watchful eyes of the City's nervous and notorious 'Robocop' riot police – as the well-armoured and robot-looking security forces came to be known.

That evening, as the light began to fade, there was not so much as a football scarf or replica shirt in sight. When in doubt find the Irish bar. I remembered that during Euro 2000 the Ingerland Lads had set up one of their headquarters in O'Reilly's, on Boulevard Anspachlaan, opposite the Bourse (the old city's treasury). Then, after a series of skirmishes, the Robocops had gone in mob-handed beneath a hail of tear gas, bludgeoning and arresting anybody they could lay their hands on before unceremoniously herding those who weren't to be sent for trial onto planes and flying them back to England. A young American couple enjoying a tour of Europe for their honeymoon got caught up in this random sweep and ended up with an unscheduled post-nuptial visit to Stansted!

O'Reilly's had been closed for the duration of the tournament. I remember standing outside its boarded-up windows the night that Turkey beat Belgium and knocked them out of the championships. Brussels has a substantial Turkish population and a sizeable number had turned out onto the street in front of the Bourse to celebrate the Turkish humiliation of the joint hosts. I tried to imagine a similar scene in London if Turkey had knocked England out: Trafalgar Square mobbed with Turks rubbing the England supporters' noses in it. There would have been a massacre. Here the Belgium fans stayed away. The few non-Turks at the party were media who performed their usual act of whipping up emotions by diving into the crowd with television cameras and bright floodlights. Not wanting a repeat of the riots involving the England fans, the city's mayor had told the police to keep a low profile the night of the Turkish victory. They could be found off-stage in large groups sitting in and around their transport, relaxed, but with helmets, shields and batons at the ready.

I was beginning to lose interest when a group of about 50 young Turks took flight down a narrow street towards the main square. A nearby French camera crew took off after them and, with little idea of what was going on, I tucked in behind. Following the mob, we moved from doorway to doorway, like a British army platoon through the streets of Belfast. Anything or anybody that got in the way was pushed over, smashed or dented. As I took cover in a shop doorway one young Turk stomped across the bonnet and roof of a new BMW parked in front of me. Glass could be heard shattering everywhere. Having ignored many other restaurants and cafés, for reasons not immediately apparent to me, the mob suddenly halted their running rampage for a focused attack on a corner-house bar. Two burly bouncers took refuge inside as the mob advanced hurling stones and bottles through the bar's windows while the startled customers took refuge upstairs. Things were getting very ugly when the unmistakable rhythm of many batons tattooing plastic shields gave the crowd early notice that the Robocops were on their way.

It was a formidable sight as they approached in flanks down several streets simultaneously, battering and scattering any of the young Turks that got in their way. Not wanting to be trapped, somehow I managed to get around the back of one rank of the riot police. From behind they were less scary. It was almost comical as the sergeant tried to keep his men in a straight line. One poor lad tripped over his shield and his helmet fell off. More like a scene from *Dad's Army* than *Full Metal Jacket*. This show of force was enough to discourage any further Turkish attacks and the mini-riot fizzled out as quickly as it had started.

Later that night I returned to the Lop Lop, one of the bars that briefly had been under siege. It turned out that there was a small group of England fans drinking there. Ever since Manchester United's 1993 'Welcome to Hell' reception by Galatasaray supporters, including attacks on players and fans, there has been bad blood between English and Turkish fans. The murder of the two Leeds supporters in Istanbul intensified this enmity. Some of the England fans had taunted some of Brussels' migrant-Turkish population during Euro 2000 with a racist chant that insulted two ethnic groups: 'I'd rather be a Paki than a Turk'. That night the young Turks had been seeking retribution. There were only seven England supporters in the bar and they rushed upstairs as the windows went in under the Turkish mob's assault. A similar story was told by Thierry de Groot, the owner of the nearby Au Pot Carré, as he brushed up the broken glass from the pavement outside his bar. 'The English were totally faultless. They had been drinking quietly, then the Turkish stormed the bar!'

This had all happened before the framework of this book had been fully formed in my mind. Then my ideas were restricted to investigations solely around ticket touting. I had hoped to meet up with Big Tommy and some of the Lads I had met in Marseilles who were supposed to be floating around the Low Countries spivving tickets. As it happened, because England went out in the qualifying stages, the ticket market slumped and Tommy stayed at home. It would not be the last time he would let me down on a field trip. As it happened I did bump into Ricky (the short-arm typist) in the main square in Eindhoven while he was doing tickets for England's game with Portugal, but he only had time for a brief conversation. We arranged to meet up some time later once Big Tommy had arrived, but because the Big Man never showed, this plan went out the window as well. That was about the extent of my inside scoop on the ticket touting during Euro 2000. Well, almost.

All was not lost as I still had my other project to work on – England's bid to host the 2006 World Cup. As ever I was on five-star hotel-lobby watch trying to track down any of the hierarchy who might have an involvement with or perspective on England's by now spluttering bid. The ITV media circus were using the Brussels Sheraton as their Belgium HQ. I had discovered this by chance when late at night, before the opening game between Belgium and Norway, I had wandered in and been attracted by the racket coming from the Piano Bar. It was the unmistakable sound of a bunch of lads having a booze-up. At first I thought it had been occupied by a bunch of hooligans. I was only half-right. 'Big' Ron Atkinson was having a bit of a session with Terry Venables, Des Lynam, Ally McCoist, David Pleat, Barry Venison and a whole bunch of ITV producers, technicians, and make-up artists. Champagne was the order of the night and it flowed like water. As the night wore on the party got louder and louder. I eventually left to the sound of Big Ron leading a chorus of 'My Way'.

After this encounter I made a point of dropping by the Sheraton at the end of most nights to check out who else was in town. Apart from that first night, expensive though it was, the Piano Bar was a bit of an oasis of calm and a good place to chill out after a long day in the field. So it was to there that I headed after running the streets with the young Turks. I arrived there about half past midnight pretty exhausted. Propping up the polished mahogany bar I ordered a beer and turned to see if any of the football famous had come in for a nightcap. I rather hoped that no one had as I was knackered and did not really want to have to try and inveigle my way into somebody's company who probably did not want to talk to me anyway.

It was then that I spotted Tony Banks sitting in the shadows by the piano in one of the leather upholstered easy-chairs. I know him vaguely as when he was minister for sport he had been decent enough to attend the launch of a book about FIFA that I had co-authored with Alan Tomlinson. He had given up his role as minister for sport to front England's bidding team for the 2006 World Cup. This was always a high-risk appointment. 'If you've got nothing to say then say it,' seemed to be Banks' philosophy. On this night he had the haunted look of a man who had swapped a seat on Concorde for a berth on the *Titanic* and had just spotted the iceberg coming. Tired though I was, this was an opportunity that I had to pursue, so I approached his table and introduced myself. Fortunately he recognised me and invited me to join him for a few minutes. I knew I would not have long, so I briefly explained my interests in him and his latest work. The date for FIFA's decision was very close and Banks promised to talk to me in greater depth and detail once that decision had been made. He then finished his toasted sandwich, excused himself and went off to bed leaving me sitting with his minder: a big, powerful-looking 50-year-old who goes by the evocative name of Ned Kelly.

Kelly, who is ex-SAS, is the boss of Special Projects Security (SPS) and had been hired by England's 2006 campaign team to look after VIPs like Banks, Bobby Charlton and Geoff Hurst who were helping to promote the bid. Kelly's main concern, however, revolves around his company's responsibility for security at Manchester United. We chatted for a while, during the course of which I mentioned my interest in ticket touting and particularly the activities of Big Tommy. When I mentioned him, Kelly laughed. 'I know Big Tommy,' he said. 'You realise he's a millionaire, don't you?' I doubted this, but did not say so at the time. Kelly took his leave and I went back to the bar. What I had not yet realised was that if Big Tommy was making a fortune, at least part of it might have been generated through his dealings with Kelly.

More than a year and a half passed before Ned Kelly's name came up again. It was a Monday morning and I was in Manchester to catch up with Big

Tommy and make some plans in the run-up towards the 2002 World Cup. Tommy picked me up in his brand-new Mercedes and we sped off towards his new offices in Newton Heath. Before getting to the office we had to drive to a downtown hotel to drop off some United match tickets for a group of businessmen visiting from Norway.

As we drove, the Big Man kept his mobile phone on audio and I was treated to a more or less incessant parade of calls about tickets. There were, however, a couple of other calls that were even more interesting. 'Tommy, have you heard about Ned? Sounds bad, doesn't it?' There was a panic on in the Manchester touting circles because Ned Kelly, Manchester United's head of security, had been suspended from all duties by the club after allegations made in a Sunday newspaper which, amongst other things, linked him to ticket touting.

Under a front-page headline, 'United Chief is a Tout', the *Sunday Mirror* went on to detail how two of their reporters – one a glamorous woman – posed as PR consultants who wanted match tickets and executive hospitality for high-rolling overseas clients. It is claimed by the *Sunday Mirror* that Kelly demanded £5,000 for two executive boxes that usually sell for £1,500 apiece and £50 each for five £28 tickets – a deal that if it had gone through would have netted him more than £2,000 profit. Allegedly Kelly then further compromised himself by telling the undercover reporters sensitive secrets about the club he was hired to protect, including a series of indiscreet revelations, half-truths and lies about some of the club's most famous players and their families. The paper also claims that Kelly made racist jibes about other clubs and their fans.

All this was a bit much from a man who was brought into the Manchester United fold in 1990, at least in part, to lead a crackdown against ticket touts. The response of the club was to suspend him immediately pending an investigation. As we drove out of town I asked Big Tommy how much of a player Kelly was. The Big Man was evasive, but it was clear that Kelly was well known by the touts and had been one of a number of Manchester United insiders from whom they harvested their tickets. A few months later I would recall this conversation when I was standing outside the Maritim Hotel in Cologne. The previous night Manchester United had 'lost' their Champions

League semi-final to Bayer Leverkusen through the away goals rule. As I waited for a taxi to take me to the airport a small, stocky man walked out of the hotel and came up to me. He was freshly pink from the shower and wore a smart open-neck pale-blue shirt, grey slacks and a blue blazer, on the pocket of which he had fastened his diagonal, blue-and-red-striped clip-on tie with the SPS logo on it. He was here as part of the security team for Sports Tours who had brought over a few hundred fans of the game. Sports Tours are independent of Manchester United but often hire SPS people to supervise their business trips.

'Anybody seen a small, drunk, bald bloke in a blazer like this?' he asked nobody in particular. 'Can't find him anywhere and we had to check out the room ten minutes ago.' He then raised his hands to ruffle his short red hair. 'Bloody hell, feels like someone's playing baseball in me 'ed. We had some bloody night last night. Started out in those bars over there,' he said, gesturing towards a row of buildings opposite the hotel. 'Bloody gay bars they were! Anyway, we soon got out. I think we had to get a taxi. Ended up in a whorehouse somewhere. I went with this bird. She gave one of the best lines I've ever heard. She said, "I use three condoms, why you no go whoosh, whoosh!" I just laughed and said, "Cos I'm pissed, luv, but keep trying!"'

The little man then proceeded to give a brief seminar that could have been entitled 'How to spend loads of money in brothels and lap-dancing clubs around the world without the wife finding out'. When he had finished I asked him if he worked for SPS and he told me he did, usually as security at Manchester United's home games. I then asked about his boss. 'What about Ned? Is he still suspended by United?'

'I saw him last Friday,' he replied. 'He'll be all right. The club has cleared him anyway I think. It were a right well-fit bird that stitched him up, you know. You know what Ned's like. He told them that he would have done or said anything to get into her knickers. Knowing Ned he probably would too! Anyway, the club believed him.'

I checked this story out with Manchester United. A spokesman would not comment as at the time of asking, because even though the club had finished their investigations into Kelly, the Greater Manchester Police had not concluded theirs. However, I gleaned enough to suggest that he would be kept on, if only because SPS had grown to be an integral part of Manchester United's security operation. Big Tommy was not so sure. It was rumoured that Kelly had further blotted his copy book by supplying tickets to a notorious Salford gangster who was serving a life sentence in Strangeways. The lifer used the tickets as sweeteners for his contacts on the outside who were still running his criminal affairs. If this were found to be true I found it hard to believe that Kelly would survive.

Back in Brussels, whether or not the Leeds–Galatasary/England–Turkey feud would have any influence over tomorrow night's encounter between Anderlecht and Leeds was something that I thought about as I made my way to O'Reilly's, itself located at the fringe of the city's Turkish quarter. O'Reilly's is typical of its genre: large, with a high, polished hard-wood bar, bare plank floor, barrels for tables, and a variety of Irish bric-a-brac hanging from the walls and ceiling. Generic fiddle-dee-dee music blends with the hubbub of a bar busy with its regular city-types, having a drink on the way home from work. I had guessed right and the bar was fuller tonight because of the many Leeds fans that had joined them.

Many sat or stood close to a big screen on which that night's European Champions League action was to be shown. For the moment it was showing *Sky News* from London. I mingled with the supporters near to the bar. Most seemed to be Category A, straight members, in town to enjoy the game, take in a few of the sights and enjoy some Brussels mussels, washed down with some of the country's famously strong beers. But there was a couple who looked to be up for a bit of trouble. I recognised one of them from my first Scum Airways trip to Munich. Leo is somebody not easily forgotten: he's tall and hefty, with a round and well-weathered beetroot for a face. Although a Leeds supporter Leo was from Leicester. He had been useful for Big Tommy when Leicester had qualified for the UEFA Cup and Leo had put the Big Man in touch with a band of Leicester Lads who had used ITL for the club's – albeit short – European campaign. The last time I saw him in Munich he was so drunk he could barely stand up. He was not much better now and neither was his shaven-headed mate. They got louder and more abrasive and insulting as the evening wore on. While the Turks provided one of the main themes for their racist jibes, anybody foreign, including the Belgians, was fair game. The bar staff – veterans of Euro 2000 – had seen it all before and called the police. Remembering the Brussels police's indiscriminate approach to disorder, and not wanting to end up back at Stansted, I made a strategic withdrawal before the cavalry come over the hill. This was a good example of how the antics of a few bad Lads can sour the atmosphere and lead to more extensive trouble. The problem with a pub full of football fans, particularly overseas, is that because club and country partisanship and patriotism are close relatives of aggressive sectarianism and nationalism, it does not take much of a spark for trouble to flare and the flames to spread. Hooliganism thrives on an 'us versus them' mentality and the demonisation of 'the other'. Once abroad there are plenty of 'them' about. Often, all it takes is for a couple of troublemakers, like Leo and his mate, to shout a few well-targeted insults, run the flag up the mast and wait for the reaction. Once this comes, other fans can get drawn in, the press, television and police turn up and from the ensuing chain reaction it is not long before there is a fully blown hooligan incident. The local papers the next day reported that there had indeed been trouble at O'Reilly's overnight with several Leeds supporters arrested. I hope this included Leo and his mate.

I got back to the hotel to discover that it was also being used by Leeds United's official travel club. They were less than impressed to find themselves cheek by jowl with Big Tommy's lot, not least because the Scum Airways package is much cheaper than their own. Stuart Priestly, the boss of Leeds United Travel, complained to me that although they ask not to be billeted with the likes of ITL, often these requests are either ignored or made impossible to implement as the independents use local agencies and book hotels in different names.

Tommy himself arrives the next morning at about 11 a.m. He marches into the lobby overwhelming the reception desk, sequestering room keys, barking out orders to his flock and dishing out match tickets. I recognise Kenny and his firm and soon Benny and most of the rest of the Munich boys file in. As soon as the Lads are checked in they are out on the beer. Kick-off is not until 9 p.m. and that leaves plenty of drinking time. Tommy tells them where to go and arranges to meet up with them at 6 p.m. back at the hotel.

He tells me that he has got another flight coming in with some customers on it and asks me to come with him to the airport to meet them. We jump in a taxi and speed off to Brussels Airport. There are half a dozen or so Lads on a flight from Leeds–Bradford, but more significantly, there are two grafters, Jed and Joey, coming in from Manchester who are going to work a scam with the Big Man. It turns out that at the Manchester United versus Sturm Graz game, they had managed to steal several VIP hospitality badges and a bunch of distinctive Champions League camera crew vests. Tommy was offering special 'executive' packages to some of his more tried and trusted Leeds clients. Jed and Joey were to do the rest and I was there to witness it.

The Leeds flight landed first and the Lads – all bomber jackets and baseball caps – gathered in the arrivals lounge as we waited for Jed and Joey's Manchester flight. I was quite happy for them to view me as one of Tommy's gofers, but as the Manchester passengers began to filter through I was startled to hear a Northern Irish accent addressing me. 'Och, John, what about you, what are you doing here?' I turned to see Brian Hamilton, the former Everton player and Northern Ireland player and manager, alongside Gerry Armstrong, another former Northern Ireland player and Brian's assistant when he managed the international side. They were in town as commentators and pundits for BBC Radio Five Live's and Eurosport's coverage of Anderlecht versus Leeds. I knew both of them quite well. While researching another project I had flown with the Northern Ireland team when they had played a World Cup qualifier against Albania when Brian and Gerry were in charge. Only the weekend before this trip I had been in Northern Ireland participating in a conference on the future of football in the Province. Brian also participated and we shared workshops and had dinner together. He looked more than a little askance at the company I was now keeping. The Leeds Lads in turn were eyeing me suspiciously. I had to usher Brian and Gerry to one side. 'Sorry, Brian, can't talk now, I'm kind of undercover, I'll tell you about it later.' They shook their heads, turned and left.

'Bloody hell, John,' said Tommy later, 'you don't half pick your moments to meet your media pals!' I mumbled an apology. Eventually, and much to Big Tommy's relief, Jed and Joey cleared customs and walked into arrivals with Jed carrying a small hold-all in which were concealed the stolen vests and passes. Tommy ordered a small fleet of taxis and we made our way back to the hotel to meet up with the rest of the Scum Airways group. We arrived in time to see the official Leeds travel club supporters being marshalled by stewards in bright blue and yellow Leeds United tracksuits cum shell-suits. Most of these fans were decked out in replica Leeds gear, most wearing either the white home or the yellow away replica shirts with the cider company, Strongbow, emblazoned across the front, all bought at full price.

In contrast there was not a Leeds scarf or shirt to be seen on the Scum Airways Lads who were mostly casually dressed in the familiar non-uniform uniform of designer shirts, dark bum-starver jackets and anonymous baseball caps. Big Tommy led us towards the Brussels metro, as the officials were herded towards their waiting coaches for their police-escorted journey to Anderlecht's compact Parc Astrid stadium. The Lads did not usually wear Leeds gear anyway because this made them easy for potential enemy firms to spot. Anderlecht's ground holds less than 20,000 and tickets had been hard to come by. Most of the Scum Airways tickets had been procured by Big Tommy on the local Brussels market and were in the Anderlecht end. The police had mounted a big operation to keep the fans segregated. They would try and prevent anybody wearing Leeds colours from getting near that end of the small stadium.

This presented Big Tommy with the strategic problem of how to get his customers on the other side of the police blockade. In addition, the VIP and press entrance was towards the Anderlecht end and Jed and Joey's 'executive' customers would need to be taken round there also. Tommy's idea was to get off the metro one stop before the ground and walk the rest of the way under cover of the darkness and drizzle that was falling from the night sky. The police were ready for this move and almost as soon as we came out of the metro station they picked us up, hemming us in on horses and motorbikes to make sure that we arrived at the Leeds end of the ground. Tommy told the Lads to break up into groups of three and four and make their way through the police lines to the other side of the ground.

It was not so easy for Big Tommy to hide his giant frame. Soon he was spotted by a police inspector from Leeds who was helping with the local crowd control operation. He was watching Tommy like a hawk. The Big Man talked to him and lied, saying that he was waiting for Billy who he had left in O'Reilly's with our tickets. The inspector told Tommy that he would radio through to Stan – Black Stan, Leeds' Football Intelligence Officer, who I had met in Munich – who was in O'Reilly's, and check whether Billy was on his way with our tickets. At this Big Tommy decided to make a strategic withdrawal. After a couple of unsuccessful attempts at sneaking through, he shouted, making sure that the policeman could hear, that he had had enough and was going to get a taxi back to the hotel.

With that he flagged down a passing taxi. Jed, Joey and I piled into the back as Tommy settled his ample body into the front seat. Tommy stabbed his finger towards the stadium and said, 'Other side of ground, other side of ground,' to a rather bemused cabby. Big Tommy was speaking in that loud, over-accented voice that monolingual Brits specialise in when dealing with foreigners. The police had many of the side streets blocked off and try as he might the cabby was struggling to make any headway. At one point, having zigzagged back and forth down a series of residential streets, we arrived back where we started and were once more surrounded by Belgian and British police. Big Tommy obviously subscribed to that school of thought that believes if you don't get through to Johnny foreigner the first time, then say the same thing again only louder. 'No, no,' yelled the increasingly exasperated Mancunian. 'Other side of ground. Anderlecht end.' The cabby spun away and tried again. After 15 minutes of mind-boggling twists, turns and reversals we were dropped off near to the far end of the ground.

Jed and Joey went off to case the VIP and press entrance while Billy and I went looking for his 20 or so VIP customers. Eventually we rounded them up and waited for Jed and Joey to return. Jed came back on his own. They had found the gate and, as he put it, 'sweetened' the attendant to turn a blind eye while they smuggled the Lads through. Joey was now on the inside waiting for the first batch of Lads. This would be done in groups of four and five. I stood with Tommy and Jed in the rain behind a hot-dog and burger stand helping to put the silver and black-starred Champions League camera crew vests on the Lads. Jed took each batch off and chaperoned them through the gate. Once inside, they were met by Joey who took off their vests, pinned hospitality badges on them and took them through to the VIP lounge where they had access to as much free food and drink as they wanted. Once in the VIP lounge Joey took back the hospitality badges and then went back to the gate and passed them along with the vests to Jed who legged it back to Big Tommy to suit up the next batch.

It looked like a perfect scam except for what seemed to be a major omission spotted by one 'executive' customer. ''Ere, Tommy, without tickets where do we sit when we come out t' hospitality lounge?' he asked as the Big Man fitted his vest. 'Don't worry,' replied Tommy, 'go straight out into the stand and you'll see the seats reserved for the players' wives. A lot of them don't turn up, especially on a dirty night like this. Just pick a seat and enjoy the match surrounded by some top crumpet!' Once the last of the batch had been smuggled in Tommy turned to me and asked me if I fancied going in too.

This was a difficult one for me. On the one hand I wouldn't have minded seeing the game and actually living the scam from top to tail would have given my research an even deeper level of authenticity. On the other hand there were legal and ethical issues. Thus far in my insider dealings with Scum Airways I had managed to stay more or less within the law. Jibbing my way into the game in the way described would have been illegal and from an academic researcher's point of view decidedly unethical. There was also my recent memory of my encounter with Brian Hamilton and Gerry Armstrong at the airport. I had, on occasion, enjoyed official press and hospitality status at Champions League and international matches. The thought of bumping into some senior UEFA official or journalist who knew me while sneaking in with Big Tommy was not my idea of fun. 'No, not really, don't fancy it for much of a game,' I eventually replied.

'Good,' he said, 'let's get a cab, have a few pints and watch the game in that Irish pub, what's it called? O'Reilly's, that's it.' And that is what we did. Joey went straight back to the airport to catch the last flight to Manchester and Tommy, Jed and I sat and watched Leeds secure a surprising 1–4 away victory, securing their passage into the second phase regardless of the result against Real Madrid in the Spanish capital in a few weeks' time.

It was after midnight before the tired but exuberant fans began to drift into the hotel bar. The Scum Airways VIPs were full of themselves. They'd stuffed themselves with food and drink in the hospitality lounge and enjoyed the game in the company of some of the players' wives. I sat talking to Tommy and

Jed about the night's events and other scams. 'I don't know how you get away with it,' I remarked.

'We get away with it because nobody expects anybody to be that cheeky,' Tommy told me, 'and because the officials are either greedy, couldn't care less, or too bloody stupid.'

Jed then proceeded to tell me about a time-honoured fiddle he had set up with corruptible officials of the VIP car park at Barcelona's Nou Camp stadium. Once in the VIP car park there was direct access to the ground via an elevator. Jed claimed to have smuggled in many carloads of fans into the Manchester United versus Bayern Munich Champions League final.

As an example of the naïvety of officialdom Tommy related a classic scam carried off during France '98. Outside of the media entrance to the Stade de France there was a poster that had pictures of all of the categories of accredited media passes with a key to what areas the holders could gain access to. These passes are easier to forge than tickets which these days are manufactured with all the hi-tech security features of bank-notes. One of the touts nicked the poster and used it to produce fully laminated replicas that were virtually indistinguishable from the real thing. They were then sold to the highest bidders. Allegedly one punter wearing one of these forged passes was found in an area on the perimeter of the pitch where only the FIFA president and close associates should have had access! I also remembered the story about England's game with Romania in Lens, when with assistance from the touts, some Lads had jibbed their way into the VIP box with Prince Charles and his sons William and Harry. When I first heard this tale I had doubted it could be true. Now, after a night spent with Jed and Joey, I could see how such a breach of security might happen.

Tommy went off to bed while I stayed in the bar listening to and chatting with the Leeds Lads. I was feeling relaxed after a good night's fieldwork when one of the veterans of Munich wandered over to me at the bar and said, 'I know who you are – you're Old Bill, aren't you?'

I took a deep breath. 'No, no. Don't be daft.' I decided I had to take him into my confidence in the way I had already done with some of the sharper Leeds boys. 'Actually, I'm writing a book about the independent travel business. Don't worry I'm not a journalist and I'm certainly not a cop.'

I do not know if this satisfied him. He wandered off to join his mates and a moment later they were glowering over towards me. Among them was the man who had asked me the Fred Pickering question on the way out to Munich. 'I knew you weren't what you cracked on to be,' he shouted over. It was a timely reminder for me that the moment that you start to feel comfortable doing this kind of work the more vulnerable you are likely to be. As my research continued, it would not be the last shot fired across my bows.

I checked out the next morning and as Big Tommy set off for the airport I made my way to the station to catch Eurostar back to Ashford. As I sped through Flanders, I reflected on my latest adventures with Big Tommy and his chums. By now, apart from the stuff about avoiding 'deleterious consequences', I had broken just about every rule in the BSA's code of ethical practice at the hub of which was the notion of informed consent. I was supposed to tell all of those I was studying what I was up to and give them the right not to participate. I was also required at all times to work within the law. I tried to imagine pulling a stolen Champions League camera crew vest over one of the Lads' heads while saying, 'By the way, you know that this is against the law, don't you? Is it OK if I write about this and publish a book with you in it?'

It was impossible for me to tell most of the grafters and the Lads what I was up to. For a start my main gatekeeper, Big Tommy, warned me enough times that I would be at risk if I did. If I walked around with 'researcher' tattooed on my forehead, most would not talk to me and I suspect a few would fill me in. Either way I would be denied the information I needed for this, I believe, important story. Unlike *MacIntyre Undercover*, a programme that thrives on controversy and condemnation, I had entered the field determined to gather material for a book that would not be judgmental. I wanted to tell the story as much as possible from the grafters' and the Lads' vantage points, in such a way that allowed readers to form their own moral positions about these mysterious worlds and the colourful characters who live in them. This, along with an acute sense of self-preservation, was as close as I would come in my work to adopting an ethical position. The rest I was making up as I went along.

# 6

## Madrid, March 2001

OUT OF THE GRAFTERS' WORLD AND INTO THE EQUALLY mysterious realm of the QAA (Quality Assurance Agency), the university sector's equivalent of the schools' inspectors, OFSTED. I had been asked to head up my department's preparation for its QAA subject review later in the year. In order to gain insight as to how QAA operated I successfully applied to become a QAA subject reviewer. Compared to infiltrating Big Tommy's operation this was a piece of cake. Once on the inside I could use my knowledge of their operation to inform the way we got ready for their scrutiny. It did, however, take my professional and personal schizophrenia to new levels as, both physically and mentally, I flitted betwixt and between stuffy university committee meetings and riotous away days with Scum Airways. What disturbed me most was the fact that increasingly I felt more at ease mixing with the Lads than posing as a QAA inspector.

Also, my university commitments were beginning to slow down my fieldwork. The next trip I could take after Anderlecht was another Leeds away game with Real Madrid the following March. Technically this was a meaningless game because by then both teams had already qualified for the next round. Nevertheless, the Leeds fans were still on a cloud, kept in the air by the unprecedented and surprising progress of their young team. Few expected them to have gone this far and nobody knew when, if ever, they would get this far again. The opportunity to see their team play the legendary Spanish giants in Madrid's Bernabeu stadium was not one lightly passed up and they signed up to go in their thousands. ITL were taking about 700. I took off my suit, shirt and tie, slipped into jeans, T-shirt and bomber jacket and headed for Gatwick.

As I came into arrivals at Madrid Airport the Big Man was there with his ITL sign held high above his head as a beacon to those others in his party who were arriving from Leeds–Bradford and Manchester. This was Tommy's biggest operation since Manchester United's excursion to Barcelona for the Champions League final in 1999. He was in full-blown travel-rep mode, barking out orders, checking lists and marshalling his troops towards awaiting buses and taxis. Being in the middle of large numbers of England football fans as they spill through an airport arrivals concourse can be a formidable and menacing experience. There is an aura of confidence and contempt about them as, like a platoon of commandos disgorging from a landing craft, they move energetically and urgently in packs, brushing aside hapless fellow travellers and discarding beer cans, playing follow-the-leader to the waiting transport. Big Tommy was too busy to bother much with me so I jumped in a cab with a couple of other lads and headed off to my designated hotel, wondering if, without hanging onto Tommy's coat tails, I would get any fresh information from this field-trip. Clearly, the Big Man was my most important gatekeeper and it was through sticking close to him that I hoped to get access to the other grafters and top Lads who were in Madrid for the Leeds match.

I was beginning to miss Billy. In Munich and in Amsterdam he had been a great informant and a good companion. Despite his chequered past I couldn't help but like him. It has been my experience that if you can get to like somebody you have a much better chance of finding things out from that person. Even people who have few redeeming features usually have one or two things about them that can be endearing. As a researcher it is important to find these spots and concentrate on them while shutting out the more heinous qualities of a potential informant's character. In doing this kind of fieldwork there is little room for moralising or political correctness. I may, in my private life, take somebody to task for being racist or sexist in front of me, but I would not dream of doing so while out in the field. If I did I would not last more than two minutes with the Lads. It does not mean that I have to pretend to adopt similar views, but it does mean that I keep my mouth shut. Through experience I have learned that information does not flow without rapport and rapport does not easily emerge without some level of friendship. Big Tommy is a good example. There are lots of things about his current operation and certainly about his past that would not endear him to polite society. Nevertheless, following my 'find something to like' rule of thumb I had grown quite fond of aspects of him and his roguish ways. I believe this helped keep the gate open to the grafters' world and lubricated the flow of information. Once again, this instrumental and, some might say, cynical approach, is probably not within the parameters of the BSA's ethical code, but without it projects like this simply could not be undertaken.

I had similar feelings towards Billy, who I had not seen for almost a year. I was disappointed when Tommy told me that he and Billy had fallen out over money and that he was forced 'to let Billy go'. An interesting way of putting it, I thought to myself. In the relatively short time that I had known Tommy his business had expanded considerably. This was achieved by broadening his target market away from Category C and B hooligan types to include more and more Category A 'straight members'. As this happened the language of the grafter was being shed for the jargon of the businessman. In this regard, as during the progress of my research, Tommy attempted to reposition himself as a legitimate and respectable businessman; street-level and unashamed spivs like Billy were becoming more important to me.

I battled in a scrum-like queue at the Hotel Convention's reception trying to check in along with about 50 other Leeds fans. 'There has been a mistake, Señor,' said the receptionist, checking her lists, 'you have to go to other hotel, Hotel Principe.' With a shrug I turned and went looking for another taxi. The Convention was on the edge of the city centre whereas the Principe was down town. If I were to have to go it alone, I thought to myself, I would be better off there, close to where any action was likely to be.

'No, Señor, we do not have you booked into this hotel,' I was told by the receptionist at the Principe, 'you must see your representative.'

Another bum steer was unfolding before me when my stuttering pidgin-Spanish pleas were interrupted by a familiar Mancunian voice from behind. 'Hey, Suggy, what you doin' here?' It was Billy.

'Never mind me, what are you doing here?' I replied. 'I thought you and Big Tommy had fallen out.'

'Not really. Just a misunderstanding. Business was slow and he didn't have much on for me so I took off to Thailand to do a few shirts. When I got back this trip was coming up. It's a bigun for him, biggest he's done with Leeds. The Big Man needed some help so he brought me in.'

'Good,' I said, 'you can start by sorting out my room. This is the second hotel I've been to and I'm not on anybody's lists.'

'Don't worry,' said Billy. 'There's a spare bed in our room. You can have that.'

It was only then that I noticed Jed, one of the grafters who had worked the VIP scam in Brussels, standing behind him. I learnt that Jed spends most of his time in Spain, usually in Barcelona where he and a Spanish partner run a small event/hospitality company – a cover for a multitude of grafter's sins, most of which are spun around the activities of FC Barcelona. According to Jed, Spain's a grafter's paradise because almost every official is bent or corruptible. Jed looks like he has just woken up after a night sleeping rough in some doorway, but his looks are deceiving. He has a sharp mind and, according to Billy, is worth a fortune. In addition to his business in Spain, Jed has dozens of properties in Manchester. Even so, unlike Big Tommy, Jed is a grafter through and through, with little or no ambition to become a legitimate businessman. Grafting gives him a good living, but more than that, he enjoys the thrill of the chase, the adrenaline rush that comes with masterminding and pulling off a scam. What a result, I thought to myself, rooming with these two should make the trip to Madrid more than worthwhile. I was right.

Jed knows Madrid well and with his guidance we spent a pleasant early evening in the old part of the city chatting while enjoying cerveza and tapas in a couple of small and welcoming tavernas, well out of the way of the gathering Leeds hordes. Post-Franco Spain is a public and friendly culture. People like to sit idly in the shade or to promenade along tree-lined avenues, parks and decorative plazas, stopping once in a while to share a coffee, aperitif, and tapas with friends and neighbours. It is, unfortunately, a culture wide open to abuse by the Lads on tour. Although Spain's coastal resorts have been the favoured destinations of British package holidaymakers for over 30 years, central Madrid is not so used to thousands of young men, many of them drunk, cluttering up its tavernas and spilling onto its walkways, disrupting the gentle flow of everyday life. Big Tommy intuitively understands this and builds it into his business plans. Later in the year, when Leeds United played Valencia in the semi-final, as the following ITL blurb clearly indicates, it was not the prospect of visiting this historic, beautiful ecclesiastical citadel that Scum Airways used to hook and pull in the punters.

Fly out bank holiday Monday morning from Manchester to Valencia. We will then transfer you to Benidorm for one-night stay in a four-star accommodation on Lavente beach in the heart of Benidorm. Relax by the pool in the sun and spend the evening in the rocking bars of Benidorm (remember the holiday season has started). On the day of the game we will transfer you to Valencia for the semi-final. Price includes flights, hotel, transfers. Match tickets (£40) can be supplied with travel.

The next morning, match day, while Jed was dispatched by Big Tommy to rustle up some more tickets, Billy and I set off in search of the Leeds Lads. Billy also had some of Big Tommy's other business to take care of before we hit the bars. We went into a bank across the street from the hotel and out of his hip pocket Billy produced a thick roll of well-thumbed English money and passed it to the cashier for counting. She thumbed through the well-used £10, £20 and £50 notes counting over £900 which she proceeded to convert into a stack of (pre-euro) Spanish pesetas. Next stop was the tobacconist where Billy made heavy weather of explaining that he wanted several thousand Benson & Hedges cigarettes in cartons of 200. Much to the bewilderment of the shopkeeper, he kept asking for 'sleeves', the grafter's term for these cartons. Eventually the peseta dropped – 'Ah si, si!' – and the tobacconist ducked behind the counter and emerged with one such carton. Listening to the Spanglish being spoken it was hard to fully interpret the transaction that followed. Billy ordered 50 sleeves and got them for about £15 a throw, which works out less than £2 per packet of 20. Back in England cigarettes were retailing at almost £5 a pack and this haul would be a nice earner for Big

Tommy once they were knocked out in the clubs and pubs of north Manchester. Cigarette smuggling has come to rival drug smuggling as the bane of Her Majesty's Customs. In 2001, in order to get an idea of the extent of cigarette smuggling into Britain, an innovative and imaginative survey was carried out. One Saturday, at all Premiership football stadia where there had been games, before the grounds were cleaned, surveyors went in and ferreted through the litter collecting all of the discarded cigarette packets. They discovered that more than a third were not duty paid. In other words they had been smuggled. It was not a coincidence that football grounds had been selected for this survey as it is among the communication networks of the fans that much of the buying and selling of the grafters' goods takes place.

I remember asking Tommy about this some months earlier and he told me that many of the Lads use their football trips abroad to stock up with cigarettes for personal use, but most importantly, in bulk for selling on to the black market. In this way many of the Lads pay their way around Europe. The football charter flights are especially good for this, he told me. 'When they've got a charter coming into Manchester or Leeds–Bradford at two o'clock in the morning with more than 200 football supporters on board, police and customs just want to get them out of the airport as quickly as possible. They don't usually bother checking bags.' Tommy took a charter for Manchester United's game with Valencia. When I asked him how the trip went he said, 'Great! I tell you, though, it's just as well it didn't crash. There were that much tobacco on board the wreckage would still have been smoking a fortnight later!'

Like so much that is traded on the black market, the main problem that the authorities face is that, by and large, the general public are quite happy to buy contraband at reduced prices. Moreover, the smugglers are not generally viewed as criminals. Rather they are often local heroes in a community where the police and customs are the villains. On one Scum Airways trip I was travelling with a small group on a scheduled British Airways flight from Cologne to London. Going through the final security check before boarding the plane two men in front of me were stopped by police and questioned because they were each carrying on board a couple of thousand cigarettes. Despite the fact that the men argued that they were for personal use, a policeman told them that he was going to inform British customs at Heathrow who would expect the cigarettes to be declared on arrival there. As I was taking my seat on the plane, another man, who had nothing to do with the two who were questioned, made an announcement to his fellow passengers. 'Listen, these two lads have just been pulled by the Germans for having too much snout, so I've told them that those of us who haven't got any cigs will take in 200 each for them, all right?' Heads nodded in approval and the cigarettes were dished out accordingly.

Contraband cigarettes taken care of, Billy and I set off to the centre of town to find the Lads. We did not have far to look. Another city and another 'plastic Paddy' pub in Calle de Espoza, a narrow street in the centre of the city. Inside some of the veterans of Munich 1860 were gathered. I recognised quite a few and felt quite comfortable in their company as they bantered Billy about 'the red scum' – his beloved Manchester United. Main topic of conversation was about the domestic game between the two clubs in Leeds at the weekend. Seems that one of United's firms had taken a coachload into a pub in the heart of the Leeds Lads' territory and given one of their firms a right pasting on home turf. This was a humiliation hard to bear and already, as the sun shone in Madrid, the Leeds Lads were plotting next season's revenge in Manchester. It was also here that I had the conversation with the Lad arrested for his Nazi mimicry in Munich's Hofbräuhaus.

I was standing next to Billy when somebody I had not seen before got up from a nearby table and approached us. He looked to be in his early 30s, with short black hair and dark eyes sunken within arching eyebrows and high, stubble-enhanced cheekbones. Billy did not introduce him, but I soon learned his name was Shane. There then followed one of the more bizarre conversations that I had been privy to hitherto.

Shane said, 'Here, Billy, how are you? Listen, can you get us a pair of trainers?'

'Yeah, I think so, give us your size,' replied Billy, 'I'm coming up your way next week and I'll bring up what I've got.'

Shane continued, 'Aye, good. What about Pokemon cards, d'you do them Pokemon cards?'

'Yeah, I do,' confirmed Billy. 'I can get you them double-sided gold ones if you like. I'll bring a load over and you can see what you want.'

So far this conversation had been interesting because it was further confirmation of the overlap in the worlds of the independent travel business, hooligan culture and straightforward black-market grafting. What was said next sharpened my interest considerably. Shane stepped closer to Billy and lowered his voice. ''Ere, Billy, can you get us any gas?' I wondered what Shane meant – amongst other things, was Billy moonlighting as a salesman for British Gas? – when from the inside of his baggy waistcoat pocket Shane produced a green plastic CS-gas grenade and, pushing it toward Billy said, 'Like this.'

How was my roommate to respond to this? I admit I was taken aback when Billy replied, 'Yeah, but I only do them in packs of 36, cost you £100, not worth dealing in ones or twos.'

At this Shane returned to his table to consult his mate, who was quietly and dextrously rolling a joint under cover of an over-large fisherman-style hat pulled low down over his ears. After a brief tête-à-tête Shane returned and said, 'Okay, put us down for 36,' before adding, 'What about stun guns? Can you do stun guns?'

I held my breath waiting for Billy's response. 'Yeah, I can get you two types. One's a fuck-off big one, about the size of a bicycle pump. Stick it into a man's chest and it'll knock him clean across this bar room! Then I can get these small ones that fit in your trouser pocket. Not as powerful, but still give you a good belt and stop you in your tracks for a while.'

Shane thought for a moment. 'Aye, right. Tell you what, get one of those fuck-off big ones for me.' Then, revealing his caring-sharing side, Shane asked, 'And can you get one of the smaller ones for our lass?' I had formed the opinion that Shane's girlfriend would be better off with the bigger stun gun if only to keep him at bay.

In less than five minutes we had gone from snide training shoes, through Pokemon cards up to CS-gas grenades and stun guns. Surely, I thought, that would be it and Billy's trading post would close. I was wrong. Shane returned to his table, had a mouthful of beer, took a long pull on his pal's joint and engaged him in more whispered conversation. He passed back the joint and walked over to us again. This time he got even closer to Billy's ear, but I could still hear the exchange. ''Ere, Billy, d'you do guns?'

Billy smiled at Shane before replying, 'Well, I can but I don't really like to, gets me involved with the wrong sort of people in Manchester, if you know what I mean. Why, what are you after?'

Shane's response was both scary and hilarious at the same time. 'Well, you see, I've got three guns. I've got a Beretta, a Webley and I've got a sawn-off shotgun. Trouble is, I buried 'em in t' cemetery in Leeds a while back and now I can't find them.' Suddenly, I had an image of Shane and his mate, like latter-day bodysnatchers, fiendishly creeping around an old graveyard at midnight digging up the dead and trying to find their weaponry. Shane was not messing about with his replacement arsenal. 'Billy, can you get us one of 'em Match 16 machine pistols?' Commonly known as an Uzi, this rapid-fire, hand-held machine pistol is the favoured weapon of the drug tsars and their enforcers. Not so good long range, but it can cut a man in half at closer quarters.

Billy thought for a moment before replying, 'OK, but it'll cost you £1,500 and it will take me about a fortnight to get hold of one.'

With that Shane returned to his partner for another conference before confirming that the price was right and that the deal could go ahead. Deal done, I found it hard to conceal my astonishment as the conversation slipped smoothly and seamlessly into talk of tonight's game. Shane and his mate still needed a couple of tickets. Billy sold them a couple of spares that would turn out to be for the seats in front of us. On reflection, of course, I have to consider that I was being set up and that Shane and Billy were just acting out a yarn for my benefit. Somehow I don't think so. It struck me as the kind of story that had to be true because it was too outrageous to invent.

Once Shane had left, I asked Billy who he was. 'Oh, that's Shane,' he told me, 'a nice enough bloke if you get to know him, but a bit of a nutter really.' I asked Billy what he thought Shane wanted the machine-gun for. 'He's big time into the Leeds drug scene and there's a lot of gang stuff going on up there. He obviously wants protection. The Old Bill are onto him too, big time. He had his photograph in the local paper a few weeks ago with a police warning for the public not to approach him, as he was violent and extremely dangerous. He's on one of those three strikes and you're out deals,' Billy explained. This was a reference to the then Home Secretary, Jack Straw's, policy, borrowed from the United States, that anybody convicted of a third felony would be put away for a very long time. 'Obviously Shane's going to go down shooting,' concluded Billy. Nice guy to go to the game with, I thought to myself.

By now it was mid-afternoon and many of the Leeds Lads had spilled out of the bars and onto the narrow streets to drink their lager in the warm, early spring sunshine. It was not long before shirts were off, bellies were out, songs were being sung and glasses were being broken. It became increasingly difficult for people to pass by without being jostled and harassed by what was now turning into a pretty ugly mob-scene. Cars were rocked from side to side and had their roofs drummed upon as they tried to edge through the increasingly unruly Leeds throng.

Billy's good at spotting potential trouble and steering his charges to places where they are less likely to fall foul of the police. He also knows when to take himself out of the firing line when trouble kicks off. Moments before the inevitable arrival of the riot police, Billy tugs my shirt and says, 'Come on, Suggy, let's get out of here. It's going to kick off any minute.' We make off down a side street and take refuge in a small tapas bar. Typically, it is a cheery, friendly place with what looks to be a father and his two daughters working behind the counter. As the wailing of police sirens competes with the mellow Spanish music emanating from the jukebox, a group of Leeds Lads burst in, seeking sanctuary from the riot police. The atmosphere in the place changes to one of menace as the 'We are Leeds' mantra rings out. The proprietor tries to quieten his new customers but to no avail. One whips off his shirt and points proudly to his fat belly which has 'Munich 58' tattooed around his hairy navel. 'Time to get off-side,' whispers my Red Army friend.

The Bernabeu is a truly magnificent football stadium, in my view the best in Europe, and probably the best in the world. It is designed with one relationship in mind: people watching football. It has a capacity of 90,000 and wherever you sit there is a perfect view of the pitch and any action on it. It looks like what it is: an amphitheatre where some of the best and most dramatic football has been played in front of some of the most knowledgeable and passionate fans in the world. Tonight's match would hardly live up to its setting, but for a game with little meaning (Leeds and Madrid having already qualified), it turned out to be better than might have been expected. Alan Smith scored first for Leeds who dominated the opening exchanges. Then came the most controversial moment of the game: Madrid's prolific striker, Raul, rose to punch the ball, Maradona-like, past a stranded Nigel Martyn. Everyone in the ground saw Raul use his fist – except, that is, the Polish referee Ryzard Wojick who awarded a goal. If this had been a meaningful game, with about 5,000 Leeds fans spread around the ground, including some of their top firms, there would have been chaos. Instead, as the teeming rain danced around them, the away fans just continued their celebrations, almost to a man taking off their shirts and, with bellies gleaming in the floodlights, singing the Leeds anthem 'Marching on Together'. The bemused Madrid fans sat stoically in their own stadium, no doubt wondering how the country that gave the world Shakespeare could also spawn the likes of this lot. In front of Billy and I sat Shane and his mate, equally impassively, passing a damp joint back and forth.

At the final whistle Billy disappears hoping to find Big Tommy outside the ground. Despite Raul's 'hand of God' goal, both sets of fans stream contentedly away from the Bernabeu Stadium, secure in the knowledge that their teams have already qualified for the quarter-finals. Many of the Leeds supporters are with the club's official travel club and have come on a day stop: fly in, take in the game, fly out. This is the travel arrangement that the police prefer as it provides less opportunity for trouble and they are more than happy to provide the returning coaches with police escorts to the airport. Like the officials, Big Tommy has a fleet of coaches waiting to take his own day-stop customers straight to the airport and the rest back to their hotels in the city centre. It is temporary chaos outside of the ground and I find myself acting as a Scum Airways steward, making sure that Tommy's lot get on the right coaches. Others, who have travelled under their own steam, take refuge from the pouring rain in one of the many small bars that ring the giant stadium. As Big Tommy's last coach pulls away I decide to join them.

As highlights from some of the night's other European ties are shown on a small TV in the corner of one bar, a rowdy, but happy, Leeds throng swill glasses of foaming lager and sing their favourite partisan songs. After rousing choruses of 'We are Leeds, We are Leeds, We are Leeds' and 'Marching on

Together', the bemused locals are treated to a new refrain which, sung to the tune of the 'Okey Cokey' went something like this:

> You put both feet in, both feet out,
> In out, in out, you kick him all about.
> You do the Jonnie Woodgate and you turn around:
> That's what it's all about.
> Oh Jonnie Woodgate, oh Jonnie Woodgate,
> In out, in out, you kick 'em all about!

The song was a dark celebration of the (at that time) alleged exploits of Leeds and England defender Jonathan Woodgate who, along with fellow Leeds and England player, Lee Bowyer, was in Hull Crown Court accused of battering and kicking a young British-Asian student, Safraz Najeib, outside the Majestyk nightclub in Leeds city centre late one Thursday night. During the first trial it was alleged that Woodgate had been seen to take a step back and leap with both feet, simultaneously landing bone-shattering kicks on the prone body of Najeib. The Lads had picked this up in the press and were now singing the praises of their young hero.

Intermittently, I had been among the Leeds Lads for more than a year and during that time two off-the-field issues had been prominent. The first was the murder of Kevin Speight and Chris Loftus on the eve of Leeds' UEFA Cup away leg in Istanbul. The second was the Bowyer and Woodgate trial. Other than the fact that they both concern Leeds, on the surface there seems to be little or no connection between the two. Underneath the surface I had come to the conclusion that they were deeply and intimately connected and the singing of the unsavoury ditty described above provides a clue to this connection.

In England over recent years, city and town weekend culture in general has become increasingly yobbish. Excessive drinking, drug taking, fighting, mugging, hooliganism and related displays of masculine aggression are the trademarks of the Saturday night yob culture that regularly has a racist dimension. Monday morning across the country the courts are full of young men of the same age and background as Bowyer and Woodgate facing charges from drunk and disorderly to grievous bodily harm. There are even more, like

121

Safraz Najeib, waking up at home or in a hospital bed, cut, battered and bruised, having fallen victim to this Saturday Night Fever.

What makes the Bowyer and Woodgate trial different is the fact that they are both high-profile and highly paid professional footballers. Different, but not exceptional. Barely a month goes by without reports of footballers behaving badly in clubs and pubs hitting the headlines. Why this should be has been much debated and I believe it is the combination of several inter-related elements. Firstly, there is the generic yobbish culture already referred to. Some footballers' off-field antics are no more than a particular expression of this. Secondly, English football, from its grass-roots amateur base to its professional apex and including fan culture, has long since been an anti-intellectual training ground and haven for heavy drinkers. Woodgate, during the first trial, confessed to drinking 'seven or eight pints and vodka and rum cocktails', a prodigious amount by anyone's standards, but not necessarily exceptional. Up and down the land on Saturday nights tens of thousands of amateur footballers head thirstily off the field for a few pints, a quick bite to eat and then back out on the town with the lads. Conversation rarely gets elevated above tits, bums, fighting and football. Any attempts to introduce more serious and intellectually challenging topics into this discourse are generally scorned. Their professional peers are brought up to have similar appetites, the major difference being that they have more time and much more disposable income to play with. In addition, through the media, young football stars are favoured with god-like status, leading some to think that they are above the rest of us mere mortals, including those who make and implement the law. As such, rather than protecting developing players from such yobbishness, professional football can propel them headlong towards it.

The debilitating and career-ruining potential of this culture has been well documented in a number of confessional biographies of famous players such as Best, Merson and Adams. Who can forget Paul Gascoigne's dentist-chair celebration (mimicking a reported episode of binge drinking during England's trip to Hong Kong) after his goal for England against Scotland in Euro '96, or young Gazza in his Newcastle shirt standing shoulder to shoulder with the fans behind the goal at St James Park. Gascoigne now does voluntary counselling work for the PFA (Professional Footballers Association), speaking to young players about the mistakes that he made, particularly of the dangers of binge drinking. There are also promising signs that the influx of foreign players and coaches along with the introduction of the football academy system is beginning to challenge this self-destructive dressing-room culture. Nevertheless it is likely to be a long time before it is totally eradicated.

As Safraz Najeib discovered to his cost, on a Saturday night in virtually every town and city in England a Lads' night out can easily turn very nasty. Whether Bowyer and Woodgate were directly involved in the alleged assault is immaterial. The point is that assaults such as this are frequent occurrences and are celebrated elements of the Lads' culture. That Bowyer and Woodgate might have been involved is enough to elevate rather than diminish their status with the Leeds Lads. Hence the Woodgate tribute song.

This sense of being 'in it together lads' – management, players, and fans – was reinforced by the untimely publication of team manager David O'Leary's book, *Leeds on Trial*, in which he confesses to the adoption of a 'siege mentality' by the club. O'Leary's book is an honest, insightful and largely interesting manager's-eye view of the on- and off-field achievements, tribulations and trials of Leeds United. It covers a similar period to my own involvement with Scum Airways and observations of the Leeds Lads. O'Leary makes some valid points which, with a little joined-up thinking, could have been used to draw similar conclusions to mine about the nature of the relationship between yobbishness and football. Commenting on the Najeib assault and the alleged involvement of some of his players he notes that at the time of the incident:

> I thought it wiser to give our players some time at home with instructions to stay with their families and rest. Yet what occurred in Leeds in the early hours of that Thursday morning was exactly the kind of incident, fuelled by excessive drinking, that you know can happen when you take a group of young men abroad. It was the risk of something like this that I'd expressly been seeking to avoid by staying at home [. . .] There is a time and a place for footballers to enjoy themselves, but enjoying themselves should not consist of getting drunk out of their minds. There is an attitude among many English

> footballers that having a good time involves precisely that [. . .] I'm
> afraid too many British players seem intent on getting legless. I know
> of a trophy-winning team whose manager noticed that after the
> celebration of one of their more recent triumphs that the only
> drunken players in the room were Brits.[1]

O'Leary failed to spot the connection between these players' boorish 'boozing culture' and the behaviour of the Lads.

As the verdict in the Bowyer–Woodgate trial approached, it was widely believed among the Leeds faithful that Woodgate would go down. This, the *cognoscenti* argued, was why the club paid £18 million for the former West Ham centre-half, Rio Ferdinand, as cover for Woodgate's impending incarceration. In the event, the first trial collapsed. After the jury had been sent out to consider their verdicts, under extremely dubious circumstances, the *Sunday Mirror* published an account of the trial containing material that should have been withheld under the law of contempt. The judge ruled that this could have influenced the jury's deliberations, dismissed them and called for a retrial.

At that retrial, while Bowyer was found not guilty on all charges, Woodgate was found guilty of causing an affray and ordered to do 100 hours community service. The verdict caused a public outcry, particularly in the British-Asian community, who were especially enraged by the judge's original instructions to the all-white jury that the offence should be in no way considered as a racially motivated attack. On 20 December 2001 the BBC news reported how, in a statement to the House of Lords, the Liberal Democrat peer, Lord Dholakia, launched a savage attack on the way the criminal justice system had handled the trial and went on to target Leeds United Football Club saying, 'We should thoroughly deplore the action of the Leeds club, its manager and its chairman in the way they seem to be handling this matter.' In an only thinly veiled reference to Bowyer and Woodgate he also fiercely criticised any 'thugs who masquerade as footballers', then, in rather extreme terms, by saying such 'Bin Ladens should be banned from playing abroad'.

In the same debate, in perhaps more appropriate and measured terms, Labour's Lord Faulkner of Worcester, a former chairman of the Football Task

Force and director of Brighton and Hove Albion, supported Lord Dholakia and argued that neither player should again be selected for England. 'However talented these players may be as footballers,' said Lord Faulkner, 'their selection for England would send the unmistakable message that every drunken lout of that sort, and behaviour of that sort, is tolerated.'

The new suits at the Football Association were obviously listening. Having dropped heavy hints that, after a series of impressive performances in the Leeds first team, Woodgate was on the verge of being reselected for England, Sven-Göran Eriksson was forced by his paymasters to do a U-turn. Maybe they pointed out to Sven that Woodgate's criminal record would rule him out of membership of the England official supporters club. In addition to his community service he may even have been eligible for a banning order under the 2000 Football Disorder Act. Either way, for non-footballing reasons, Woodgate would not be going to Japan in 2002. 'Jonathan Woodgate has served his punishment and, normally, that would have been enough,' Eriksson told BBC Radio 5 Live. However, Eriksson had been persuaded that this was not a normal case, adding, 'At the same time, there are certain rules for fans as we are trying to make the image of British football better abroad. It should be the same for players.'

Leeds chairman Peter Ridsdale was furious, and complained bitterly that Woodgate was being restrained from doing his job by the FA. 'A fan is not allowed to go because if they have committed an offence that might lead to a violent offence at a football match, then their travel is quite rightly restricted,' fumed Ridsdale. 'But I don't believe anybody is suggesting that if Jonathan Woodgate was in the England squad then there would be any danger of him getting involved in affray again.' Not for the first time the Leeds chairman had missed the point. He was right to suggest that Woodgate's inclusion in the England squad would not have been a threat to national security, but that was never the issue. The issue was about symbolism and Woodgate serving as a role model for the Lads to strut their stuff in England and abroad.

Ridsdale might have saved his breath. A few weeks later, Woodgate made his chairman look very foolish when he went on a drinking spree with his mates in Middlesbrough and finished up in hospital with a broken jaw. Woodgate claimed it was the result of over-exuberant horseplay with his friends, but others suspected that he had been involved in another nightclub fracas. The injury caused him to miss Leeds' vital series of final Premiership games and once more cast his future at the club in grave doubt. Woodgate had only just finished his community service. Summing up at the end of the second Najeib trial, Mr Justice Henriques looked at Woodgate and told him, 'I have little doubt that you have learned a great deal.' The Judge should have saved his breath too.

Earlier in the year the Leeds United managerial hierarchy, including Ridsdale and O'Leary, had, in my view, made another mistake when they had tacitly condoned their team's collective head-shaving before their crucial Champions League away game with Valencia. They intended this as a gesture of support for Lee Bowyer, whom they believed to have been unjustly suspended for this important European tie by UEFA after a disciplinary commission had viewed video evidence of an off-the-ball clash between him and Valencia's Sanchez. But consequences do not always follow intentions. At this time Bowyer was yet to be cleared of the attack on Najeib.

Like hair, it seems some memories are shorter than others. I was a longish-haired teenager in the '60s and '70s and lived in terror of fellow youths with close-cropped hair. Before the David Beckham-style skinhead became a chic fashion statement, it was an essential accruement of the skinhead uniform. This was a time when along with football hooliganism and 'queer bashing', (and terrorising people with long hair), 'Paki bashing' was a key component of this always nasty and sometimes Nazi subculture's domain activities. The skinhead look may subsequently have been adopted by less menacing style vultures (ironically, nowhere more so than by the gay community), but skinheads and the skinhead mentality have not gone away. This look remains a dominant image for National Front bully boys as it does for Leeds' and other clubs' hard-core Lads. Regardless of the intentions of a club trying desperately to shed its image as racist, the team's ritual head-shaving and management's, at least, tacit support of this, at a time when the Bowyer–Woodgate trial was in abeyance, gave out all the wrong signals. No matter what the club's players and officials thought, the Lads interpreted their team's shorn pates as a vindication of their aggressive and racist style of support.

Although not formally structured as such the Leeds Lads are at the centre of a loosely connected travelling subculture that both helps to create and revels in the club's growing reputation, both on and off the field, as the new hard men of Europe. The hard-core Lads are the ringleaders who plan the trips and mastermind the trouble. They are surrounded by an inner circle of foot-soldier Lads who are always up for a scrap and are happy to be led into battle. Then there is an outer circle of supporters who do not travel bent on trouble but still like to be on the fringes and share in the aggressive 'having a laugh' antics of the hard-core and their foot soldiers. When trouble starts and the police and cameras move in, these camp followers – or lads with a small 'l' – are as likely as anybody to get a hiding and get arrested. Then, there are the large numbers of peripheral supporters who want little or nothing to do with the central activities of the Lads' brigade, but who, whether they like it or not, by doing things like shaving their heads, taking their shirts off, waving them and bearing bloated bellies, taking part in assertive and aggressive chanting, are guilty of providing succour and cover for the serial troublemakers. Of course there are many other kinds of Leeds fans who travel abroad who are not in any way connected to the gratuitous, macho and ethnocentric displays and rituals described in this book, but they tend to get lost in the crowd. After the Madrid match, for instance, a headline in *El País* declared, '3,200 hooligans de visita en Madrid'. The Lads had made their mark and Leeds United's reputation was once more tarnished.

As I have already argued, for many of the Lads, Scum Airways trips are like stag weekends or enhanced Saturday nights out. They are experiences where social barriers collapse, identities are masked and/or exchanged and (almost) anything goes. This sense of being on the edge of control is accelerated through drink and/or drugs. While this can help to make the party happen by lowering inhibitions and heightening emotions, it can also help events to spin wildly out of control. The Lads do not come to the carnival as neutrals. They come armed with hang-ups about their masculinity and their national identity. They come possessed by ideologies that are racist, sexist, ethnocentric and xenophobic. The space and freedom for adventure, particularly of the Lads variety, can come at a price. If this Laddish Saturday Night Fever is dangerous at home it is potentially fatal when taken and exaggerated on tour abroad.

There can be little doubt that the Leeds Lads who were murdered in

Istanbul did not directly provoke the violence that was meted out against them. Turkish sources claimed that some Leeds supporters had desecrated images of the country's national hero, Kemal Atatürk, abused the Turkish flag and harassed a number of women in the square where the murders took place. Billy, who was with them, swears that none of this was true. 'They were just "baloonin'", you know – having a few drinks, having a laugh,' he told me. But by transporting the ethos of Saturday night in Leeds, Doncaster or Bradford to Istanbul, the Lads put themselves at extreme risk. Indirectly their baloonin' provoked a predictably aggressive response in a country also noted for its intense national pride and male bravado, as well as strongly conservative sexual mores.

The Lads may define their public displays of drunken camaraderie as 'just having a laugh', but they cannot control how this is interpreted in other cultural settings, particularly one as otherworldly as Turkey. The Lads may express contempt for foreign police, but without their protection – as was the case in Istanbul – they are very vulnerable to the kind of attacks that led to the death of Christopher Loftus and Kevin Speight. In these circumstances, once trouble starts retribution is brutal and indiscriminate. In no way does this excuse the Turks' deadly reaction, but it does help to explain it.

As I stood in the bar in the shadow of the Bernabeu listening to some supporters of Leeds United sing their sick song, it occurred to me that what I was witnessing in ways better than any of my or O'Leary's words, summed up the dark side of the relationship between a club, its players and its fans. This was to be my last trip with the Leeds Lads as their shaven-headed team – minus Bowyer – would be edged out by Valencia in the semi-finals. I had met some good people, even amongst the Lads, but there was a nasty and aggressive side to many of them that I was both wary and weary of and on balance I was glad to see the back of them. I drained my glass and left.

For the record, while Lee Bowyer was acquitted at the second criminal trial, at the time of writing, backed by his family, Safraz Najeib has filed civil proceedings against the Leeds player. More than two years after the deaths of Loftus and Speight, on 1 May 2002, a Turkish court found Ali Umit Demir guilty of their murders and he was sentenced to 15 years in prison. Another 19 accused men were found guilty of a variety of lesser charges and fined and sent to prison for three months. Demir has appealed his conviction.

I managed to take in one more Champions League game during the 2000–01 season, however, the final in Milan. As insurance, in case either Manchester United or Leeds made the final (or indeed both), I had applied to UEFA for media accreditation. I knew that Big Tommy's ticket prices would be beyond my means and I was thrilled when my application to UEFA was accepted. While the absence of either Manchester United or Leeds rendered the trip more or less useless for the focus of this book, it was wonderfully relaxing to head off to a game on the continent without having to look for trouble or meet and hang out with spivs or hooligans. As I wandered around the city's splendid and spacious piazzas, soaking up the party atmosphere created by the milling and mingling Valencia and Bayern Munich supporters, I wondered if it would have been so friendly if either of the English clubs had made it through. Somehow I doubted it.

Not for the first time (or I hope the last) I felt both lucky and fraudulent as I took up my halfway-line seat in Milan's terrific San Siro stadium. I was sitting next to one of Britain's greatest living sports journalists. This to me was an amazing coincidence because two years previously at the final I had sat in a similar seat in the Amsterdam Arena waiting for Real Madrid to take on Juventus and then just as now he had been in the next seat. He never spoke to me in Amsterdam but in Milan he broke his silence. We were both standing and taking in the pre-match entertainment. The game had been branded by the Milan organisers as 'L'Opera del Calcio' – the opera of football. The pre-match entertainment concluded with the orchestra and choir of Milan's La Scala opera house performing a selection of arias. 'Nessun Dorma', the anthem of Italia '90, boomed around the cavernous stadium. The legendary journalist at my shoulder, famous as a man who does not waste or mince words, turned to me, took the large half-corona cigar out of his mouth and, in a gravel-like Scottish accent, spoke to me for the first and last time, 'What a load of bollocks for a football match!'

I nodded in agreement, before replying, 'Yeah, but at least it's better than three years ago in Amsterdam. Remember then we had had to suffer Boyzone!'

The game itself was a turgid affair, only enlivened by the post extra-time penalty shoot-out which, of course, the Germans won. After the game I headed for the five-star Hotel Savoy where all the UEFA executives, media big-shots and sundry football VIPs were staying, to see if I could pick up any interesting FIFA/UEFA gossip. The usual suspects were there, including some non-football celebrities who were having a ball, boozing, clubbing and rubbing shoulders with the football *glitterati*. As I trudged back to my own two-star hotel I reflected that anonymous, Neanderthal football fans were not the only middle-aged men that behaved badly abroad.

ENDNOTES
[1] O'Leary, David, *Leeds United on Trial: The Inside Story of an Astonishing Year* (London, Little Brown & Company, 2002) pp. 167–69

# 7

## Bangkok, July 2001

THROUGHOUT MY RESEARCH THAILAND WAS A PLACE THAT KEPT cropping up in conversation with Big Tommy and the other Manchester grafters, particularly Billy. I had been led to believe that, amongst other things, Bangkok was the main centre for trade in fake replica football kits. It was to Thailand that Billy often disappeared for some Rest and Relaxation and to top up his stocks of replica shirts, CDs, computer games and God knows what else. It is also one of the main centres for the production and distribution of narcotics. There were also lots of indirect comments that led me to believe that at least some of the Manchester grafters were movers and shakers in the drug business. I was not sure how far I wanted to go down this particular road, but it seemed sensible that at least I should go and check out this city as soon as the opportunity presented itself.

As luck would have it at the end of the 2000–01 football season both Liverpool and Manchester United organised end of season tours to Singapore and Thailand. These tours are neither rewards for the players, nor are they serious tune-ups for the following season. They are public relations exercises undertaken to extend the market reach of ambitious global businesses like Liverpool PLC and Manchester United PLC. After a hard slog in the Premiership, Champions League and other competitions, the last thing a professional footballer needs in June is a tour of South-east Asia. He needs all the time he can get between seasons to rest, recover and spend precious time relaxing with family and friends.

To illustrate this point, it's worth me recalling a heated exchange between Gerry Armstrong – then the assistant manager of the Northern Ireland senior international side – and three of his senior players on the way back from a game in Armenia in May 1997. Armstrong asked the three Premiership players for their passports. The IFA ((Northern) Irish Football Association) had agreed a one-match post-season tour to Thailand. Armstrong explained that the players would receive £900 for their efforts and have five days Rest and Relaxation at a Thai beach resort. They flatly refused to give up their passports. Using strong language, they complained bitterly that for giving up such precious off-season time, £900 was an insultingly low offer. They argued that the tour would generate much more money than this and the whole point of it was not preparation of the national team, but to pour some cash into the IFA's meagre coffers. As they contemplated ten days of intense heat and humidity in Singapore and Thailand, I am sure that many of Liverpool and Manchester United's players would have felt the same way.

Anyway, Big Tommy told me that there were a bunch of Manchester's top Lads going to Thailand and that he would be going with them. He said that they were off to stock up on shirts and that it might be interesting for me to see first hand how this end of the snide rag trade worked. By now my shoestring research budget had just about snapped. I was desperate to go to Thailand with Big Tommy and the Lads, so I needed to do some creative thinking. Perhaps I could pay for the trip by smuggling a suitcase full of replica kits? The thought did cross my mind, but even my generous interpretation for my profession's ethical code would not stretch that far. Instead I thought of a more credible means of supporting the trip. The first World Congress for the Sociology of Sport was scheduled to be held in Seoul, Korea, at the end of June just before the Manchester United tour of the region. The following year Korea was to co-host the World Cup finals and the conference organisers were keen for delegates to offer papers on the World Cup theme. I submitted a paper about the bidding wars associated with how FIFA awards the hosting of its premier competition. At the same time, through the British Sociological Association's Sociology of Sport Study Group, I applied for and got a travel grant from the UK Sports Council. This way I could fulfil my commitment to the Sports Council by participating fully in the conference and break my return journey in Bangkok where I hoped to catch up with Big Tommy and his troops.

Naïvely, at the time I did not realise Seoul is about as far away from Bangkok as London is from New York. The cheapest flight I could get meant that I had to fly to Seoul from London via Bangkok and Taiwan – 38 hours door to door. I did not get to see much of the South Korean capital as I was committed to spending most of my time on a university campus at the edge of the city. I did manage to spend one night down town trying to get some flavour of the place in anticipation of possibly returning the following year for the World Cup. A fascinating place for the cultural tourist, but I am not sure what the Lads would make of it. It is the only place in the world that I have been where I have been invited for a meal and not recognised a single thing on the table. I wondered how the dogs of war would get on with dog for lunch.

One thing the Lads would have in common with their Korean hosts is aggressive, competitive heavy drinking. As I walked out the back of my hotel at about 11 p.m. one of the first things I saw was two drunks fighting outside of a bar. It is hardly surprising the way they binge drink. I was amazed by some of the special offers advertised in the hotel bar. Not your pound a pint stuff here. Instead, customers were invited to have a special deal such as six beers, one bottle of Scotch, a bottle of vodka and a bottle of any other spirit, not to take home but to sit and drink at the table! I looked on in astonishment as in groups of threes and fours young men and some women bought into these deals and proceeded to indulge in drinking competitions, getting hammered in less than an hour. I cringed thinking of the likely effect of this practice on the Lads should England play here in the future.

In contrast, despite its own exoticness, Bangkok I found to be a much more hospitable and less culturally impenetrable place. From afar it appears to be an ultra-modern city, with huge 40- and 50-storey glass and concrete apartment complexes, hotels and office blocks bursting out of the verdant flood plain. But like most other South-east Asian cities that ultra-modernised when the Tiger economies were roaring, Bangkok's skyline is deceptive. Beneath the canopy of the city's raised network of highways, in the cracks, crevices and shadows of this megalopolis, there flourishes the other Bangkok, a more medieval citadel, with its temples, bamboo dwellings, elephants, *tuk-tuks* (sort of motorised rickshaws) and river taxis.

Bangkok is a massive, sprawling city of more than 12 million people. I arrived at the beginning of July, catching the tail-end of the monsoon season. The Chao Phraya River that flows through the centre of Bangkok was fast-flowing and swollen murky brown, as were the many tributaries and canals that wriggled among the city's shanty towns, temples and skyscrapers. Large ferries ploughed up and down the main river as smaller, sleek and swift river taxis sped past like exotic water insects, disappearing into the bowels of the city down one or other of the river's smaller arteries. In the surrounding streets a cacophony of sound emanated from Bangkok's infamous bumper-to-bumper traffic. To reduce such street-level stress the Thai government built a network of elevated highways, but because these are toll-roads they are barely used by the locals who seem to prefer to battle it out for free in the chaos and smog down below.

One of the more dangerous things that a visitor can try is crossing one of the main street-level thoroughfares in Bangkok. These roads are generally three or four lanes each way. They criss-cross the city via crossroads and traffic lights. The ebb and flow of traffic is halted for several minutes at a red light. This causes a huge build-up of cars, buses, lorries, *tuk-tuks* and motor-cycles. While they wait for a green light, the motor-cyclists all filter to the front of the grid, revving their engines loudly. When the light changes the traffic moves with the force of a river dam breaking. It roars forward led by 50 or more bikers burning rubber like the start of a motor-cycle grand prix at Brands Hatch. Not a time or place to chance crossing on amber.

All cities have their market places but Bangkok itself is a giant market place. Every pavement, every alleyway, every inch of wasteland is occupied by somebody making, faking, fixing and selling something. There is no obvious limit to the range of stuff for sale on the streets: high-tech computer components and software; clothing for all wardrobes; songbirds in cages; elaborate Buddhist icons, spices and all manner of edible (and to me inedible) foodstuffs, including fried locusts, huge juicy grubs and baked, black scorpions. The spicy smells and noisy pandemonium of this limitless market place blend with the sound and smog from the traffic, and the sweet, fetid monsoon air, giving Bangkok a unique flavour.

South-east Asia is where more than 90 per cent of the world's counterfeit produce comes from, and, as one *farang* (Westerner) told me, 'Bangkok is the bootleg capital of the world.' The working motto of Thailand could easily be 'you design it, we'll copy it'. Anything from suits to sophisticated pieces of computer technology can be found and purchased on Bangkok's counterfeit market. The emergence of so-called designer fashion – the kind of apparel for which the display of the company logo is at least as important as the quality of the fabric and costume design – has given a huge boost to Bangkok's renowned counterfeit rag trade. Nowhere is this expansion more evident than in designer sport and leisure wear. Alongside long-standing top-range labels like Ralph Lauren and Hugo Boss, there has grown a huge market in polo-shirts, T-shirts, sweat-shirts, tracksuits and replica football shirts bearing names like Puma, Umbro, Nike and Adidas.

Mike Royalance is Adidas UK's Trademark Protection Manager. A considerable proportion of his job is dedicated to identifying fake products. Mike is a kind of snide detective, who works alongside Trading Standards, Her Majesty's Customs and Excise, and the police in tracking down and eradicating the counterfeiters. This is now recognised as such a huge problem for the sportswear industry that companies like Umbro, Nike and Adidas work closely together within the framework of ACG (Anti-Counterfeiting Group) in a collective attempt to stamp out the illegal use of their labels. In the case of the snide football gear, they also work closely with the big football clubs.

Mike told me that there is no limit to the ingenuity and cheek of the counterfeiters. 'Anything we make, almost before it's on the clean market, they've copied it and it's being knocked out in street markets and pubs and clubs up and down the country.' Sometimes the fakers will go as far to produce goods that Adidas and its competitors do not even make themselves. I remembered one of my first encounters with Freddie in Manchester when I was trying to track down Big Tommy. He had Hilfiger watches for sale at a time when Hilfiger did not produce them themselves. 'There seems to be no end to their cheek,' Mike told me. 'I've seen mobile phone covers, watches, jewellery, the lot all with our logo on. The worst I've ever come across is a set of Adidas knuckledusters!'

The main counterfeit market though remains in sports clothing. 'Ten years or more ago,' explains Mike, 'most of this gear was produced domestically in sweat shops in the north and Midlands. Then the quality wasn't up to much – cheap and cheerful – and you could spot a snide a mile away. Nowadays 80 per cent to 90 per cent of it is produced abroad, almost all of it in the Far East in countries like Indonesia, Singapore, China, the Philippines, and Thailand where most of it comes from.'

Now not only is there more of it, but also it is of much better quality. In the beginning most of the stuff used to be straightforward copies. A grafter could take a particular shirt to a Thai tailor and ask him to copy a couple of hundred. The tailor would take his best guess at the design and quality of material and produce an order of forgeries that would look fine from a distance but that would not usually stand up to closer scrutiny. Today, however, they don't just fake the design and the logo, but they also use virtually identical materials, so much so that some of the better stuff cannot be detected as counterfeit by look and feel alone.

Emulating bank-note security devices, several leading companies have gone so far as to have holograms embedded within their products, making them more difficult to reproduce. Difficult, but not impossible, as the counterfeiters themselves are conversant with the latest computerised textile techniques. Mike tells me that even though they now use computer technology to scan and test samples of suspect produce, 'but even the computers can't spot the difference between the best fakes and the real McCoy'. At the 2000 Sydney Olympic Games such was the concern of the Organising Committee over counterfeiting that they used DNA taken from the saliva of an unnamed leading athlete and incorporated it into a special ink to be used in all official products sold at the Games. Officials could then distinguish the real from the fake by using hand-held scanners.

The problem is that all it needs is for somebody who works in the factory where the genuine article is being produced to steal the design and the specifications of a given item and an identical product can be manufactured in another sweat shop around the corner. More sophisticated organised criminal gangs steal the latest products from international trade fairs and sometimes have large quantities on the market before the genuine article is released. In 1999, for instance, Reebok's prototype DMX shoe was stolen from a display stand by a Chinese gang. The counterfeit shoes were on sale in Eastern Europe and Russia within weeks, long before their official release by Reebok.

To add to the difficulty of the task facing the snide detectives, these modern counterfeiters also replicate the products, labelling, tagging and packaging down to the smallest detail. They have even gone so far as to replicate the paperwork that is used to support the manufacture and distribution of legitimate merchandise. In one particular case the only way the snide detectives identified a shipment of 5,000 items as counterfeit was when they checked back though the chain of paperwork and discovered that this was a limited edition and Adidas had only produced 1,000 of them in the first place. These counterfeiting operations are now so thorough, Mike tells me, that some major high street retail outlets have been conned into buying large quantities of counterfeit produce.

Interestingly, the fakes not only have to be good enough to fool the snide detectives, they also have to be as close to the real thing as possible or discerning customers in the black economy won't buy them. For instance, many counterfeit football shirts end up on the backs of school children. For them, worse than having no replica kit at all is to be fingered by their mates in the streets or at school and be accused of wearing a snide.

In South-east Asia the counterfeit market serves three types of customers. First, and of least importance to Mike and the rest of the snide detectives, are ordinary tourists who go to places like Bangkok on holiday and pick up a new wardrobe for themselves and faked gifts for their friends and relatives. Then there are lone carpetbagger grafters like Billy, Alehouse, Mick and their mates who visit Thailand for a bit of Rest and Relaxation and come home with a couple of suitcases jam-packed with snide CDs and computer games and fake replica football kits. The latter, Mike explains, can be picked up for less than £2 in Thailand and peddled back in England in the usual places for £20–£25. If Billy can pack 200 shirts in a couple of hold-alls and turn them around in Manchester's pubs and clubs he stands to earn himself a cool £4,000.

I remembered sitting in Big Tommy's office for the first time and him proudly pointing out the framed Manchester United shirt on the wall which had been signed by his hero, George Best. 'Yeah, but you know it's a snide, don't you, Tom?' asserted Billy.

'Bugger off, it's genuine,' huffed the Big Man and the two proceeded to have ten-minute argument over whether it was or was not snide. From where I sat it looked real enough to me. Billy went to his house around the corner and returned with a counterfeit Manchester United shirt, which to me looked and felt perfect.

This kind of one-man smuggling is more of an irritation than a serious problem for the big sporting goods companies, particularly when compared to those big-time crooks who buy in bulk and shift in big volume. This is where the boundaries between the counterfeit textile business and organised crime become very blurred. Some of the techniques used to shift counterfeit gear from South-east Asia and penetrate the British market are exactly the same as methods used by the drug cartels to move narcotics around the world. To counteract this the snide detectives have to deploy the same techniques as the drugs squad, including using undercover agents. Mike told me the details of one big operation that they had managed to infiltrate. The operation was organised by a Thai family from their base in Geneva. In Thailand 300,000 fake Adidas 'units' (the term used for any product) were run up and packed into a container before being driven to Singapore. From Singapore they were shipped to Rotterdam's free port area and held in a bonded warehouse for several weeks, out of the reach of Dutch customs, before being shipped on to Spain. According to Mike, a corrupt Spanish customs official cleared the cargo after which it was sent back to Holland. Spain is in the EU and goods cleared by customs in one EU country are generally waved through by the customs officials of another. Thus it was relatively easy for the shipment to be freighted from Holland to the UK and taken to Manchester for distribution. In another case customs intercepted a consignment of counterfeit apparel that had been shipped from Holland to Liverpool in flower boxes.

The UK is one of the biggest markets for counterfeit sportswear, alongside Japan and the USA. In the UK the main centres for import, manufacture and distribution are in the north and Midlands with Manchester and Leicester being the most important cities. It is mainly from there that much of the snide gear that ends up on market stalls or in pubs and clubs in Liverpool, Leeds and Glasgow comes from. Through his work for Adidas, Mike knows the main players in this network very well and describes most of them as likeable rogues. 'For them,' Mike tells me, 'it's not wrong, it's just part of a way of life that has been going on for generations. They think that they're just doing a job like anybody else. Some of them even send me Christmas cards!'

This is one of the many problems faced by the snide detectives when trying to bring such people to justice. Neither the grafters themselves, nor the majority in the communities they provide for, see that there is anything wrong with what they do. On the contrary it is viewed more as a public service than as a crime. I once sat in a pub in north Manchester waiting for Big Tommy and Billy and within 15 minutes had been offered the purchase of cigarettes, football shirts, meat joints and a set of German steel carving knives. This was obviously standard business and nobody batted an eyelid. It was rumoured that in some neighbourhoods on Merseyside, the grafters operated like milkmen, delivering contraband booze, cigarettes and perfume to the doorstep.

In one form or other something like the black market has probably been around since before recorded history. Its modern form has its origins in the twentieth century's two world wars when, during times of scarcity and hardship, enterprising non-combatants, through theft and other forms of corruption, would find ways of supplying food and luxury goods not readily available through rationing. These spivs were the predecessor of the likes of Big Tommy and his chums and, like the current generation of grafters, were held in some regard in their communities.

This kind of trade is also attractive not just because of the huge profits that can be made, but also, much to Mike's lament, because the punishment for getting caught is usually very light. Get caught with a couple of kilos of heroin at Bangkok's Don Muang Airport and, if you're lucky, it is ten years in the notorious Bangkok Hilton. The authorities' approach to the snide market is considerably less strict. It is not in the interests of the faltering Thai economy for them to crack down on the counterfeiting industry that keeps people in work and brings money in. Get caught with a suitcase full or even a container load of the latest Manchester United strips and the worst that tends to happen is that you have your gear confiscated.

Sanctions are not much more severe at the UK end. Customs will seize and destroy such contraband, but often do not prosecute. Officially, counterfeiting and smuggling are criminal offences that can be punished with five- to ten-year custodial sentences, but rarely are such cases brought to trial, and when they are the maximum sentences have been between 12 and 18 months. It is much more usual for culprits to be cautioned and sent away with a £50 fine. Mike complains that most of the big fish that he is after can afford expensive lawyers who often advise their clients to demand a trial at the crown court. They know full well that the prospect of a long and complex trial that eats far into the court's already stretched budget is not appetising for the authorities. Thus, charges in such cases are often dropped. When they do get into court the usual defence of accused traders is that of due diligence. They claim to have taken all reasonable precautions to make sure that the stock that they imported was genuine. According to Royalance, the standards of counterfeiting are now so high, defence lawyers argue, that often the likes of Adidas and Nike themselves cannot easily detect fakes of their own products. 'What chance does my client, a humble market trader, have your honour, when the companies themselves find it hard to tell the difference between fakes and the real thing?'

Eventually I suggest to Mike that because legitimate brands use child labour and sweat shops, buying fake gear that is produced in similar conditions does not trouble the consciences of too many consumers. I also put it to him that one of the problems with getting the authorities or anybody else to see these kinds of activities as criminal is that the real product is over-sold and over-priced. Aggressive marketing and the constant changing of kits and related designer sportswear styles put an unreasonable burden on less well-off families who have to buy expensive clothes for their fashion-conscious children. If the likes of Billy, for instance, can supply a counterfeit Manchester United shirt which in all dimensions is an exact copy of the real thing, then surely he is providing a community service?

Not surprisingly, Mike rejects the 'Robin Hood' argument. For a start he argues that the genuine product is of a higher quality. He also believes that it is unfair that companies like his should spend millions developing a high-quality product only to see the counterfeiters produce inferior versions for sale on the black market. Mike also contends that this kind of trade is not only illegal and damaging to legitimate business, but it is also almost seamlessly connected to other, more sinister kinds of organised crime. 'Some of the most violent and experienced criminals in the country have realised the huge fortunes that can be made from counterfeiting.' To reinforce his point, he offered several examples, one involving a major seizure of counterfeit goods at a warehouse in West Yorkshire.

One evening, Trading Standards officers along with police posing as warehousemen took delivery of the four wagon-loads of counterfeit sportswear that they had been tipped off to expect, and arrested the drivers. They were about to shut down the operation when a fifth wagon, unrelated to the first four, pulled up at the gates blaring its foghorn. The driver had been held up in traffic on his way up from London and seemed desperate to have his cargo unloaded that night. Thinking that they had nothing to lose, the police duly obliged and when they opened up the container they discovered that it too was packed with counterfeit gear. When this driver was arrested he showed signs of wild panic, unusual for a relatively low-key, snide gear bust. Eventually the driver broke down and explained to police that he was driving for a London mob that, among other things, peddled drugs around the city's casino gambling circuit. He was meant to drop off the snide gear in Yorkshire, get paid off then drive across the Pennines to Liverpool and use the money to pay for a consignment of heroin and cocaine that was badly needed in the Smoke's casinos. According to Mike, using the profits from the clothing black market as a grubstake for drug dealing and other more serious felonies is not unusual.

Counterfeiting can have even more sinister connections. Mike claims that in Northern Ireland loyalist paramilitaries control both the counterfeiting and drugs markets and use them to finance their terrorist campaigns. Angela, Manchester United's Trademark Manager, shares Mike's views on this. She once went to a market in Ulster and had to be protected by heavily armed police as she searched for fake Manchester United gear. The RUC (now the Police Service of Northern Ireland) had warned her that she would be at serious risk from the paramilitaries if she attempted to investigate them alone. Mike's and Angela's views are supported by the National Criminal

Intelligence Service (NCIS), who reckon that 60 per cent of the organised crime gangs involved in counterfeiting are also drug traffickers.

In another, different kind of case, Mike tells me of his personal involvement in a bust on a sweat shop in the heart of Leicester's Asian community. Early one morning he was with police and customs as they broke down the door of an ordinary-looking terraced house. Once inside they found it had been extended backwards to accommodate dozens of sewing stations and rack after rack of counterfeit designer clothing. As they were about to leave one of them heard a noise coming from the attic. When they investigated its source they found 20 illegal immigrants cramped in the roof space. It turned out that since their illegal entry into Britain they had been held in the house and used as slave labour in the sweat shop. This was justified as a somewhat indeterminate means of paying for their illegal journey into the country.

'So you see, this is not a victimless crime,' claims Mike, airing a view shared by the UK's Consumer Affairs Minister, Kim Howells, who asserts that 'counterfeiting is often the tip of the criminal iceberg. There are links between counterfeiting and organised crime and it is often used as a means of laundering money gathered by drug dealers.'[1]

The snide detective's job has not been made easier by a complex trade war that has been going on in the world of high street fashion. Companies that manufacture and sell designer products rely on creating an impression of exclusivity. It is not an exaggeration to suggest that the brand name has become more important than the product itself. This exclusivity of image is linked to both price and the public's perception of the status of the shops that retail a given commodity. It is also linked to carefully controlling the numbers of products released into a given market. Levi Strauss, for instance, like to see limited editions of their jeans that they have supplied directly on sale for £40 a pair in top boutiques in London's Oxford Street. They do not like to see bulk quantities flogged at £25 a pair, squeezed between fresh veg and kitchenware in a supermarket in Basingstoke. This is precisely what happened when companies like Tesco and Asda started to send their buyers to factories in South-east Asia that make Levi's products under licence, to buy up surplus stocks. Levis then went on sale at approximately half high street prices in

Tesco and Asda superstores in the UK. Levi's went to court and for the time being this particular practice has been halted. Nevertheless, there is still a huge market in 'grey goods' (as these products that fall somewhere between the legitimate and black market are called) and the big sportswear companies are particular victims of this trade.

To muddy the waters further, in addition to grey market goods, there are goods that come from the parallel market. For instance, a global company like Adidas will have generic global products, but for marketing reasons these products may be unevenly distributed from one country to another. Also there may be specially adapted products and designs for different markets. In both cases there can be huge price differences in Adidas's products sold in different countries. Thus it can make commercial sense for a retailer in England to source his Adidas stocks more cheaply from warehouses in Spain rather than going directly to Adidas UK. With grey and parallel goods competing with the real thing, it's no wonder the consumer gets bewildered. This plays into the hands of the counterfeiters who exploit the market confusion to peddle their snide gear.

The development of Internet technology has been a nightmare for Mike and his colleagues. There are now hundreds of web sites, mostly emanating from South-east Asia, that offer to sell the widest variety of fake designer and replica products. One such site, Kitshirts.com, trades on the anti-big-business theme:

> Welcome to the world of soccer shirts. We have a wonderful selection
> of replica football shirts for adults and children all over the world.
> With more than 150 teams to choose from we hope you will find the
> team you are looking for . . . We can provide the latest high quality
> football shirts at wholesale prices . . . Why pay ridiculous prices for
> the same merchandise?

The site used to advertise Manchester United products, but the club threatened Kitshirts.com with legal action if they did not remove advertisements for their shirts from the web site, which they promptly did. The likes of Liverpool, Leeds, Chelsea and England are all still displayed prominently.

It is the counterfeiting dimension of Bangkok that I have mostly explored. I arrived in the city on Monday having arranged to meet Big Tommy on Thursday when he was scheduled to fly in, a few days ahead of Manchester United's game with the Thai national side the following Sunday. He has promised to show me around the corners of the fake replica shirt business in Thailand, but with time to kill I decide to do some exploring of my own. Looking at my map I see markets dotted everywhere, one bearing the endearing name of Thieves Market. But I don't have to go there to get a flavour of what is on offer. In the evening, as stall after stall is erected along all of the city's highways and byways, I join the ebb and flow of the masses to see what is for sale. An Adidas top here, a Manchester United shirt there, Levi's everywhere. I head to one of the many indoor markets occupying the ground floors and basements of some of the city's tallest buildings. There are hundreds of small tailors and haberdashers, selling all manner of clothing, most with signs posted offering to replicate any make, any style and any number of clothes that you bring in. 'Suit you, sir. What about a Hugo Boss three piece, Calvin Klein denims, or some of Adidas's latest lines?'

On the way back to the hotel I decide to walk through a maze of backstreets in which are found a warren of workshops making, faking and repairing goods of all kinds. In the steaming evening heat, most have their garage-type doors thrown wide open to let in as much air as possible. Inside some are men labouring furiously over lathes and workbenches, fixing or mending some piece of machinery or car part. Inside others are women running material through humming sewing machines or sitting cross-legged on the floor hand-stitching other garments. This is mainly small-scale stuff. Outside Bangkok's centre and in some of the smaller provincial cities and towns there are thousands of operations much larger than these backstreet sweat shops, where whole factories are given over to the mass production of counterfeit garments. Manchester United actually employ local lawyers who in turn hire undercover agents to try and hunt out these big illicit operations. Then United's snide detectives work with the Thai police and try to have these factories closed and the counterfeit produce confiscated. The problem is finding squads of police that can be trusted to do this work. Often, a factory is identified, but before it is raided, the owner is tipped off and the place gets cleared before the police turn up.

Of course Bangkok does not appeal to the Lads just because it offers cheap shirts and moody suits. It is also the capital of the global sex-tourism industry. I had thought that Amsterdam was the ultimate Lads paradise. I was wrong. Bangkok makes Amsterdam look like Eastbourne. Bangkok and the nearby seaside resort of Pattaya are twinned sin cities. The latter used to be a quiet fishing village. In the 1960s and 1970s the Americans developed it as a recreational resort for their troops fighting in Vietnam. The soldiers took advantage of their time away from the fighting to drink, take drugs, have sex and listen to rock and roll. Young girls from impoverished peasant families from rural Thailand and neighbouring Laos and Cambodia were drawn or sent to Pattaya and Bangkok to service the troops. After the Vietnam War, some American servicemen with fond memories of their R and R there returned to Thailand and opened up girlie go-go bars. It would be an oversimplification, however, to conclude that the Americans invented the sex industry in Thailand. Certain classes of women in Thai society have long since secured their futures through engaging in a variety of mistress/master relationships and by working a paternal hierarchy to their own advantage. Thailand is the gateway to South-east Asia and as trade with the west grew in the nineteenth and twentieth centuries these practices began to embrace relatively wealthy foreigners or *farangs*. Hence, the country has a long tradition of a variety of forms of prostitution that the American intervention accelerated and made available for extensive tourist consumption.

Whatever the history, if it is in-your-face, cheap-and-cheerful sex for sale that you want, Thailand is the place to find it. If there were any Lads in town they were bound to be in or around the main sex-tourism neighbourhoods of Nana Plaza, Soi Cowboy or Patpong. For the rest of the week it was these neighbourhoods that I patrolled, sometimes in the company of Jim Hawker, an English journalist from the *Bangkok Post* who knew the Bangkok vice scene like the back of his hand. While for the most part my searching for the Lads would prove fruitless, watching and listening to Jim I did learn quite a lot about the city's sex trade. I began my expedition in Patpong Market, the traditional centre of the flesh industry in Bangkok. There you will find strip-joints cum go-go bars in abundance. These are lap-dancing disco joints where a punter can sit and have drinks while watching flocks of numbered naked

145

and semi-naked girls dance on bars and in cages. Jim explained that if one takes your fancy you can order her by number and have her sit naked on your lap. In some of these places, if you want you can pay for oral sex on the premises. Otherwise you can pay a small 'bar tax' to the owner of the place and take the girl back to your hotel and negotiate separately with her for other sexual favours. In some cases these girls are rented out of these bars for weeks on end, as permanent companions for tourists.

Most of these girls are from rural Thailand or nearby countries such as Laos, Myanmar, Cambodia, Vietnam and even China. Apart from a few stock phrases – 'Wot your name? Where you from? Love you long time!' – most speak very little English. One of the saddest sights I saw several times in Bangkok was that of flabby, balding, middle-aged *farangs* standing in lines at cash machines with their diminutively pretty consorts waiting behind them. In the most extreme cases tourists have been known to marry these girls and take them back to their homes in Europe and North America, often with disastrous consequences for both parties. Pretty though many of the bargirls are, I found it hard to imagine what it might be like to hang out with them for a week or more, let alone marry one and bring her back to England.

In other less public places you can find live sex shows featuring men and women, men and men, women and women, transvestites and anyone, animals and people; it's a seemingly endless variety of stage-managed perversions. Everywhere there are massage parlours outside of which languish packs of beautiful young Thai girls inviting in passers-by for a laying on of hands. It can be really intimidating for a lone tourist like me. I had just finished a long and hard football season myself and I was in training for a marathon. I was full of aches and pains and was very attracted to the idea of a full body massage; I was too scared, though, to have one in Thailand for fear of being compromised.

Instead I restricted myself to window shopping – all in the service of research, of course – and eventually escaped the heat for a cold beer in what appeared to be a respectable bar. Patpong is close to the city's business district and the Cosmos Club was full of Thai and European white-collar workers having drinks after work. It was over 90 degrees and very humid and after my walk my shirt was damp with sweat. As I took up my stool at the bar a pretty young girl tastefully clothed in Thai costume came to my left side and asked me did I want a drink. I asked for a Carlsberg and she then asked the waitress behind the bar for the beer. In exchange for this service she received a chit from the waitress which she then took to a cashier at the other side of the bar. I learned later that this was a ritual practised in most of Bangkok's bars. For each drink that punters like me were helped to purchase, the bargirl received a tiny percentage – roughly 1 per cent – of the sale as a bonus. The accumulated bonus helped supplement the pittance they received for wages at the end of each week. Another girl approached from my right side with a damp, terry cloth, white towel and proceeded to pad the sweat from my brow. Then (reminiscent of the final scene in *Ice Cold in Alex*), as I took the first sip of my Carlsberg, I was approached from behind and, with expert hands, another bargirl began to give me a neck massage. It doesn't get any better than this, I thought, when I noticed the large TV screen above, which was showing edited highlights of the previous season's English Premiership football!

The Cosmos Club became my favoured watering hole as I awaited the arrival of Big Tommy. It was cheerful, orderly and the service was very pleasant without being overtly erotic. It was in the Cosmos Club that I met John and Mark, two brothers from London. John was a disc jockey and his brother was a partner in a successful Bangkok-based marketing firm. It turned out that they had both been involved with the Chelsea Headhunters in the 1970s and 1980s. They had moved to Thailand to get away from serious hooliganism and some of its nastier spin-offs. It was John who first told me about Hickmott, or Icky as he called him, the Chelsea hooligan ringleader who had been given ten years' imprisonment for his exploits with the Chelsea Lads in the 1980s. John told me that, like himself, Hickmott had ended up in Thailand and owned a bar in Pattaya called the Dog's Bollocks. Pattaya is affectionately known by Bangkok's ex-pat community as Patpong-on-sea. This extract from one web-based travel guide gives a good flavour of the place:

> With its murky sea, narrow, rubbish-strewn beaches and streets packed with high-rise hotels, Pattaya is the epitome of exploitative tourism gone mad. But most of Pattaya's visitors don't mind that the

place looks like Torremolinos or that some businesses still dump their sewage straight into the bay – what they are here for is sex. The town swarms with male and female prostitutes, spiced up with a sizeable proportion of transvestites and planeloads of western men flock here to enjoy their services in a rash of go-go bars and massage parlours for which 'Patpong-on-sea' is notorious.[2]

It is not surprising that Hickmott has based himself in Pattaya, as this area of Thailand is rapidly replacing the coastal resorts of southern Spain as the Costa del crime. Criminal gangsters from England, Russia, Germany and Japan have discovered in Pattaya a cheap, convenient and relatively surveillance-free environment from where they can run their global rackets. Almost half the bars, cafés and restaurants there are Western-run, specialising in English newspapers and home-from-home menus of English breakfasts, hamburgers, chips and the like. Unsurprisingly, Pattaya is also one of the main centres for making counterfeit sportswear, particularly fake replica football kits.

It was from outside the Cosmos Club, on Thursday afternoon, that I called Big Tommy on his mobile phone, fully expecting him to be either at his Bangkok hotel or Don Muang Airport. To my horror when he answered he was in his car somewhere just outside Stockport. Something had cropped up and he was not coming. Stiffed again, this meant that I was out on a limb until returning home on Monday. I tried to conceal my disappointment and asked him if he had any intelligence on the whereabouts of the Manchester United Lads for whom I had been searching without any success since my arrival. He told me that they were down in Pattaya and would be coming up to Bangkok at the weekend ready for the game on Sunday. 'But listen, Suggy,' warned Big Tommy, 'be careful with them. They're not like the Leeds Lads. They don't like strangers nosing about and they wouldn't think twice about doing you if you cross them.' I thanked him and slunk back into the bar to finish my beer.

Big Tommy not coming was a big blow to me. He knew where the Lads would be and was to have been my secure escort into their circle. Without Tommy I was flying blind and I still had not tracked down my quarry. I was annoyed with myself for not figuring out that the Lads would have made straight for Pattaya. It was now Thursday evening and I decided that if they were heading to Bangkok over the weekend that it was now too late for me to head to Pattaya in search of them. Instead, hoping that they would come to me, I spent Friday and Saturday trawling through bar after bar in some of Bangkok's sleaziest neighbourhoods. What followed could only happen in Bangkok.

It is another hot and steamy afternoon in the Thai capital and before setting off on my trawl of the city's low life, I had taken refuge in Larry's Dive Bar, just off Sukhumvit Road, between Nana Plaza and Phrom Phong. The bar gets its name not because it is rundown and seedy, but because Larry, its owner, is an enthusiastic scuba diver. The large, airy saloon is decorated with fins, wet suits, diving masks, air tanks and other maritime memorabilia. Larry's is a good refuge. It is quiet, particularly in the afternoon, cool and hassle free. The service from the pretty waitresses is attentive and comes with no strings attached. For your money you get a cold beer and a warm smile, which is not an invitation for you to pay for 'extras', and are left alone to drink and think in peace. It is a good place for me to sit, contemplate and scribble down my field notes.

The bar is empty except for another *farang*, a huge man who sits two bar stools away from me. He is wearing shorts and a red checked lumberjack shirt open over a pale green T-shirt. He must have been 6 ft 6 in. and there is not much fat contributing to his enormous bulk. Maybe he's a baseball pitcher, I wonder, because he wears his baseball cap with the peak at the back. This is one style statement that I cannot abide, but I'm not going to tell man-mountain this, particularly as his menacing presence is accentuated by the multiple lacerations covering his face, as if he had recently been flung through a car windscreen.

I watch as he drains the last of his Screwdriver and orders up another. 'Hey, buddy, can I get you another beer?' he asks me in a deep, American voice. I look up from my note pad. This is not a man to offend so I accept his hospitality. 'My name's Steve,' he says, stretching his enormous paw towards me. I grasp his hand as firmly as I can, half-expecting to have it returned like a boneless rubber glove. My hand comes back more or less intact and I introduce myself, trying not to stare at his recently carved face. As if reading my thoughts, Steve says, 'Sorry about the way I look, man,' and proceeds to explain how he received his injuries, throwing in his life story for good measure.

Steve is Canadian, originally from Toronto. After finishing college, where he majored in engineering, he went north to Yellowknife on the banks of the Great Slave Lake in the North West Territories to work in mineral extraction. The weather was brutal, and the work equally hard, but he made a fortune. He made so much that three years ago, when he was only 34, he had enough money to keep him comfortable for the rest of his life. So Steve quit the mining business and took off around the world in search of excitement. He ended up in Thailand, where he has been for almost two years.

'Yeah, man, this is a great place but it can fuck you up big time,' growls Steve. 'After six months I got myself a Thai girlfriend. Not a bargirl, but a proper Thai girl from a big, powerful family here in Bangkok. They're great women, man, but don't double-cross them – they've got tempers like wildcats. That's how I got all cut up. She found out I'd been with another Thai girl and went nuts. She attacked me and scratched my face to bits.' It is hard to imagine this colossus being set upon by what I imagine as his diminutive, doll-like girlfriend. I can only sympathise with him. After just a week I here I have concluded that staying faithful in Bangkok for several months would test any man's resolve. 'Yeah, man,' he continues, by now slightly slurring his words, 'now I gotta get out of town cos her family are after me. Gonna head down to Waheen. Wanna come with me?'

The thought of going off with him to the tropical paradise has a certain appeal, particularly as so far I have endured a largely fruitless and futile week hanging around the city waiting for Big Tommy to turn up. But Steve's a stranger and a pretty weird one at that, with a posse of Thai kick boxers on his tail. Too risky. 'Er, no thanks, Steve. Got work to do here in Bangkok,' I said, 'let me get you another drink.' What he told me next confirmed turning him down was a good decision.

Steve looks unsteady on his bar stool. 'Yeah, man, and I just got bitten by a snake,' he says.

'Jesus,' I say, 'you've not had a lot of luck lately. Do you know what kind of snake it was?'

'Yeah, man, it was a king-cobra,' he tells me. Holding out his giant right hand palm down he shows me two clearly visible fang marks on the fleshy webbing between index finger and thumb.

'Wow,' I say, 'I thought king-cobras were deadly poisonous? You should get to a hospital.'

At this he laughs. 'Don't worry, man, I already got the antiserum [antidote].'

I think about this for a moment, then say, 'Steve, was this an accident, you getting bitten by a snake?'

'Hell no. You can get it done over in Chinatown, gets you real fucked up, like a real first-class high, better than any drug – and they sell you the antiserum, so you're safe enough. Wanna try it? I'll take you over there right now if you want.'

I have done a few foolish things in my time, but the prospect of paying to be bitten by a deadly poisonous snake is way out of my risk-taking league. 'Er, no thanks, Steve. I'll stick to beer if it's all the same to you.'

Steve buys me another beer and explains that he does crazy things like this because he is bored, 'Bored out of my fucking skull, man!' Since taking early retirement he has been everywhere and done just about everything. He's started running out of experiences, hence the stunt with the cobra.

I am about to suggest that if it is kicks he is after he should take a trip with Scum Airways next time there's an away game in Istanbul, but his taxi turns up. He eases himself off his stool and walks unsteadily towards the door. 'Don't forget to take the antidote,' I remind him as he stumbles into the awaiting cab. As the taxi edges its way towards the Sukhumvit Road, Steve just smiles back at me and pats his shirt pocket. Of course, this story could have been the product of a deranged mind, but intuitively I felt that Steve had been telling the truth.

I often wonder what Steve's doing now, if he is still alive. Probably gaffing Great White sharks or playing Russian roulette with a revolver and five bullets. As I watched him go that day I hoped that I would never get that bored.

I left Larry's Dive and set off on a by now familiar and seedy trail. No sign of the Lads on Friday, but on Saturday I got lucky. As usual, I had started out by searching Patpong, but found no evidence of them there. Then I moved onto Soi Cowboy without so much as seeing a Red Devil tattoo or Manchester United scarf. Finally, around about midnight when I had just about given up hope, I went to Nana Plaza, which happened to be just around the corner from my hotel, and there they were.

Nana Plaza is a courtyard around which are three floors of different kinds of bars: soft on the ground floor; medium on the first floor; and hard-core pornography on the top. I walked into the ground floor of the square and heard them before I spotted them. Once you have heard it for the first time, the roaring and raucous banter of a mob of English football fans in a foreign bar is unmistakable. The Manchester United Lads are in the first go-go bar that I come to, about 20 of them, mostly very thickset and in their 30s or 40s. Not a Manchester United shirt in sight, but I know right away that these are the Lads Big Tommy was talking about. There is a certain menace that hangs over them, which, for all of their loud laughter, screams out 'don't fuck with us'.

The Big Man's warning about how dangerous these Lads can be is at the forefront of my mind as I take a deep breath and walk into the open-fronted bar. I take up a good position, leaning next to the cash register with my back to the counter so I can watch the Lads and eavesdrop on their conversations. The company is scattered in threes and fours around the bar with bargirls mingling amongst them. Next to me one of the younger ones is trying to fend off one of the bargirls. He's drunk and having difficulty with his words, but manages, in a slurred Manchester accent, to mumble, 'Nor, I don't want to gor with yah cos I luv me wife . . .' How gallant, but, after the next exchange, I wonder how long his resolve to fidelity had lasted down in Pattaya.

One of his mates, a squat man in his mid 40s, sweating profusely, comes up to order a drink at the bar. While he is waiting he turns to me and asks whether I am in town for the United game. When I tell him I am he asks me if I have been in Pattaya. I tell him no and he proceeds to tell me what I had missed. 'Hey, it were fucking magic. Been down there all week. The other night we went in t' go-go bar that had about 50 bargirls in it. We bought the fucking lot, didn't we? Took 'em back to our hotel and shagged the lot of them. It were great. In our room we had a bowl of condoms and a bowl of Viagra.

Fucking great it were!' He also tells me about a run-in that they had with a Chelsea firm in the Dog's Bollocks which made the trip even more worthwhile. With a beaming smile on his bulbous, red, glistening face, he turns and waddles back with his beer to his mates. Quite the catch for a pretty young Thai girl.

Suddenly a spontaneous rendition of 'Glory, Glory Man United' breaks out leaving the Thai girls looking somewhat bewildered. In another bar across the passageway a foolhardy English tourist, not realising what he is up against, stands up and starts singing 'Who the Fuck are Man United?'. At this one of the younger United Lads, who I later learn is called AJ, gets off his stool and walks over to the bespectacled heckler who has returned to sit with his girlfriend. In a strange display of chivalry, AJ removes the heckler's glasses and punches him hard in the face, knocking him to the floor. Before things can go any further, security guards move in and escort the heckler and his girlfriend out of the complex. On the way out, surrounded by security, he continues his tirade against Manchester United, sending AJ into a fury. 'Specky bastard!' he shouts after the foolhardy *farang*. Then turning to his mate next to me at the bar he explains, 'I only took his specks off because he was with his girlfriend. Then, once he's surrounded by security, he starts again, don't he! Well, he's just cost the speckies of the world thousands, cos next time a specky has a go I'll smash his glasses all over his face.'

I cannot quite remember how but I end up talking with AJ. He is nobody's fool and after a while I can tell he suspects that I am not just the average ground spotter on a particularly exotic away day. I take a chance and let him know something of the book project that I'm working on. AJ is a well-educated man who had been an undergraduate at Manchester University before dropping out to join the grafters' game. He reads quite widely and has read most of the pop-sociology on football hooliganism. It was 1 a.m. in a Thai go-go bar and I found myself having a discussion about the quality of academic writing on fan cultures in Britain with a Lad who has just knocked somebody else senseless for insulting Manchester United! We argued about the merits and failings of the work of people like Bill Buford, Eric Dunning, John Williams, and Tony King. AJ got to know the latter when he was researching for his book, *The End of the Terraces,* in and around Old Trafford.

I feel that AJ could be a promising informant and to further establish my bone fides with him, I drop a few names, including Big Tommy's. At this point AJ insists on introducing me to their ringleader, the legendary Rocket O'Connor. He's another big man, not quite as heavy as Big Tommy but not as flabby either. Rocket's wearing a sleeveless vest that reveals the full bulk of his muscular arms and shoulders. Not a man to be crossed, I think to myself as he walks over. 'Who the fuck's this?' he asks AJ with no trace of friendship in his voice. 'This is John,' replies AJ, 'he knows Big Tom and he's writing a book about grafters and that.'

This definitely does not impress Rocket. 'Aye, well, Big Tommy's losing the plot, in't he, working with those Leeds cunts. Come on, AJ, we're goin' back to the hotel.'

Obviously there is no love lost between Rocket and Big Tommy, something that I resolve to follow up once I get back home. AJ says that he is going to stay for a while. During that time he tries to persuade me to come back to their hotel with them. They are staying at the Arnora Hotel, a short trip away by *tuk-tuk*. On the way from the hotel, AJ tells me, the gang had hailed five *tuk-tuks* and paid the drivers double to have a race to Nana Plaza.

The eager researcher in me is tempted to go. After all, I have just made contact with my target group and have lots more to find out. AJ seems to be a potential gatekeeper but after such a short encounter I cannot be certain that I can trust him. After all, it had been him who had assaulted the heckler. But it was Rocket who worried me most and I remembered Tommy's warning about the potential ruthlessness of these people. I decline his offer, at which point AJ suggests that we meet up the next day at their hotel and go to the game together. He tells me that they have a bunch of counterfeit press and VIP passes and that I can use one of them.

My sense of self-preservation was even stronger in the cold light of the next morning so I decided not to chance a day out with Rocket and his henchmen. Anyway I already had a ticket and after nine days working the streets of Bangkok I just wanted a hassle-free day before flying home. Before going in the stadium I wandered around the ground to see if there were any touts about. The *Bangkok Post* had claimed that the 60,000-seater Suphachalasai Stadium had been sold out and that tickets were being sold on the black market at treble the face value. Such is the scale of United's popularity in South-east Asia that two days earlier more than 30,000 Thais had turned up just to watch United train! There were a few Manchester touts outside offering tickets, but there were few takers as demand was lower than that claimed by the papers and just before kick-off they were lucky to get face value.

Inside, the stadium was just about full, mainly with borderline-hysterical Thai teenagers in replica Manchester United shirts who screamed every time Beckham or Giggs got the ball. The Manchester United snide detectives that attended this game said later that for them it was a mirror image of one at Old Trafford. In Manchester they try and spot fans wearing counterfeit shirts whereas for the game in Bangkok they had trouble spotting anybody wearing a Manchester United shirt that was not fake. I was one of the few people in the ground who appeared to be supporting the home team. Against all predictions – the local press forecast a United win by three or four goals – the Thais came back from Roy Keane's first-half goal to tie the game 1–1. The game itself was a bit of a joke, however. It could not have been otherwise, having been played in Bangkok's searing afternoon heat and humidity. It must have been 100 degrees in the shade and on the pitch there was no shade. Anyway this was neither about football nor the professionals who played it. This was about expanding United's market reach in South-east Asia. Judging by the crowd and the press coverage, for the suits of Manchester United PLC, the tour had been a huge success.

As I made my way back to the hotel for my last night ashore, I wondered how England would fare in this heat and humidity the following year should they qualify for the World Cup finals? Realistically they would have to beat Germany away the following September if they were to stand any chance of going through. As part of his business development, Big Tommy was trying to break into the England away market and this would be his next trip. It would also be mine.

ENDNOTES

[1] 'Britain labelled as world counterfeit capital', *The Observer*, 6 June, 1999

[2] *Excite Travel: Pattaya*. http:/travel.excite.com

# 8

# Five Past One, September 2001

I GOT BACK FROM THAILAND AT THE END OF JULY AND ALMOST immediately I was off on my travels again. This time, thankfully, it was a family holiday, spending three days in Paris and a week in Agde in Southern France's Languedoc region, on the Mediterranean coast. At first it felt weird wandering around a cosmopolitan city like Paris, visiting art galleries and museums, and dining out in fine restaurants. During my last half a dozen trips abroad I had become so used to patrolling low-life dives that this sudden immersion in urban civilisation came as a bit of a culture shock. Sitting at a pavement café on the Champs Elysées, sipping wine and watching suave Parisians and tourists parade by, I had a sudden urge for an Irish bar and a pint of lager with the Lads!

A week's Rest and Relaxation in the sleepy medieval cathedral town of Agde was enough to cure me of my Laddish longings. It was not long after I was home, however, that I was jolted back into Big Tommy's world. It was a hot afternoon in mid-August and I was walking my dog, a Golden Retriever called Captain, in Friston Forest on the edge of the Sussex Downs when my mobile phone hummed in the pocket of my shorts. Big Tommy's voice sounded harsh against the birdsong and breeze rippling through the forest's beech, pine and sycamore trees. 'Suggy, it's Tommy here. What the fuck did you say to the Lads in Bangkok?'

Suddenly my mind raced back to Thailand. Big Tommy was obviously unhappy and I immediately knew I had made a big mistake dropping his name to Rocket and his mob in Nana Plaza. 'Er, can't remember too much,

Tom,' I haltingly replied. 'I managed to find the Manchester United Lads eventually. Like you said, they'd been in Pattaya. Stumbled across them in a bar. I wanted to let them know that I was OK, you know, come off as one of the boys who knew the score and that. I thought if I dropped a few names, let them know that I knew a few of the top Lads, like you and Billy and Jed, then they'd feel more comfortable about me hanging around with them.'

'Fucking hell, Suggy,' Tommy hissed, 'that's the last thing they'd think with a bloody stranger wandering in who seems to know too much about their business!' Then his voice softened a little. 'Look, John, you've got to be careful. You've no idea who you were dealing with there. Real bad Lads. One of them would be on the top three of the most wanted list of any police force in the country. I got a call from Rocket about you as soon as they got back. D'you know what they thought?' Before I could answer he told me. 'They thought you were undercover Old Bill. They wanted to take you back to their hotel and cut you up!'

All of a sudden it was not so warm and it seemed to me that the birds had stopped singing. 'Bloody hell, Tom. I hope you put them straight!' The last thing I needed at this stage of my research was the word to go round the Lads' networks that I was an undercover cop. 'Yeah, I told Rocket that you were sound,' Tommy replied. 'He seemed to accept it, but I don't think you'll be able to go away with the Man U Lads in the near future.'

The spectre of the MacIntyre bust loomed once more. What with undercover NCIS spotters, investigative journalists and pop-sociologists all trying to penetrate their turf, the Lads were getting very jumpy. I was especially worried in case anybody decided to dig into my background. It would not be long before they found out that though now retired, my father had been a career policeman on Merseyside and had spent almost ten years in the Special Branch. I did not want anybody putting two and two together and making six. Months before, during a quiet moment in Amsterdam, I had purposely let this slip to Billy, just in case it came out later. I thought that by freely admitting that my dad had been Old Bill it would be less likely that I would be suspected of being a policeman or informer. This was the *Alice Through the Looking Glass* life I was now leading.

In the short term at least I was not planning to go away with the

Manchester United Lads, but at the end of the following week I was scheduled to take a trip with Big Tommy to Munich for England's crucial World Cup qualifier against Germany. This was to be the Big Man's first England venture. Just as with the clubs, there are many England supporters who want little or nothing to do with the official, FA sponsored and monitored, supporters' schemes. This means that there is a large market for the independents. There are a few independents that operate mainly out of London and the South-east that cater for England's away games, but nobody was systematically working the north of England. Having cut his teeth on the Champions League, Big Tommy was trying to get into and corner this market, and Munich was his first England adventure. I wanted to experience this new venture, as it would add a new and important dimension to this story. I was worried that by compromising Big Tommy with Rocket and his gang might have screwed up my access.

'Listen, Tom, I'm sorry if I dropped you in it with Rocket and the Lads, but how are we fixed for next week? Are we still on for Munich?' I asked penitently. 'Yeah, that's okay. You should be all right there. There's hardly any of the Man U Lads that bother with England so you should be safe enough. Just stick close to me, we'll share a room in the hotel if you like.' At one level, the researcher in me was mightily relieved, because my access was still secure. At another, the human level, I was less happy as it meant that yet again I would have to stick my head in the lion's mouth. I thanked him and made arrangements to meet at Manchester Airport the following week before turning off my phone. I took a deep breath, patted my dog and strode off towards the Eight Bells, a welcoming country pub in the picture-postcard village of Jevington. Captain needed water and I needed a pint and some thinking time.

Whether or not Rocket really did want to 'cut me up' was a moot question. Officials at Manchester United that know him describe him as a thug and a thoroughly 'nasty piece of work'. They have no love for the independents in general, but seem to particularly despise Rocket, who has an office above a chip shop only a couple of hundred yards away from Old Trafford. It had been obvious in Bangkok that he and Big Tommy were rivals and that there was a bit of bad blood between them. I made a few enquiries in Manchester and through a friend of a friend got to AJ, the Lad who had belted the 'specky bloke' in the bar in Nana Plaza. According to AJ, Big Tommy was just trying to protect his own back. Tommy wanted to put me off tracking down AJ or Rocket once I came home in case they told me stories about Tommy that made him look less of the Big Man that he postured at being. Either way it was a salutary and timely warning that I needed to watch my own back.

Just over a week later I found myself at 5 a.m. in the departure lounge at Manchester Airport mingling with ITL's first England customers. While they were a mixed and motley crew, I could tell straightaway that this would not be the usual Scum Airways trip. To begin with there were some women, lots of replica England shirts, hats and scarves. The men just did not have the menacing demeanour of a firm. I recognised one chap from the Midlands who had been on the previous year's Manchester United trip to Amsterdam and Eindhoven. He had a crew of Villa and Wolves supporters with him, but they likewise did not display the glowering aggression of a firm. No doubt there would be laddish behaviour but there were, as far as I could judge, no Lads on board for this trip, so at least this leg of the journey promised to be trouble free.

This would be my first trip away with England for the Scum Airways project, but I had been amongst the England away support on many occasions since and including their games in France '98. Forests have been felled to supply the books and articles that have been written about England's football supporters. I do not intend to recover all of this ground, but I do have a few of my own observations on the nature of England fans, particularly when they travel overseas, that will have a bearing on the following narrative.

The social and regional make-up of England's travelling support is complex. England fans are predominantly male and equally predominantly white. As in other walks of life, women are featuring more and more in the ranks of England's away support but, given that at least 50 per cent of England's population are female, their number remain disproportionately minuscule and they are very marginal to the mainstream of England's fan subculture. This relative absence is, in part, caused by the fact that fan cultures in general, and the England fan culture in particular have been colonised by certain kinds of men. England football provides them with opportunities to celebrate and reinforce traditional masculine identities: ones based on physical prowess and an unquestioned working-class patriarchy generated in the labour-intensive, urban, industrial economies of the last century. Neither in the workplace, nor at home do such social and economic conditions still prevail. There remains nevertheless, for a certain type of men, a need to hang on to this muscular, factory-floor, barroom image of manliness. Supporting England for some, then, is a male preserve through which the rituals of this fading form of masculinity can be acted out. The shaven heads, the bulging and tattooed muscles, the ritualistic aggression and real violence that are associated with the England fan culture at home and abroad are, at least in part, expressions of a distinctively English masculine identity crisis. What is at issue is not the absence of women in the midst of Ingerland; rather it is the celebration of that absence through the exaggerated, Neanderthal displays of manliness that always accompany England's forays abroad.

That England fans abroad are predominantly white is linked to another crisis that overlaps with the crisis of masculinity; that is a crisis of national identity. As I was writing this book Queen Elizabeth, the Queen Mother, was laid to rest. That her lying in state and her funeral caused such a public display of affection is a lasting tribute to her memory. I believe it happened also because it gave 'the people' one of only a very few unambiguous opportunities to celebrate 'the nation' in a way that was a memoir to that nation's past. A past when Britannia did rule the waves, the sun never set and to be British, even if you lived in a slum in Salford, was to be somebody. This is a Britishness that no longer reflects the multi-ethnic and pluralist democracy that we currently abide within. Notably there were few black, Asian or other ethnic faces filing past the Queen Mother's coffin in Westminster Hall. Other than the monarchy, sport is one of the few institutions that encourages, even demands, displays of national fidelity and, as 'the national sport', in this regard football bears a particular burden.

This is a burden that has become heavier at a time when, on the one hand, a sense of British national identity has been eroded by forms of political devolution in Scotland, Wales and Northern Ireland, while on the other, the sovereignty of the nation – in parts or as a whole – is called into question by the increasingly ominous presence of the European Union. When England won the World Cup in 1966 the flag waved at Wembley and in the streets thereafter was predominantly the Union flag. A legacy of imperial arrogance maybe, but his was a time when most English people were happy to consider themselves British first and English second, believing that being English was at the core of being British. Today the number of Union Jacks unfurled at international matches is far less than those bearing the cross of St George, the English flag. This is a sign that many are no longer secure with the notion of Britishness and this notion is rapidly being replaced by Englishness as the core national identity of the fans.

This is not a post-modern, inclusive Englishness; rather it is a defensive, exclusive, and distinctively Anglo-Saxon national identity. It's adoption by a core of England supporters makes supporting England – that is going to England games and mixing with other England supporters – very difficult for non-whites. It is a form of nationalism that feeds upon difference and the fear and loathing of anything or anybody foreign.

Together, an aggressive, posturing, pre-modern masculinity along with a pernicious strain of English nationalism frame the ideology of many who follow England abroad. While perhaps only a hard-core of Category C hooligans deliberately mobilise this ideology into violence, from what I have seen on the fringes of serious hooligan incidents in places like Marseilles, Brussels and Charleroi, it remains the central belief system of a large number of so-called ordinary fans. As such when trouble flares, like oxygen to a flame, they can be quickly drawn in. Even if they are not directly involved, often the way many English fans disport themselves, within the trappings of English nationalism, for the overseas authorities, makes them indistinguishable from the thugs so they get mopped up anyway. It is this portrayal of Englishness and the ideology that underpins it which, more than anything else, lies at the root of the problem of the so-called English disease.

As a sociological explanation for English hooliganism the preceding analysis is, I hope, both succinct and plausible. The problem with it is it is wrong, or at least incomplete, because it misses the essential point that the Lads are what they are because they enjoy being that way. To a large extent I share the view of reformed ex-hooligan Dougie Brimson who, commenting on the value of sociological theories of hooliganism that attribute causality to alienation and working-class angst, writes:

They were wrong. At least in part. For whilst it was true that the majority of people involved in hooliganism were working class, that was simply because football was the working-class game, but many were reasonably well educated in decent, stable employment. More importantly, very few, if any, were searching for anything other than a good time. And that was exactly what hooliganism was providing, week in, week out.[1]

'Crisis? What crisis?' I hear the Lads ask. Like pigs in a sty, they are extremely comfortable wrapped in their masculine, misogynistic, xenophobic and Anglo-Saxon identities. Going on the piss with the boys, using brothels, giving blacks, Asians, Turks, and other groups a hard time, taking on their mob, having a ruck with the police, all contribute to an adrenaline-fed high that staying home, putting in 9–5 at the office, and doing a share of the ironing can never equal. For the Ingerland Lads, hooliganism abroad, and everything that goes with it, is a fun-filled way of life. Leave the other stuff to the new men.

The English FA need to consider this as they embark on their noble attempts to gentrify the game. Further, they must be more sophisticated in the way they understand and manipulate the sounds and symbols that surround the national team. I think it is unfortunate that at a time when across Europe the far right is beginning to stir once more, the English FA should, albeit unwittingly, aid and abet the promotion of the aggressive version of Englishness described above and so favoured by the far right. The England team kit has developed in such a way that, more and more, it resembles the flag of Saint George and fans are actively encouraged to bring and wave Saint George banners at England games. It is not for nothing the far-right BNP has adopted the flag of Saint George to promote its political campaigns in England. Meanwhile, the FA-sponsored supporters band warms up the crowd with 'Rule Britannia' and the overture from *The Great Escape* while outside a pub nearby the Lads practise their favourite anthem. Beginning softly with 'With Saint George in my Heart' and finishing with a rousing blast of 'No Surrender to the IRA'. Some argue that the symbolism of the nation's patron saint should not be surrendered to the far right and that its co-option by the

FA and England supporter groups is a positive step in its reclaiming by moderate opinion. I am not so sure that the existing right-wing meanings associated with the cross of Saint George can be so easily erased and over-written by self-styled, democratic, English republicans. On the contrary, I believe that it will encourage more and more neo-fascists and fellow travellers to join team Ingerland's rank and file.

Contrary to the views that some apologists hold, it is not just about a few extremists, rather it is about the central meanings associated with being an England fan abroad. Nick Lowles, co-editor of *Searchlight*, the international anti-fascist magazine, agrees.

> While the Fascists might exploit the nationalism of some English supporters abroad, the sad truth is that many young men that follow the national team do not need the involvement or direction of racist groups to express their own bigotry and xenophobia. Time and time again they have proved themselves more than capable of performing the role alone.[2]

In fairness to the FA, they are attempting to reform the nature of England's away support, to make sure that 'official tickets go only to decent fans' as Nick Baron, the FA's marketing manager for England fans, puts it. 'We're trying to dilute the fanbase and move away from the idea that all England fans are shaven-headed, beer-bellied, tattooed thugs.' One method used has been the reformation of the England Members Club which in the past, it is believed, was hijacked by significant numbers of active hooligans who were then able to get their hands on official tickets. The FA shut the club down and reopened it, this time vetting all applicants and rejecting those who had been subject to a football banning order, and/or had been convicted for violence or public disorder within three years of the application. Cleaning up the England Members Club will not have much impact on the thousands of England fans who choose to travel alone or who prefer to use the services of Big Tommy and his ilk. The plain fact that there are usually thousands more fans prepared to travel to England's away matches than there are official tickets made available presents a huge problem for the authorities.

At the same time it is a good business opportunity for Big Tommy and his cronies.

Munich's Olympic stadium holds 60,000, of which the English FA's official ticket allocation for the match against Germany was only 10 per cent. It was estimated, however, that by trains, planes and automobiles, more than twice that many fans would make the trip to Bavaria and that thousands would be seeking out tickets on the black market. The NCIS had identified this as a high-risk game. Mark Steel, an NCIS spokesman, said, 'People should be rightly anxious about this game. It's clearly got all the elements which we recognise as making it potentially a high-risk game with trouble. It's a high-stakes game, involving qualification for the World Cup. It's on a weekend in a place which is cheap and easy to get to. Tickets are reasonably plentiful for those prepared to pay the price. There's the old-fashioned enmities between the two countries, at least as far as some of their fans are concerned. And both countries have a well-known hooligan problem.'

He might also have added that the kick-off was at 8 p.m. giving the Lads plenty of time on Saturday to get well tanked up on strong German lager. The NCIS's intelligence also suggested that many of England's top hooligan gangs were targeting Munich for a gathering. It was believed that firms from the likes of Chelsea, Leeds and Millwall had called a truce to take on the Germans on their own soil. 'Many people regard this as World War Two in reversal,' commented one police officer, 'with us invading them and taking them on in their own stadium.' To make matters worse, the German authorities had information that neo-Nazi German hooligans, associated with clubs such as Hamburg, Hansa Rostock and Hertha Berlin, had likewise called a truce and were hatching a plot to mount attacks on England supporters on their way to and in Munich. It promised to be an interesting weekend.

As it turned out, Big Tommy's first England venture had attracted few of the heavy mob. Once in the international departure lounge I sat with Big Tommy and asked him about this batch of customers. He agreed that there were, 'No Lads on this trip, only straight members.' He went on to explain that not many of the firms from the big northern teams bother with England. The English national team has never been as well supported in the north of the country as it is has in the south. In part this has been because of the location of the national stadium in London which also hosts the headquarters of the English Football Association. Also, there is a long-standing myth in northern football circles that players from northern teams have been under-represented or discriminated against in successive England squads. In general it is just a particular football version of a general northern view that the wealth of the nation is produced in the grit and grime of the industrial north before being siphoned away for the benefit the soft, southern underbelly. Supporters of the likes of Manchester United, Liverpool and Everton, do support England, but in the past they have tended to do so at home or in local pubs rather than following them overseas. This may be changing, particularly as players from northern clubs are now representing England in significant numbers. Possibly the only positive thing to come out of the catastrophic failure to construct a new national stadium has been the FA's decision to host England games at Premiership grounds around the country. This has given the national team more regional exposure and has encouraged and may be encouraging a more representative supporter base.

Another reason why the top northern firms tend not to travel with England away is that all or most of their energies are dedicated to supporting and fighting for their clubs, particularly those clubs like Manchester United and Liverpool that are seasoned European campaigners. In such cases the Lads have plenty of opportunities to show out for causes that are much closer to their homes and hearts than England. It is obvious that many, if not most, fans that actually follow England abroad are not supporters of the country's biggest and best-known clubs. Many a time I have sat in a stadium waiting for an England match to kick-off and passed the time by studying the club names on the hundreds of flags and banners that adorn the stadium. Teams of the stature of Hull City, Bristol Rovers, Scunthorpe United, Swindon Town, Bournemouth, Doncaster Rovers, Cambridge United and Brentford are usually well represented whereas it is rare to see many references to the biggest Premiership teams.

Most smaller clubs have no memory and little or no prospect of performing away on the European stage. With nothing much better than an away game at Crewe to excite them, the prospect of going abroad and strutting their stuff globally with England is a tantalising one for supporters of the League's small fry. According to the NCIS some of the worst troublemakers at England's overseas games are associated with clubs from the lower divisions. There are some significant exceptions, particularly from teams based in London, most notably Chelsea, West Ham and Millwall. In addition, Leeds have always had a strong, reactionary England following. Not only do they swell the ranks of regular England supporters, but they also send their top firms and these form the vanguard of the English hooligans.

Big Tommy introduces me to a group of Manchester City supporters who are coming with us. It turns out that they are his new neighbours. He tells me proudly that he has just moved into a new £150,000 house in Prestwich – North Manchester's Nob Hill. This is an important stage in Tommy's journey towards respectability. Most people born and raised, like Big Tommy, in Cheetham Hill could only dream about owning a house in Prestwich. He is now a proud family man with a big house and two cars. To crown his social elevation not only has he become a member of the area's Round Table, in 2001–02, Big Tommy was invited to become its chair, an honour that he delightedly accepted. Now a real pillar of the parish, Big Tommy is not the first and will not be the last shady dealer to use illegitimate or semi-legitimate means to earn the trappings of respectability.

Big Tommy's neighbours are immensely likeable Man City anoraks. A couple of them, Neil and Stew, make regular contributions to the City fanzine, *Bert Trautmann's Helmet* – named in honour of their club's long-serving German goalkeeper. He joined City after serving a stint as a prisoner of war, after deserting from the Wehrmacht during the Second World War. They spend most of the journey arguing about Manchester City and winding up Big Tommy because of his affiliations with Manchester United. They are not hard-core England fans, but are looking forward to a trip during which they can combine a bit of shopping and sightseeing with what is to be a memorable England encounter. They are just the sort of people that the FA is targeting in their campaign to dilute England's fan culture. With no real rogues to infiltrate (yet) I find their company a breath of fresh air compared with some of the Lads I have had to fall in with on previous Scum Airways adventures.

With in excess of 10,000 England fans travelling to Munich it is highly unlikely that they will all be such good ambassadors as my new comrades. Invoking clauses in the revised Football Disorder Act, British police monitoring UK ports and airports detained or prevented around 50 suspected hooligans travelling to Germany. Committed hooligans are extremely resourceful and you can be sure that if 50 were detained hundreds more made it through to the continent. Many would have travelled to European destinations other than Munich. Once in places like Paris, Amsterdam or Brussels they could relatively easily make their way to Munich through a variety of border crossings. But they do not always get away with it. The same day that I was flying to Munich 8 men aged between 29 and 41 suspected of hooligan links were stopped at Birmingham international airport as they tried to board a flight to Prague in the Czech Republic. The previous day another 23-year-old Wolverhampton man was likewise prevented from using this particular back-door route to Munich.

Some of the most serious pre-match disturbances happened hundreds of miles away from Munich in Frankfurt, which was being used as a staging-post by hundreds of England fans. The nature of this skirmish illustrates well the contagious and inclusive nature of hooligan events. On this particular occasion, most, if not all, of the England fans did not come looking for trouble. On the contrary, the Frankfurt police said that the fighting was instigated by approximately 450 German hooligans who gathered around the city's main railway station looking for suspects. They did not have to look too hard as a group of about 100 or more England fans – big lads, shaved heads, tattoos, England shirts – spilled out of a pub, not, according to them, looking for trouble, but looking like they were looking for trouble, according to neutral observers. The German hooligans started to chant insults and the usual broadsides of glasses, bottles and chairs began to fly before the riot police moved in. More than 20 English and 40 Germans were arrested.

Munich itself was relatively quiet. We had a coach laid on from the airport and checked into a small but stylish three-star hotel on the edge of the city centre. Big Tommy was too busy ducking, diving and dealing tickets to have me nosing around so I decided to go and do some sightseeing with the 'City til I die' delegation, most of whom had by now donned official replica sky-blue club shirts for the expedition. Munich is unmistakable as the Bavarian capital.

I had not noticed so much when I had been trailing around with the Leeds Lads on my last visit, but the old city of Munich is impressive. Its architecture betrays elements of Gothic, Renaissance, Baroque and neo-classical influences. The city boasts wide streets flanked by three- and four-storey buildings displaying intricately sculptured façades. Pedestrian walkways connect luxurious shopping centres to cobbled squares and high-spired churches. There are dozens of *Bierkellers* and beer gardens complete with lederhosen and oompah bands. It is also a city with a cosmopolitan feel and flavour, a major industrial, business, and tourist centre with shopping facilities that match those of Paris and London.

Stew is interested in the city's political history, particularly the events surrounding the Second World War. Unlike some of the neo-Nazis on the Leeds trip, he wants to see the sights out of genuine historical interest and the rest of us tag along. We take the underground from our hotel to Marienplatz in the city centre. It is a warm but overcast day, and our first visit is to the Neues Rathaus (New City Hall) which dominates one side of the square. Stew explains that it was here in 1933 that Hitler took one of his major steps to seizing overall power in Germany when he stormed in with his Nazi supporters and took control of the Bavarian political administration. I had been there with the Leeds Lads almost exactly a year before and watched them drink themselves stupid in the Rathaus's elegant courtyard. 'Wouldn't have got away with it in 1933,' I thought to myself.

In the square itself a stage had been erected and musical equipment was being assembled in preparation for a concert planned to entertain the fans who would almost certainly be drawn towards Marienplatz in large numbers. It had all of the essential features of an Ingerland bridgehead: lots of bars with out-of-doors drinking facilities, plenty of space for a pitched battle and enough exits to make a getaway should things get too hot. In the bars surrounding the square and in nearby streets, forward detachments of the English invasion were beginning to set up camp and already the occasional refrain of 'Ingerland, Ingerland, Ingerland' pierced the busy Friday afternoon hubbub.

Next stop was to have been the Hofbräuhaus just around the corner. The proprietors had obviously learned something from their encounter with the

Leeds Lads. In the porch guarding the entrance to this massive stone beer hall, two big men in black, with trademark bouncer's earpieces, checked identification on the way in. I handed one my passport. 'I'm sorry, sir, you can't come in today,' he said in methodically German-accented English. 'No English are allowed in,' he said before handing me back my passport. I had some sympathy with this strategy of blanket exclusion, but still felt that somehow my civil rights were being violated. So I asked why not. 'Because you are English, and with you there can be trouble,' he replied unblinkingly. I drew breath to argue, but then thought better of it as a bunch of already drunken English fans staggered past, one stopping to relieve himself up against a nearby wall.

There were still 36 hours to go before the match and there was a sense of gathering menace in and around Marienplatz. We decided to jump back on the underground and across town to the Englischer Garten (English Garden), the largest public park in Germany and a quiet oasis in the middle of Munich. Somebody had read that the England manager, Sven-Göran Eriksson, had been running in the park each day while the team had been based in the city, and the Manchester City crew thought that it would be a laugh if we could find him there and have a word about tactics for tomorrow night's game.

No sign of Sven, but the walk in the park was pleasant enough before it started to rain. The Englischer Garten is close to Muchener Freiheit, one of the city's livelier areas for bars and restaurants. We had something to eat and went for a bit of a pub-crawl around the local bars. It was great fun as we mingled with the locals, sharing drinks with them, talking football and generally getting along famously. So this is what normal fans do, I thought to myself, and what a pleasant difference compared with a night on the town with the Lads.

By 10 p.m. people were beginning to get weary and we decided to make a move back to the hotel. By now the late afternoon drizzle had turned into a torrential downpour. By the time we made the underground station I was tired, wet and very tempted just to go back to the hotel and get my head down. But I had to remind myself that I was here to do research and not simply to enjoy the match and its build-up. Reluctantly I bade farewell to my new friends and got off the U-Bahn once more at Marienplatz.

I suspected that if there was to be any action on the eve of the match it would be in and around the main square. However, as I walked from the station the rain was dancing hard off the cobbled streets, making it impossible for the public displays of aggressive nationalism that usually prelude any violence. Marienplatz itself was virtually deserted. By now I was getting soaked. I chanced my arm at the Hofbräuhaus once more, but with the same result: no English wanted here. I wandered around the corner and found another, smaller restaurant and *Bierkeller* that was open to all comers. Judging by the décor and furnishings, it was obviously a respectable and up-market place that probably would not have been subscribed to by too many England fans had the bars and cafés around the square been able to operate their outdoor facilities. As it was, any nearby place that was open, dry and sold beer had been descended upon. This was packed with an uneasy mixture of Germans, regular Friday-night customers out for a quiet drink and a meal, and what appeared to me to be a sizeable detachment of Millwall's firm.

After I had managed to fight my way to the bar, I took my drink and found myself a corner in a large room at the back of the place to stand and watch. What I saw was not a pretty sight. Almost to a man the Lads bore the trademark uniform: shaved head, bulging muscles, beer bellies and tattoos. They were swilling down large steins of Hofbrau – the locally brewed, strong lager – like prohibition was about to be declared. Once in a while the Ingerland mantra would break out. This would be followed by the standard hummed and scat-sang repertoire of the themes from the pro-British war epics *The Great Escape* and *The Dambusters*. The dumbfounded German customers looked on as the Lads accompanied the latter by standing on chairs and tables with arms outstretched, mimicking the flight of a Lancaster bomber. This brief rendition of wartime tributes was wound up with a rafter-shaking chant (to the tune of the Cuban revolutionary folk song 'Guantanamera') of 'One Bomber Harris, there's only one Bomber Harris, one Bomber Harris, one Bomber Haarrrrris, there's only one Bomber Haarrrrris!' This was sung in celebration of the British RAF commander who masterminded the carpet-bombing campaign towards the end of the Second World War that saw cities like Cologne and Dresden razed to the ground and Munich itself devastated. Hundreds of thousands of German civilians lost their lives. Just in case any of the locals were missing the point, 'If you all hate Germans, clap your hands' was one chant that got straight to the heart of it.

I later heard tell that in another courtyard-style beer hall England fans had occupied the upper gallery while the Germans sat in the square below. One of the England fans was adept at making replica paper aeroplanes and he made several spitfires and sent them spiralling down among the Germans. The proprietor complained so the origami aficionado made Messerschmitts instead. Before he launched them he set fire to their tails, sending them down in flames into the midst of the Germans.

All in all, what I witnessed was a shameful display that made me feel sick and ashamed to be English. I was pondering the difference between this scene and the cross-national camaraderie that I had experienced only an hour or so earlier with the Manchester City crew when one of the Lads broke off his singing and came up to me and grabbed me by the shoulders and I froze. He looked me straight in the eye and said, 'Are yer all right?'

Straightaway I knew that I was being sussed out. So, in a broad Scouse accent I replied, 'Yeah, mate, sound, sound. It's a good laugh tonight init! Fucking Krauts.' With that he kissed me on the forehead and turned to his mates and said, 'He's OK,' and went off to join them. I wanted to bolt but I stayed on for a few minutes longer so as not to arouse further suspicions.

As soon as I felt it was safe I made my exit during a full-blooded rendition of 'No Surrender to the IRA'. I was a bit confused by what had happened. I was sure that the English police would have undercover spotters in and around Munich looking for firms like this. I reasoned that they would look just like the rest of the Lads. At 40-something with longish greying hair, put me in a suit and I might get away with undercover work among city financial fraudsters, but amongst the Lads I stuck out like a sore thumb. It was unlikely that the police would use anybody looking like me for this kind of undercover work.

I mentioned this incident to Big Tommy over breakfast the next morning. 'Ah, Suggy,' he said, 'No, they wouldn't have thought you were English Old Bill, but they might have thought that you were a German police spotter.'

'Of course, you're right,' I told him, 'that's why he asked if I was all right. He wanted me to reply to hear my accent, to check if I was German or not.'

'That's right,' said Tommy, 'and as soon as he heard you were a Scouser he knew you couldn't be, so he gave you a bye ball.' The German police that I had seen tended to be in their 30s and with longer hair than their English counterparts. Tommy's explanation made perfect sense and I was to get another confirmation of this later in the day.

It was now Saturday morning and the 'City til I die' crew were off to do more sightseeing and some shopping. I arranged to meet them later in an open-air beer garden in the market place behind the Frauenkirche, Munich's fifteenth-century cathedral. Big Tommy was off to the airport to meet Stiles, one of Tommy's London equivalents, who runs his own independent travel business. Stiles is a well-established carrier of England's irregulars and I was interested in meeting him. We took a cab back to the airport. On the way Tommy explained that Stiles had a charter coming in, the second of the day. Stiles caters both for the Lads and for regular fans, or straight members as Tommy calls them. For a big trip like this, if possible, he likes to keep the two distinctive types of supporters segregated. 'This flight we're going to meet's full of mainly straight members,' he explains, 'but he had one come in this morning with Chelsea's top firm on board. Right bloody nutters that lot. Wouldn't be right to mix them with the ordinary punters.'

At the airport Tommy introduces me to Little Jimmy, a grafter who works the Arsenal scene. He's waiting for the flights to come in too. Jimmy's got a board full of a variety of enamel England badges that he sources for about 10p and knocks out at around £2 apiece. Makes good money doing this at the Arsenal and at England and has recently cornered the Glasgow Celtic market. He sets his stand up near to the coaches awaiting the latest shipment of England fans and as they pour out of arrivals, badges sell like hot cakes.

Stiles arrives and Billy introduces me to him as one of his Scouser mates who is helping him out on the trip. Unlike Big Tommy who, with his close-cropped hair, baseball cap and casual sportswear look, could easily pass himself off as one of the Lads, Stiles looks more like a man who has come to Munich shopping for antiques. He is about 5 ft 10 in. and slim, in his early to mid 40s, bespectacled with longish mouse-coloured hair. Stiles is wearing a blue lightweight, blazer-style jacket and grey slacks and has an expensive-looking shoulder bag hanging by his side. For him, this trip is strictly business and it is a business that pays him handsomely. In many ways Stiles is Tommy's role model. An ex-hooligan who has made big money and earned a measure of respectability around travel. Tommy and Stiles first 'met' in 1981 on opposite sides during the Battle of Deansgate when a hundred-strong Arsenal firm were ambushed by Big Tommy and 150 United at Manchester's Deansgate Station. 'It raged for about three-quarters of an hour. There was blood and bodies everywhere by the time the Old Bill moved in.' Stiles has what Tommy craves, that is ATOL (Air Travel Organisers' Licensing) status. With ATOL accreditation Stiles not only has a globally recognised emblem of approval, but he can also charter his own planes via the CAA (Civil Aviation Authority) without having to go through an agent. Stiles also owns two prestige villas in the Caribbean. Not bad for a Lad who started out fighting on the terraces of Highbury with the likes of Big Tommy and United's Red Army.

Stiles is with another man who is introduced to me as Mark. He is likewise casually dressed for business. Mark runs an extremely successful ticketing agency in London. The late Stan Flashman's claim was that he could get a ticket for any event, anywhere, any time. Mark's business makes the same claim. Big Tommy tells me later that Mark clears half a million a year on tickets for Wimbledon alone (that's the grand slam tennis event and not the Crazy Gang!), but says that he is also a big player in the football ticket market. Of the 10,000-plus England fans in for the game, about 4,000 are seeking tickets and it promises to be a good day for Mark and the other spivs.

Once all the punters are shepherded to the right coaches Big Tommy arranges for Stiles, Mark, he and I to have lunch later. This will be good for me to sit and listen to three of the country's top football grafters and spivs have a natter over lunch. I am disappointed when we get back to town and Tommy has second thoughts. I can tell he is worried, thinking that because Stiles and Mark do not know what I am really doing, they might get onto some subjects that he would rather I did not know about. Tommy's been a great gatekeeper and informant, but I am not so naïve to believe that he would let me know about everything that he is into. Instead he decides we should go and track down his neighbours in the beer garden next to the cathedral market. There are no more than a few rows of wooden trestle-like picnic tables with bench seats seating about eight people on each side. Beer is sold from a central bar where an orderly queue is constantly moving past a serving hatch out of which burly bartenders dispense stein after stein of foaming lager. It is a jolly and friendly place, close to Marienplatz, but far enough away to avoid the attention of most of England's supporters. Surrounded by Germans, we sit in the shade of a tree talking football and keeping the pressure on Big Tommy, the only Red amongst us.

Soon we are joined by a couple of Germans, a father and his teenage son from Berlin who are likewise in town for tonight's match. We talk with them mainly about football, but the wailing of sirens interrupts our conversation. Something is kicking off somewhere. 'Ya,' said the older German, 'we were in a bar in town with lots of English fans. It was attacked by a gang of German hooligans. They came in through the door, but they left through the windows!' The German police had warned that a large gang of neo-Nazi German hooligans from all over Germany was descending on Munich to confront the English. If our friend's account was true, so far the score in the hooligan war was 1–0 to England.

Tommy's mobile chirps for the umpteenth time. He has a coachload making its way from Frankfurt where they had arrived from Manchester on a morning flight. The passengers are mainly Chelsea supporters based in the north of England. Chelsea north-west is another market that Big Tommy is keen to develop. He tells his courier where we are drinking and asks him to join us. Eventually the courier turns up with a couple of the Chelsea boys in tow. This little firm is a different kettle of fish altogether from the Manchester City crew, and much closer to the stereotypical louts described above. Already pretty drunk, they begin a shouted and slurred rendition of 'Ingerland, Ingerland, Ingerland'. What has hitherto been a pleasant afternoon pre-match drink begins to turn sour as their partisan noise attracts other England fans in the neighbourhood. Saint George flags are raised and soon we are part of the island of little England. It could go off at any moment.

My new Manchester City friends decide to leave. I am in two minds about what to do when Big Tommy's mobile rings again. 'Who's in town? Icky! Where is he?' asks Tommy. 'Right, OK. We'll be right over.' 'You're gonna love this, Suggy,' says Tommy, turning to me. 'Hickmott's in town from Thailand. He's in a bar over by the station with Chelsea's top firm. Lets go!' With that we drain our glasses and leave, taking the remnants of Chelsea north-west with us. I am looking forward to meeting a legend that I only read about or heard tell of in Bangkok.

The bar is a large *Bierkeller* on the far side of the main train station. As soon as we walk inside I sense it is the wrong place for me to be in. The cavernous beer hall is full of Lads with the casual hooligan uniform. This mob look particularly uniform, as most of them are wearing trendy dark blue and white Hacket polo shirts with 'The Dog's Bollocks' embossed across the shoulders. Obviously Hickmott has had a snide batch made up in Thailand and brought them to Munich for his troops to wear. As we stand in the beer line waiting to be served, I can feel eyes boring into me. Big Tommy senses it too. 'Listen, Suggy,' he whispers, 'I don't think you're safe here. You stick out like a sore thumb and they're all watching you like hawks. I think you better get out.' Remembering my Bangkok near miss, I do not need telling twice. I am not that desperate to meet Hickmott and, arranging to meet Tommy later, I slip away.

I need to get rid of some of the lager first so I pay a quick visit to the gents on the way out. While I am relieving myself I notice a calling card on the windowsill in front of me. I pick it up and it reads as follows:

> British National Party
> Put British people first
> Crack down on crime
> Stop racist anti-white violence
> Save the £pound
> No more asylum seekers

Tolerant bunch. I push my way to the door. Outside a group of Chelsea Lads have spilled onto the pavement and are busy abusing any non-whites who are unfortunate enough to be passing. I finger the BNP card in my pocket. What was that about racist anti-white violence? Contemptuously, I stride through them and cross to the other side of the street.

I stayed near to here with the Leeds Lads on that first Scum Airways trip. I remember that the Schiller bar is just around the corner and decide to check the place out. I find, though, that I cannot get near to it. Police in full riot gear have cordoned it off. Along with a group of nosy passers-by, I take up a vantage point just behind police lines. Outside there are a gang of English Lads drinking and taunting the police. Occasionally a glass or a bottle flies through the air towards the police lines. For their part, though, they are massed in large numbers, the police show admirable restraint, seemingly content to let the drunken English let off steam until the time comes to usher them towards the Olympic stadium. One fan, however, gets a little too cocky and gets too close as he shouts abuse and throws a half-full beer bottle at the riot police. All of a sudden the ranks part and a 6 ft 6 in. bear of a man in combat trousers and dark leather bomber jacket sprints through the gap and snatches his baiter, dragging the man back behind police lines like a rag doll. He gets a ripple of applause from the audience for his trouble. There is somebody who will not need a ticket tonight.

As for the game itself, I have to confess I went to it as a researcher, but left it as a fan. At first, of course, it was business as usual when Germany's lanky striker, Jancker, swooped to score on six minutes. When Owen equalised six minutes later the massive England crowd went wild with joy. And when Gerrard thumped an unstoppable 25-yarder passed the hapless Oliver Kahn to give England the lead just on half-time, if the stadium had had a roof it would have lost it. When Owen's second went in early in the second half we went berserk. Even I was singing 'Ingerland, Ingerland, Ingerland' now. When Owen netted his hat-trick in the 66th minute (and all that) there was a mighty roar from the ecstatic English. Emile Heskey made it 5–1 and we celebrated, but it was more like delirium. None of us had ever been there before, and anyway, how can you ratchet your emotions up from ecstasy? It was wonderful to be in the Olympic stadium at the end and look up at the giant illuminated scoreboard and see 'Germany 1 England 5'.

The next day, we hung around Marienplatz, killing time before heading to the airport. It was lunchtime and there was a bunch of hungover middle-aged England supporters sitting around. They were staring intently at the town hall clock. As the little hand reached one and the big hand five they began to hail passing Germans: 'Excuse me, what time is it?' Unwitting victims to their own humiliation, some would reply, 'Er . . . it is five past one,' causing their inquisitors to double up roaring with laughter. Cruel but fair.

Given the number of hard-core firms from both countries in town for this game, while there was violence, and although much of this went unreported in the wake of England's famous victory, it was not on the scale that had been predicted. The heavy rain of Friday night undoubtedly kept people off the streets and without opportunities for provocative public displays the Lads' chances of confrontation with police or other fans were minimised. Had it been a warm and sunny evening, I believe there would have been a great deal of trouble on Friday night. Then of course there was England's stunning and massive victory. Having seen their national team humbled in their own back yard, few German hooligans had the stomach for a fight. As for their English counterparts, they were too busy celebrating to go looking for one.

In the cold light of day talk began to turn to England's final qualifying game with Greece at Old Trafford in a month's time. It was impossible for Greece to qualify and all England needed was to draw to be certain of finishing top of the group. Anything less and the Lads would have their atlases out planning for a winter campaign somewhere on the Eastern front. 'We're bound to screw it up,' said Neil. 'We come to bloody Germany and stuff the Krauts in their own back yard, but I bet we lose at Old Trafford.' We all agreed that this could not be ruled out as England rarely miss an opportunity to miss an opportunity. True to form the Greeks scored first midway through the first half. Sheringham equalised, but the Greeks scored again and try as they might England just could not find an equaliser. We were just digging around for our thermal underwear, when deep in stoppage time along came *that* free kick. The whole of England held its breath as Beckham stepped back, looked up, paused and, well, bent it like Beckham into in the top corner. The nation's roofs lifted off. (I believe even some Scots cheered, but I would not bank on it.) I too leaped in the air and jumped for joy when Beckham's shot hit the back of the net.

As an England fan I was glad that we had made the finals, but what was more important to me was that England were off to Japan and so was Big Tommy. I had first come across the Big Man during France '98 and it was fitting that I would close the book on him in the 2002 World Cup.

ENDNOTES
[1] Brimson, D., 'Fans to a change' in *Hooligan Wars*, ed. M. Perryman (Edinburgh, Mainstream, 2001) p. 198
[2] Lowles, N., 'Far out with the Far Right', in *Hooligan Wars*, ed. M. Perryman (Edinburgh, Mainstream, 2001) pp. 119-20

# 9

## Big in Japan, June 2002

THE WORLD CUP IN JAPAN TURNED OUT TO BE A MUCH MORE worthwhile field trip than I had dared to hope for. At the outset I wondered if there would be enough new material for me to gather to justify the trip. For a start, even though Scum Airways were doing cut-price packages for the Far East, it was by no means certain that Big Tommy would be Big in Japan by making the expedition himself. This was mainly because, to begin with at least, the ticket market was so uncertain. Japan, where England were based, is not just a long way from home, it is also notoriously expensive. Stories of having to pay £10 or more for a pint in Tokyo had scared off a lot of England fans. The French, Germans, and the rest of the European qualifiers were even less enthusiastic about converting their precious euros into yen. As ever the Irish were exceptional and would travel in their thousands, following their 'boys in green' to the ends of the earth if necessary, even if it meant re-mortgaging their homes. In contrast, the collapse of the Argentine economy and growing impoverishment in Latin and Central America meant that only a few of the most wealthy grandees could follow their teams to Japan and South Korea. In the months building up to the start of the tournament the rest of the world seemed decidedly lukewarm about the prospect of spending time and lots of money sweltering in the Orient perilously close to the monsoon and typhoon seasons.

Unlike the situation for France '98, when many football associations, particularly those from Europe, had lobbied FIFA for additional tickets, for

2002 a lot of federations sent back portions of their allocations. So too did several of the big sponsoring companies, claiming not to be able to afford to put together VIP packages for clients and employees. With so many tickets allegedly available at face value from official sources it was hard to see how the touts could make their usual killing on the World Cup. In addition, because of the scandal that had exploded over the disastrous system of distribution of tickets for France '98, FIFA had vowed to put in place for 2002 a fair, efficient, hooligan-secure and, above all, tout-proof system for ticket allocation. As it turned out FIFA's handling of the ticket distribution for Japan and Korea was worse than that of France and largely because of this the touts would clean up.

In February 2002, when I met him in the Loaf – a chic new café and wine bar built into a railway arch in Manchester's Deansgate station – Big Tommy did not know this would happen and was sitting on a strong fence, undecided whether or not to make the trip. Six months previously we had agreed that I would fly out with him and a few other grafters to hang around with them in Japan while they worked the tickets. Unless he could be sure that he could make good money, Big Tommy would not travel. Through slurps of cappuccino, he told me that he was trying to get together the £35,000 bond that he needed to put up to secure his ATOL licence, making him 'fully legit' and able to hire his own planes without having to go through a third party like Stiles. A few years ago when he was still one of the Lads he might have gone just for the hell of it. Now he was a wannabe businessman and going to the Far East for what might turn out to be little more than a very expensive jolly was off the agenda. 'Anyway,' he went on, 'I've got a big Round Table do the day after the Sweden game and I've got to be here for that, so I'll probably come out on the following Monday.'

Tommy's 'wait-and-see' approach did not suit me, as I needed to plan ahead. Besides, I had come unstuck with Big Tommy's flexible plans in the past and I could not be sure whether he would actually go to Japan at all. As I was committed to write this chapter around World Cup 2002, I decided to gamble and booked with him there and then. He lifted his mobile and ten minutes later I had committed myself to a £2,000-plus two-week package that included flights to and from Tokyo, a Japan Railways pass, an internal flight from Tokyo to Sapporo where England would play Argentina, accommodation, and a ticket for England versus Sweden.

'What about Argentina?' I asked him.

He told me that it would be cheaper to get a ticket for this high-demand game out there. Little did I know then how right he would be, but not for any reason that Big Tommy anticipated.

Months before I had mentioned to Big Tommy that rather than just being one of his regular customers, if I did go with Scum Airways to Japan it would help me if I could be given a few menial tasks to perform. I explained that having a minor operational role and allowing me to be perceived as part of the firm would help me get closer to any action that might take place. He said that he would think about it, but nothing more was said until towards the end of May. Less than a week before I was scheduled to depart for Japan the Big Man called me at home. 'John, do you still want to do a bit of work for me?' he asked.

'Sure, Tom,' I replied, 'what is it?'

He asked me to take some tickets over to Japan and give them to some of his customers. Some would come to my home address by registered post, the others I would have to pick up in London on my way to Heathrow Airport the day of my flight to Japan. Big Tommy told me that Emma, his secretary, would fax me the details of the London pick-up over the weekend.

So long as the work did not involve me in actually buying and selling tickets I figured that I would be acting within the law, and within my increasingly flexible ethical code, so I agreed. I reasoned that it would be worth the risk as not only would it give me a role within the firm, but it would also give me a hands-on feel for the global touting scene. Two days later the postman called at my house with a registered brown paper envelope for which I signed. Inside I discovered nine tickets in total: four for England–Sweden; one for England–Nigeria; two for Ireland–Cameroon; and two for Ireland–Saudi Arabia. The promised fax had not arrived by the time I had left home for London and Heathrow. As my train rattled its way towards Victoria I called ITCL and spoke to Emma to find out where I had to go in London to pick up the rest of the tickets. 'You've got to go to a place called "Mission Impossible" [I kid you not],' she told me. 'There will be a package for you to pick up there.'

Mission Impossible is located near Bond Street Underground station behind Debenhams's Oxford Street department store. I dragged myself and my luggage through a thin drizzle down Marylebone Lane until I found the company's discreet, double-fronted, opaque-windowed offices opposite O'Connor's Irish pub and next to a Danish laundry – a front for the clandestine headquarters of an international spy ring if ever I've seen one. I buzzed Mission Impossible and explained my presence to a disembodied intercom before being let in. Inside at the front two pretty young women were working busily at their stations, checking monitors and answering phone calls, while a bespectacled middle-aged man sat at his desk in an open room behind them. I wondered if he was M and which one of the ladies was Miss Moneypenny. One of the women rose from her desk, shuffled through some papers and handed me a white envelope containing my orders. I expected to be told to memorise the contents before eating them and to be issued with a cyanide capsule. Instead I was politely shown the door and ushered out into the rain.

I caught the Heathrow Express from Paddington and during the short journey to the airport examined my latest haul. It consisted of four tickets for Ireland's game against Germany, giving me 13 tickets in all to deliver. The envelope also contained a list of people and places to whom and where I was to deliver the tickets. World Cup tickets had printed on them either individual names or organisations they were first issued to. I was intrigued by the sources from where this batch of tickets came. Three of the England tickets had individual names on them and had likely been sold on to the touts by members of the official England Members Club. The two remaining England tickets were issued to the English FA – that is tickets assigned to FA officials as distinct from those allocated to the England Members Club. Likewise, four of the Ireland tickets had come from the Football Association of Ireland and the remaining four from the Czech Republic's FA. As I photographed the tickets I thought to myself that FIFA's claim to have a watertight and tout-proof system for distributing tickets for 2002 was beginning to look a little overstated.

My first drop was to be at Heathrow where I was to deliver six tickets to a woman from Sligo who was taking her son to Ireland's three qualifying-round games. I was supposed to meet her at the check-in desk for Sri Lanka Airways.

the airline that Big Tommy was using to get most of his customers into and back from Japan. No sign of her there, so after half an hour I went through into the departure lounge. I had been given her mobile number by Emma, but could not get through. I stood in a bar called the Metro Café and called Emma in Manchester to ask her what to do. 'She's just phoned me,' Emma told me. 'She's sitting in some place called the Metro Café.'

I looked up and saw a woman with a mobile phone in her hand sitting at a table ten feet away from me. She caught my eye and I smiled at her and the young lad with her. 'It's OK, Emma,' I said, 'I've just found her.' I sat at the table, introduced myself and, as instructed, asked to see some identification. Having established that she was indeed my Sligo contact, I handed over the tickets. After a little small talk, I took my leave. Mission one accomplished.

There were two reasons, as far as I could see, why ITCL were using Sri Lanka Airways. First and foremost flights were cheap and this meant that Big Tommy could undercut many of his competitors. Secondly, and of equal importance to some of his customers – the Lads – the journey to Japan was a two-legged affair via the Sri Lankan capital, Colombo. A flight between Colombo and Tokyo was less likely to draw the attention of anti-hooligan security agents than a direct flight from London. While many if not most of Big Tommy's World Cup customers were 'straight members', there were still a few Lads hoping to get to Japan via Scum Airways. The Sri Lanka route would suit them better than a direct flight.

The scale of the anti-hooligan operation for World Cup 2002 was bigger than anything previously mounted and finding ways to outwit British police, immigration officials, the NCIS and their Japanese counterparts challenged the Lads' ingenuity. Two weeks before the start of the tournament they had felt the full force of enhanced football-disorder legislation when more than a thousand of them had been ordered to surrender their passports to their local police stations to be held for the duration of the tournament. The NCIS published a league table showing which clubs the banned supporters were affiliated to. I was not surprised to see Leeds in third place with 66 but still more than 30 behind Stoke on 98 who themselves trailed Cardiff City on 112. The latter is an astonishing statistic given that most of the Cardiff thugs' banning orders came as a result of offences committed against supporters of rival English clubs. However, when it came to international games some of them were more than happy to join forces with the English Lads because they knew that by following England there was a better chance that they could vent their own warped Celtic xenophobia and wage war on foreign soil.

Of course for every one banned there are ten others equally as bad who just have not been caught and some of these would be trying to get to Japan. Even the loss of a passport could not guarantee that those banned would not travel under false passports. Living in a subculture where forged tickets, counterfeit clothes, drugs and even guns were routinely bought and sold, getting hold of a false passport would not be difficult. Particularly given that for most of the Lads who were trying to get to Japan, all roads there led through the 'bootleg capital of the world', Bangkok. When I had been in Thailand almost a year earlier I had wondered if many of the Lads would use it as a bridgehead into Japan for the World Cup the following year. Unlike in Japan, the accommodation was cheap as was the beer and the seedy sex. Whereas the Japanese were over-prepared for an English hooligan invasion, the Thais were characteristically laid back about the arrival of a few more beer-bellied sex-tourists. 'If all of their documents are right, we have no reason not to let them in,' said Deputy Immigration Police Chief, Major General Ukrit Patchimsawat. 'We expect no trouble.'

And, of course, unlike Japan, Thailand had Patpong-on-Sea, alias Pattaya, and Pattaya had the Dog's Bollocks and its proprietors, the two Chelsea Headhunters, Steve Hickmott and Chris Henderson who, according to a *Sunday Mirror* article of 5 May, were facilitating the movement of more than 100 English hooligans through Thailand to Japan. This included liaising with local criminals to get match tickets and, if necessary, false identification for those who may be on lists of undesirables supplied to Japanese immigration by British authorities and the NCIS.

It seemed that there were at least two of these lists operating. The first, the official banned list referred to above, required the surrender of passports and, unless those banned had acquired false passports in the UK it would be impossible for them to leave for Japan or South Korea. This may keep at home the first wave of hooligans. There would be many others who the police suspected of hooligan-related offences, but who did not have convictions, or the 'right sort' of convictions to get them on the official banned list. On this basis a second list was compiled that could not be used to prevent suspects from leaving Britain, but once supplied to Japanese and South Korean authorities could be used by them to turn back those deemed undesirable. This could be a quite arbitrary instrument. In Japan I met a Huddersfield Town supporter who complained bitterly that immigration police had sent his friend back to Britain when he had arrived at Tokyo's Narita Airport. 'It was all to do with something that happened in Germany. He was in a long queue waiting patiently for a taxi in Munich when this bloody Kraut jumped the queue and stole his taxi. He kicked the cab door in frustration and was seen doing this by German police. He was arrested, but released after questioning. He's never been in any other bother, but because of that he got sent back. It's not right. I know that there are loads of real villains that have got through, yet my pal gets sent home.'

Later, Big Tommy told me that 40 Lads he knew had gone via Thailand and South Korea to the England versus Argentina game in Sapporo. Some heavy-duty Category C hooligans had made it through, but eight were refused entry and spent four days in a Japanese prison before being deported. With Icky and Henderson's help, the Lads who passed through the Dog's Bollocks stood a good chance of avoiding the same fate.

The *Sunday Mirror*'s story went on the wire and was soon picked up by Channel 11, an enterprising Japanese television station, who sent a reporter and camera crew over to Thailand to check out the story and find and film activities in the Dog's Bollocks. 'Where Dog's Bollocks?' the reporter says to his boss. In this case, 'Between dog's legs' is not the right answer. The Dog's Bollocks is off South Pattaya's sea-front on Soy Yamoto, in a concentrated area of strip joints, sex clubs and sundry go-go bars with equally endearing names like the Legless Arms, Playpen-a-go-go, New Hot, Lazi Pig, and right next door, Nice 'n' Sleazy-a-go-go. The Channel 11 team arrived at the open-fronted bar, which was jammed with the Lads and a sad collection of bargirls. When they tried to go in to film they were aggressively ejected. Instead, they went next door and started to shoot footage in Nice 'n' Sleazy-a-go-go. Suddenly half a dozen *farang*s who had been drinking in the Dog's Bollocks burst in and attacked them, roughing them up and squirting them with pepper spray. Later, using security videotapes, some of the assailants were identified, including 47-year-old Steven Hickmott, who was arrested and charged with assault. Icky got off with a fine and told reporters that he would not be going to the World Cup. Instead he was off to the Philippines for work reasons.

Bryan Drew of the NCIS had said: 'We intend to stop anybody intent on causing trouble from entering Japan. There are plans in place and we know what's going on in Thailand.' Do we indeed? By 28 May, only days before the first match between France and Senegal, the Thai police were confidently able to report that of the hundreds of British hooligans holed up in Pattaya only a handful remained, the rest having made their way successfully to Japan. Don't bet against Icky being with them. Evening all.

The down side of the Sri Lanka Airways route was the interminable length of the journey. Ten hours to Colombo, with a ten-hour stopover, followed by another ten-hour flight to Tokyo via the Maldives. And when Sri Lanka say 'economy class', they mean it. We were crammed in like sardines and I needed the ten-hour stopover in Colombo to straighten out my aching six-foot skeleton. Rather than staying in the sweltering airport, those of us travelling on to Tokyo were shipped out to a local hotel for a bit of Rest and Relaxation. The Oceanic Beach Hotel was about an hour away. I was given a ground-floor room with a king-sized bed, French windows, and a veranda that opened onto a tropical beach and the Indian Ocean. Maybe I should stay here and watch the World Cup, I thought to myself. After a couple of hours' sleep, I showered and went to the bar for a drink. It was there that I met Luke.

The open-fronted hotel bar looked out towards the beach and the ocean. Dressed in shorts and a fully open Hawaiian shirt, Luke was wandering around between the bar and the beach. In fact, Luke rarely ever stood still for more than ten seconds so I nicknamed him 'Jumpy Luke'. I was sharing a welcome glass of cold Lion beer with Steve and Mick, a couple of fellow World Cup travellers from Redhill in Surrey. They were definitely 'straight members' and I explained to them a little bit of what I was writing about. When Mick spotted Luke he said to me: 'See that bloke? He was sitting near us on the plane. He told us that he was a tout.' My interest in the wandering stranger increased immediately.

Eventually Luke meandered up to the bar and started to talk to us. I was trying to think of a devious ploy that might get Jumpy Luke to talk about his touting when, in response to Mick's question about what games he was going to watch, he said: 'Not sure if I'll see any, man. I'm a ticket tout.' Straightaway I dropped a few names, asking him if he knew any of the touts who had passed my way in the last few years. He knew of Big Tommy but had not met him. He also knew most of the London movers and shakers, but said he preferred to hang out with the Scousers 'cos they stick together and help each other out more than the Londoners or Manchester geezers'. He said he had 50 tickets on him and hoped to pick up more once he got to Japan.

Jumpy Luke turned out to be quite a character and the most hapless ticket tout I had ever met. He did not just tout around football, but also did other sports, especially boxing and the Olympics. He told us that he had been in Salt Lake City, USA, for the Winter Olympics where he had been arrested three times for 'scalping' – an American term for ticket touting. He had got off with fines for the first two offences, but the third time he had been sent to prison. 'Yeah, man, spent five weeks in a fucking orange boiler suit! Thought I was gonna get away with another $50 fine, but I had this bitch of a prosecutor. Kept telling me to stand still and all that shit. Well, I couldn't take that, could I? I had to give her a right coating, didn't I? Called her a fucking slag and that. Then the judge sends me to fucking jail!' Who says justice is blind?

At this point Jumpy begins to roll a joint. 'Want any blow, man?' he asks us.

'Er, no, Luke,' I reply politely, remembering the bold statement on the disembarkation card that I had filled in on the plane: 'Import and export of drugs punishable by death'. I learn later that he had bought the cannabis with him on the plane, and that he may have even had some cocaine on him. The four of us agree to have lunch together in the hotel restaurant. It is buffet style, which suits Jumpy Luke because he can keep going up and down, refilling plate after plate of food, almost none of which he eats. The highpoint of the meal comes when I spot some local vermin – a cross between a chipmunk and a squirrel – jump up onto the cake trolley and leisurely begin to munch its way through one of the desserts. As I am reaching for my camera, the chef comes out of the kitchen and shoos it away. Then he turns and sees me trying to get a photograph of the cake-munching rodent. The chef apologises for ruining my shot and, rubbing his fingers and thumb and making a strange 'tut tut tut' noise, begins to try and coax the creature back to the cake trolley. 'Don't worry,' the chef tells me when the creature scurries off, 'he will be back soon.' Before the chip-squirrel has a chance to return to finish his pudding a bunch of strapping Irish lads, who are likewise on their way to the World Cup, demolish his favourite dish.

Jumpy Luke has been sitting down for all of five minutes, which is way too long for him. 'Gonna get a taxi into town,' he announces. 'Gotta get some pills.' Off he goes. Two hours later he returns, proudly announcing that he managed to buy some valium across the counter at a downtown pharmacy, before wandering off along the beach smoking another joint. Luke's the last to arrive for the minibus ride back to the airport. By now, full of uppers, downers, and inside outers, he is looking a bit worse for wear. I ask him why he was so late. 'Met some guys on the beach, man. They knew where the local brothel was and took me there. Trouble is I fell asleep. Only woke up five minutes ago and had to leg it back to the hotel to get my stuff.' Once we are in the departure lounge, Jumpy tries to sit next to me at the bar, but he keeps falling backwards off his bar stool, scattering his crumpled money all over the place. After I have caught him for the third time, I suggest that he goes for a lie down on one of the lounge couches – which is what he does, passing out almost immediately. It's the first time I have seen him still all day. Later, on the flight to Tokyo, he tries to skin up in the smoking area at the back of the plane, but reluctantly agrees not to continue when Paul from Huddersfield reminds him about drugs and the death penalty. Almost inconceivably, Jumpy sails through immigration at Narita Airport and melts away to spread more chaos among Tokyo's masses. By remarkable coincidence – given that there are more than 18 million people living in the Japanese capital – I bump into Jumpy ten days later walking along the street in Ginza. 'Hey, man, how you doin'?' asks Jumpy. 'You sorted me out good style on the way over. I was really out of it. You're not going to believe this, but I spoke to me mum and she said she saw me on the BBC news, being carried off the plane, I think it was by you or Paul. The news said something about drunken England fans arriving in Japan!'

Tokyo dwarfs any other city that I have been in, including New York. It sprawls around Tokyo Bay like a high-rise Legoland, a mass of corporate skyscrapers and high-rise apartment blocks interconnected through a concrete and steel network of flyovers and bridges. No city this size should work, but Tokyo does and wonderfully well. It is orderly, spotlessly clean and is serviced by a transport system that makes its UK equivalent look pre-mediaeval. If a train is more than a minute late it is considered to be a national disaster. Many England fans had opted to stay in one of Tokyo's capsule hotels, where £20 per night bought them a coffin-sized chamber among a stacked honeycomb of others. Usually Japanese businessmen, who have either been working or drinking late and are not able to make it home and back in time for the office at 8 a.m. the next day, resort to these facilities. I expect eventually to spend long enough in a coffin and did not fancy the near-death experience of a capsule hotel. Instead, my ITCL package included a room in the Tokyo Urishima, a modest hotel in the Kachidoki district. As it turned out my room was not much more than coffin sized, designed for four footers not six footers, but it had a bed, a small desk and a bathroom, which were all I needed.

Other than the hotel's regular Japanese clientele, the Urishima is packed to the gills with Irish and a few English who are mostly Big Tommy's customers. I recognise one of the English as Jim, a nasty piece of work who I had met in Munich. He is a Chelsea fan from Stoke and claims to have paid Big Tommy £7,500 for a five-week trip. Between them, Stoke and Chelsea had 118 supporters banned from travelling before the World Cup finals. Jim is one who slipped through. 'Don't know how I got out the country, really,' he boasts without much prompting. 'Got a record as long as me arm – burglary, GBH, drugs – the lot. Flew to Spain first, then on to Austria, then we came first-class to Tokyo.' Unsurprisingly, Jim tells me that they will stay for the qualifying games and if England go through they will head off to Thailand for a few days for some R & R before returning to Japan for the knockout stages.

Otherwise it is going to be a dull World Cup for Jim and his little firm who are struggling to find trouble to start. To begin with there are few natural enemies in Japan for them to pick a fight with. The Argentinians have not travelled and there are relatively few Germans about. The Swedes and the Danes are likewise few and friendly, and the Nigerians are even fewer and friendlier. No joy either with the locals who are the friendliest of the lot, most of whom have adopted England as their number-two team.

Also, the usual European-style venues for trouble are not available in Tokyo. Most Japanese bars are tiny. Most of the larger bars that I found were several floors above street level. None of them open out onto broad squares or circuses, the favoured battlegrounds for hooligans abroad. The only potential flash-point that I could find was in Roppongi, the nearest Tokyo has to London's West End. O'Mally's Irish Pub was right next door to The Frog and Toad, its English equivalent, and there was a small plaza outside in which the Irish and English mingled and tried to out-sing one another. There were a few muffled renderings of 'No Surrender to the IRA', from the likes of Jim and his ilk, but only a few joined in and the song soon petered out.

Jim and the Lads head back to the hotel, disappointed not to find a first-night ruck down town, but resolve to have a go at the Paddies in the Urishima. The Japanese get most things right, but sometimes miss the obvious. For instance, if you are interested in making money and have 200 thirsty Irish in your hotel, you do not shut the bar at 10.30 p.m., which is precisely what happened each night in the Urishima. Undeterred, the Irish (and the English) simply headed next door to a 24-hour convenience store and stocked up with multiple cans of lager and bottles of whisky and vodka, which, without any objection from management, they proceeded to drink in the hotel lobby, usually until it was time to go into breakfast at 7 a.m. the following morning.

When Jim and his crew get back the Irish are in full voice. I watch from afar as the outnumbered English engage in a bit of what on the surface appears to be friendly competitive singing. I had seen these Lads operate in Munich and feared that this was just a prelude to trouble. I edge closer and overhear Jim rallying his troops. 'Come on, Lads. All right there are only five of us, but they're just a bunch of Paddy wankers. We can take 'em easily.'

Sociologists are supposed to record and make sense of social life, not change it, and one of the first rules of sociological method is that when you are in the field you should do nothing to disturb the natural flow of events. I had lived and worked in Belfast for 14 years and both of my children had been born in Ireland. I have a real liking for the Irish. Listening to these English scumbags planning violence against them sickened me and I decided to tweak history. I spotted one big, fresh-faced Irishman called Seamus among the throng who also seemed to be keeping his eye on Jim and his fat friends. I gave him the nod and we went around the corner for a chat. Seamus used to be a bouncer in Dublin and now runs his own security company. He is used to spotting trouble and troublemakers. I told him what I had heard. Seamus thanked me and went back to usher his company away from Jim and his crew. I went to bed hoping that nothing had happened.

The next day I met Seamus again. 'Hear what happened last night?' he asked me.

'No,' I replied.

'It was that bastard that you tipped us off about, pulled a knife on us, didn't he? He ran at us, but he was so gargled the fucker kept dropping the knife. One of our lads is in the Garda [police] back home and he had an emergency number for the local cops and he called them. By then yer man had sloped off to his room. The police came, found him and searched his room. Turns out that it wasn't a knife at all but a bloody cut-throat razor!'

'Jesus,' I said, 'did they deport him?'

Seamus just laughed. 'Nah, you're not going to believe it. He told them that he needed it for shaving, so they let him off. I ask you, who do you know who still uses a cut-throat razor in this day and age?'

Jim had been warned, however, and one more brush with the law would see him on the next plane home.

Watching the games on television was a bit of a problem in Tokyo as very few were screened on free-to-air TV. Most fans could not afford hotels with cable television and were forced to roam the streets looking for a bar with a TV – of which there were few. Those who could get in made Roppongi's Tokyo Sports Café their headquarters. It was roomy, with several bars, a dance floor and multiple TV screens. It became a particular favourite for the English as in between games the DJ played mainly English records that had become football anthems. At around £6 a pint, lager was not cheap, but it did not seem to stop the fans from drinking it in great volume. At my first visit I thought that if there was going to be a kick-off it would be here. The usual suspects were all in place – shaven-headed, beer-bellied and tattooed England fans; a generous sprinkling of Jonny foreigners; a posse of tooled-up police massed at the entrance; and the usual invasion of television cameras and bright lights to stir up the cocktail.

Contrary to my fears, it did not kick-off, not that night nor any other that I was there. Instead, it reminded me of a 1960s love-in with football and music sharing the centre. This was most graphically illustrated the night after Japan's opening game with Belgium. It was 2–2, but the hosts should have won, having had a third goal unjustifiably disallowed in the dying minutes. That did not spoil the party atmosphere in the Sports Café. When I got there, long after the final whistle, the dance floor was packed with English, Belgian, Swedish and Japanese fans. The latter were a mixture of youth culture – big, bright hair, painted faces and replica Nippon shirts – and young suited-and-booted businessmen on their way home from work. They leaped, danced and hugged their way through a multi-national and global celebration of Indian food and football, the noisiest rendition of Fat Les's 'Vindaloo' that I have ever heard. A combination of high costs and a police crackdown meant that there was not a critical mass of Category B and C hooligans to spoil what was turning into a global, multi-national and multi-racial carnival. In this atmosphere even the cross of Saint George was beginning to lose its sinister BNP connotations. If this went on I was going to have to revise my view of England supporters abroad.

I was in Japan for two reasons. The first was to gather material for this book. Secondly, there had been a significant upsurge of political intrigue and in-fighting inside the FIFA family. Ever since Sepp Blatter had been elected president in highly dubious circumstances in Paris in 1998, he had faced underground opposition from some of the most powerful figures in world football, including UEFA's heavyweight president Lennart Johansson. The collapse of ISL – FIFA's marketing partner – the bankruptcy of German media magnate Kirch – the television rights holders for the World Cups 2002 and 2006 – and the whistle-blowing claims of the vice-president of the African Football Federation (CAF), Farah Addo, that he had been offered a $100,000 bribe to vote for Blatter in 1998, together had wounded the beleaguered FIFA president and caused these underground rumblings to burst to the surface. Then the FIFA general secretary, Michel Zen Ruffinen, published a 30-page dossier, backed by a further 300 pages of evidence, stating that Blatter had been severely incompetent and sometimes fraudulent in the way he had handled FIFA's finances. Under Blatter's leadership Zen Ruffinen claimed that the organisation had misdirected or lost tens of millions of pounds. Backed by a majority of the FIFA executive the president of CAF, Isa Hayatou of Cameroon, was persuaded to stand against Blatter who sought re-election in Seoul on the eve of the World Cup finals. If Blatter had been the CEO of any other public or commercial multinational, on the basis of his abysmal four-year record in charge of FIFA he certainly would have been fired. Instead the FIFA membership re-elected him with a significantly increased majority. Something was smelling very rotten and shortly before I had left for Japan it was agreed that Alan Tomlinson and I should update our last book on FIFA – *Great Balls of Fire* – and republish it in paperback under a new title, *Badfellas: FIFA Family at War*. While I was in Japan mainly for this book, we agreed that I should also try and reinvigorate some old FIFA sources. It was not until I was in the field doing this that it occurred to me that the two projects were in fact connected.

The most obvious connection is tickets. Few would argue that from an organisational point of view the 2002 World Cup was an almost total success, except, that is, for the fiasco over tickets. To begin with, if you could get them, the tickets were too expensive: £75 for the cheapest ticket for the qualifying stages, rising at each stage to as much as £350 face value for the final. This might have been OK for the high-earning Japanese, but it was too much for the relatively poor Koreans and those fans who were flying halfway around the world to follow their teams. On top of the thousands of pounds spent on travel and accommodation, English fans, for instance, who wanted to see every stage of the competition, would have to shell out a minimum £1,500 just for tickets. These prices were set by the joint Japanese and Korean WCOC (World Cup Organising Committee) to whom all of the ticket revenues were to accrue. They were way out of the range of the fabled 'ordinary fan' and it reminded me of a comment made by Alan Rothenberg, a US member of the FIFA executive. When challenged in Paris about the excessive price of tickets for South Korea and Japan, he shrugged his shoulders and simply said: 'Watching the World Cup live is not for the ordinary fan. That's why they've got televisions.'

The price of tickets was bad enough and the system for their distribution was worse – unless you were a tout that is. Keeping in mind that the hub of the grafters' world that I have been investigating is Manchester, it was an astonishing coincidence that the contract for producing and distributing World Cup tickets was awarded to Byrom Consultants, a small British company with its headquarters in Big Tommy's back yard, Cheadle Hulme, south Manchester. Buying, selling and distributing tickets was to be done on-line via FIFA's ticket website, but by the time the first game kicked off in Seoul some fans who had been allocated and had paid for blocks of tickets, still had not received them. As many as 10,000 tickets allocated to England fans had not arrived before their intended recipients had left for the Far East. It was chaos in Korea and Japan as nervous and angry ticketless fans battled with FIFA and local bureaucracies to get their hands on the precious tickets. As the early games unfolded it became obvious that large sections of some grounds were not full. This might be expected for some of the low-demand early games, like Saudi Arabia versus Cameroon, but not for high-demand matches like Japan's opening game against Belgium or England's first match against Sweden. The Japanese WCOC was furious as each empty seat meant a loss of revenue. In total the shortfall was estimated at two billion yen which would have to be made up by the ten local prefectures responsible for the stadia. Likewise the fans were frustrated and furious. Before Japan's opener, at a ticketing centre in Saitima, one indignant fan grabbed a hapless ticketing official by the lapels and threw him headlong through a plate-glass window.

Against earlier predictions the confusion and chaos over tickets meant that World Cup 2002 would be a bumper event for the touts after all. As ever there seemed to be no shortage of tickets for them. Big Tommy had told me earlier in the year that World Cup tickets would not be a problem. As indicated by the provenance of the tickets that I had brought over, tickets were flowing freely to the touts from the usual sources, including many overseas football federations. He also claimed to have a high-profile contact who would be able to get tickets out of the back door of Byroms. In fact this did not happen because the person in question (who cannot be identified for legal reasons) came under police investigation following a number of allegations not related to Byroms, but including the illegal supply of tickets. Certainly the touts were harvesting tickets in bulk. Spivs, mainly from London, Manchester and Liverpool, were out in force outside all of England and Japan's games. An editorial in the *Daily Yomiuri* suggested that FIFA should cut out the middlemen and give all of the tickets to the touts at the start of the competition. At least the touts sell the tickets outside the grounds where the games are to be played, the paper went on to argue.

The touts did not have it all their own way, however. One, named John James, was arrested at Narita Airport when it was discovered that he had almost 200 tickets on his person. The tickets were confiscated and he was sent packing back to England. This caused an unforeseen panic for another John James whom I met on the road a few days later. This innocent and likeable lad from Birmingham was staying with a mate who was working in Tokyo. He had come over for the first two games, but like me would leave before the England–Nigeria game. He had a spare ticket that he would sell once in Japan. He got back to his friend's apartment one day to be told that his mother had been on the phone in a right state. She knew that he had a spare ticket and when she heard that a John James had been deported for ticket touting she thought it was her son of the same name. I hope he was wearing his vest when he called his mum to calm her down.

My own ticket situation was interesting, not to say perilous. I had one for England versus Sweden and a spare for England versus Nigeria that I would not be using, but I did not have one for the coveted England–Argentina game. This was the hottest ticket of the preliminary rounds and in Tokyo the cheapest on offer were around £500. With Big Tommy yet to put in an appearance, I was beginning to worry that even though I had a flight and hotel booked in Sapporo I would not be able to afford to buy a black-market ticket to see the game itself. Then I met Charlie and my luck changed.

With not much happening on the Scum Airways front I decided to devote a few days to the FIFA beat. As ever the biggest problem is getting well-placed and well-informed insiders to talk. Before leaving England I had contacted New Zealander Charlie Dempsey and asked him for an interview in Tokyo. Charlie is an octogenarian, ex-pat Scot, who was president of the Australasian/South Pacific confederation of FIFA, Oceania. Charlie's moment in the sun, or more accurately his eclipse, came in July 2000 when as a member of FIFA's 24–man executive committee he was required to vote on who should host the World Cup finals in 2006. It eventually boiled down to a straight choice between South Africa and Germany. The Oceania executive had advised Charlie that if this was the case he should vote for South Africa. Instead, claiming to be under too much pressure from both the Germans and the South Africans, Charlie decided to abstain. Germany won the ballot by 12 votes to 11 and Blatter, himself a German–Swiss, was relieved of the potentially embarrassing duty of having to make a casting vote. Charlie was vilified by the global paparazzi and resigned as president of Oceania, losing his various positions within FIFA. But FIFA likes to keep its fall-outs within the family. In a slick move, after he had been re-elected at the Seoul congress, as the last item of business Blatter proposed honorary life membership of FIFA for Charles Dempsey. Was this Blatter's way of keeping Charlie quiet about the 2006 affair, I asked myself? This was a man I needed to talk to.

I tracked Charlie down at the FIFA HQ hotel, the Westin, in Tokyo's Ebisu district. Built on the site of the old Sapporo brewery, the Westin is standard FIFA five-star stuff: black marble floors; towering Doric columns; sweeping ballroom staircases; gold and mahogany trim; and overstuffed coaches for overstuffed officials in a cavernous lobby. I put a call through to his room on the off chance that he may be in. Surprisingly he was and he invited me up to talk with him. Charlie had a suite of rooms to himself. He looked diminutive and slightly frail as he sat in the middle of a Chesterfield couch watching a game on TV. We talked for about an hour and a half, mainly around themes related to my FIFA work. Towards the end of our conversation we talked about football and England's relatively poor performance against Sweden. Before I left Charlie asked me if I was going to watch England play Argentina. I told him that I hoped to, but added that I was not yet sure that I had a ticket. 'Would you like me to put your name down for one?' he asked me.

'Well, if it's not too much trouble,' I replied, 'that would be great.'

He asked me for my passport number, which I had in my pocket, and the telephone number of my hotel, promising to call me the next day to let me know if he had been able to secure my ticket.

Having successfully worked the hierarchy, I left the Westin with a lighter step than when I had arrived and headed back to Roppongi to see if there was any action with the lowerarchy. I got back to my hotel around midnight and, as usual, walked into a full-scale Irish ceilidh. Thus, I was still lying in my bed nursing a headache when the phone went. It was Charlie, and he said the magic words: 'That's OK, John. I've put in for a ticket for you for the Argentina game and it should be all right.' I could not thank him enough, but before I put the phone down he said, 'Are you going to today's game?' The game in question was Japan's long-awaited opening fixture with Belgium in Saitima.

'Er, well, no, Charlie,' I replied, 'I haven't got a ticket.'

'Would you like me to put in for one for you?' he asked.

'Of course, if it's not too much trouble . . .'

He told me he would call me back and sure enough half and hour later he did. 'That's fine,' he said, 'only problem is you will have to come with me on the FIFA VIP coach.'

I could not believe my luck. Not only would I get to see the co-host's opening match, but with luck and a little help from Charlie, I would also have the opportunity to mingle with many of the top brass that I needed to speak to with regard to updating the FIFA story.

So it turned out. In the FIFA VIP lounge just behind the Tribune d'Honeur I was able to work the room full of FIFA notables, grabbing soundbites and making future appointments with key figures as they sipped fine wine and nibbled delicate parcels of sushi. I had been investigating FIFA for a number of years and as I surveyed the room it occurred to me that there were probably more crooks here than in any single place I had been in on the Scum Airways beat. It was only a short escorted walk to the best seats in the house to watch Japan and Belgium play out a thrilling 2–2 draw. My seat was slightly to the left of the halfway line, below the Japanese Prime Minister and members of the Japanese Royal Family, and within touching distance of legendary former players like Franz Beckenbauer and Michel Platini. On the way back into town Charlie asked me if I was going to watch Ireland against Germany in Ibaraki the following day. 'Er, well, I wasn't, Charlie. I don't have a ticket.'

'Would you like me to put in for one for you?'

'Well, if it's not too much trouble . . .'

Ibaraki is a good two-hour drive from downtown Tokyo. I sat at the back of the comfortable, air-conditioned FIFA VIP bus around a large card table laughing and joking with Charlie and several other FIFA blazers from the Cook Islands and countries in Oceania and the Asian confederation. As we got closer to Ibaraki's Kashima stadium, out of the window I could see thousands of green, white and gold bedecked Irish trudging through the evening heat towards the stadium. I began to feel guilty about the position of privilege that I now found myself in. I suppose I could justify it on the grounds of access and research, but I still felt a bit of a fraud. Not that this seemed to be bothering anybody else on the bus, especially the representative from Singapore who had his wife and four children with him: twin daughters about 12 or 13; and a couple of toddlers about four and two years old respectively. All lifelong football fans I'm sure. After more of the same in the VIP lounge, during the game I sat just to the right of the senior officials from German Football Federation. It was worth the trip just to see the smugness vanish from their faces when Robbie Keane smashed in Ireland's last-gasp equaliser. On the way back to Tokyo, Charlie told me that he would no longer be going to the England versus Argentina game because one of his grandchildren in New Zealand was ill and he was returning home. This made me slightly anxious since the VIP match tickets were given out inside the VIP lounge and without a VIP accreditation pass I doubted that I would get in to retrieve my ticket. Charlie told me not to worry and introduced me to Stephan, the FIFA official charged with the responsibility for distributing the complimentary VIP tickets. Stephan instructed me to go to the Sapporo Park Hotel, FIFA's HQ in Sapporo, the morning of the Argentina game and ask for Alex Soosay who would give me my ticket; he gave me Alex's mobile phone number.

Sapporo is about 500 miles north of Tokyo and, after an uneventful flight, I arrived mid-afternoon on 6 June – the day before the Argentina game. I still had lingering worries about my ticket and I decided to try and get my hands on it there and then. After checking into my own hotel, I set off to find the Sopporo Park, exploring the town en route. Sapporo is a ski-resort city that was host to the 1972 winter Olympics. The mountain air was fresher and cooler than the fetid and smoggy heat and humidity of Tokyo. Using the excellent municipal underground system, it was easy for me to find the Sapporo Park Hotel which is on the edge of Nakahjima Park, opposite the Kerin Brewery and Beer Garden and adjacent to Nakajim underground station. Inside the lavish and spacious lobby, I found the FIFA welcome desk and asked for Mr Soosay only to be told that he had finished for the day. I would have to wait until the morning and along with thousands of other England fans, spent the rest of the evening pounding the streets of Sapporo trying to find a bar with a television. I think there were only about three in the entire city and each of those was absolutely packed out. I gave it up as a bad job and headed back to my hotel. After breakfast the next day I telephoned Alex using the number given to me by Stephan. Much to my relief Alex confirmed that he had a ticket for me and told me to return to the Sapporo Park and pick it up. It was then that a modern fairytale began.

I presented myself at the FIFA desk and a pretty Japanese receptionist in a smart, pale-blue suit escorted me up to the sixth floor and the FIFA offices where I met Alex. He was seated behind a small desk with a stack of multi-coloured match tickets in front of him. He checked his list and saw my name next to the allocation for Mr Dempsey. He then shuffled though his pile of tickets and passed one over to me. At last I had it in my hand and could relax. Then he said: 'Are you going to take the other three also?'

'What other three?' I asked, my heart quickening as I remembered that Charlie had actually told me that he had put in for two tickets for me. Alex told me that Mr Dempsey had requested four tickets in total and asked me did I want to take the rest. I was tempted, but was worried that Charlie had promised them to other people who would come for them later. 'No, I'd better not,' I said, 'what if somebody else comes looking for them?'

'You are the only one who has come,' replied Alex. 'I think it is best that you take them.' I had the distinct impression that Alex wanted these tickets off his hands and he would not take no for an answer. The remaining three tickets were in an envelope downstairs at the FIFA reception desk and he instructed my escort to take me there and give them to me, which she duly did. The envelope with Mr Dempsey scrawled on it in black felt-tip was at the bottom of the pile. As she flicked through the stack of envelopes I saw one with 'Col. Qadaffi' printed on it. Better not give me his by mistake, I thought to myself!

Stuffing the Dempsey envelope in my pocket I went and took a seat in the corner of the lobby. I needed to think. Half an hour earlier, I was not even sure that I had a single ticket. Now I had four tickets for the best seats in the house which, at least judging by Tokyo black-market rates, could be worth up to £1,000 each. The last thing I could or would do was sell them. If they were traced, not only would this reflect very badly on me, but also, more importantly, it would be hugely embarrassing for Charlie, my benefactor. Already the British press was calling for the blood of one senior FIFA executive member whose personal allocation of tickets had been sold on the black market by Beverly Hills-based ticket agency appropriately called Razor Gator. According to the *Daily Mail* and the *London Evening Standard,* tickets for England–Argentina with a face value of £100 each had been bought on the black market by England fans for £700 apiece. They bore the name of Mohammed Bin Hammam of Qatar whose reputation was already badly tarnished. It was Bin Hammam who was accused by Farah Addo, as reported in an article in the *Daily Mail* on 30 April, of being the man who offered him the $100,000 bribe to vote for Blatter in 1998.

These were shark-infested waters and I was staying on the beach. I only had one choice: I would have to give the tickets away. How ironic, I thought to myself. I had spent two years following ticket touts, watching them exploit innocent fans and now, with the project coming to a close, I found myself with three spare tickets for the hottest game in the tournament so far and I was going to give them away. Big Tommy would have a fit and maybe because of this I was feeling very pleased with myself. I was still worried that someone else may come to collect the tickets. By now it was noon. I had arranged to interview Emmanuel Maradas, the editor of *African Soccer,* in the FIFA hotel at 2 p.m. I went back to the FIFA desk and told them that I would return at that time to check if anybody had come looking for tickets allocated to Dempsey. I returned at 2 p.m. and again at 3.30 p.m. and nobody had come looking. With kick-off scheduled for 8.30 p.m. local time I decided it was time for me to start playing fairy godmother.

You would think it would be easy to give away the best seats for England–Argentina, wouldn't you? Well, it wasn't. Obviously I could not risk giving them to people who would themselves sell them on to the highest bidder. I had to find people who I could trust to take in as my guests. This ruled out the massed ranks of the shaven-headed, beer-bellied, tattooed, no-surrender brigade. I began to wander the streets of Sapporo, looking for likely suspects. After an hour without success I was feeling dispirited and irritated. The day before I was having anxiety attacks in case I could not get a ticket, now I was feeling the same because I could not give them away! I decided to head back to the FIFA hotel, by now hoping that someone had come to make a claim on the extra Dempsey tickets. I was about two blocks away when I literally bumped into another Charlie, a lad from Basingstoke that I had met briefly in the Tokyo Sport Café the week before with his mate Cully. 'John, isn't it?' he said.

'Hey, Charlie. How the hell are you? Are you going to the game?' I asked him.

'No,' he said, 'can't afford a ticket, and wouldn't do it on principle anyway. Don't mind a few quid on top but the touts are looking for ridiculous money. Cully's just paid £300 for one in the England end, and that was cheap. I'm going to try and find a bar with a TV and watch it there.'

I looked him up and down. He was tall and slim, had a decent haircut and was wearing smart jeans and a clean black T-shirt, without a tattoo in sight. 'Charlie,' I said, 'I think your luck's just changed.' I explained what had now turned into a predicament for me and asked him if he would like a ticket. Charlie just stared at me in disbelief. I told him that he would have to come with me to the FIFA hotel for a final check and that if nobody had come calling for the tickets one of them was his. I could sense the nervous tension in him as I approached the FIFA desk for the final time. By now the receptionists all knew me and anticipated my question. With a little bow one said, 'No one come for tickets for Dempsey.' I thought Charlie was going to explode. We walked out of the hotel and he was in a state of shock. 'I don't believe this,' he said. 'I need a beer. Come on.'

We found a small café and ordered a couple of bottles of ice-cold Carlsberg. As we gulped down the cool amber liquid, Charlie told me an almost unbelievable story of his own. The previous day he had taken a train to the nearby Mount Tengu. He had hiked to the top of the mountain where there was a Buddhist idol in the form of an 'imaginative long-nosed goblin'. Charlie told me legend has it that those who rub the idol's nose will have good fortune. 'I rubbed it as hard as I could and wished for a ticket for the England–Argentina game. Blow me, I wander into town and bump into you. If either of us had been 30 seconds earlier or later, we would have missed each other on that corner. It's amazing!' I think Charlie's since converted to Buddhism.

By now it was getting on for six o'clock. I told Charlie that his penance for getting the free ticket was that he had to help me find two more worthy recipients. 'That will be easy,' he said, but an hour and a half later, after we had circumnavigated the Sopporo Dome a couple of times without finding a pair of suitable suspects, he had changed his mind. There were lots of touts buying tickets and lots of Ingerland and Japanese fans looking for them, but none looked likely candidates for the Tribune d'Honneur. I was beginning to lose heart when I spotted a rather anxious-looking married couple standing among the crowd outside the England end. He was dressed in a clean, short-sleeved England top and she was dressed casually smart in pink T-shirt and cream slacks. I approached them and said: 'Excuse me, do you have tickets?'

The man eyed me suspiciously. I did not blame him. Many of the touts were Scousers like me and likely as not he was thinking that he was about to get stitched up. 'What's it to you?' he asked guardedly.

'No, listen to him,' interrupted Charlie, 'this could be the luckiest day of your lives.'

Still sounding suspicious the man told me that he had a ticket that he had got through the England Members Club, but that his wife had not. They were going on holiday after the game and they could not afford the touts' prices. As things stood, Gina, his wife, was going to have to wait outside the ground while he, Andrew, went to the game.

'OK,' I told him. 'I know you're going to find this hard to believe, but I want you to sell your own ticket for face value and I will take you in as my guests on these two FIFA VIP tickets.'

With that I produced the two tickets from my waistcoat pocket. I could read Andrew's thoughts. He obviously remembered *Jack and the Beanstalk* and was thinking that he had one definite, legitimate ticket in his hand that he was being asked to sell to be given two tickets that he could not be certain were the real McCoy. There again, he did not want to leave his wife outside the ground. Charlie came to his rescue. 'You've got to trust him. I didn't believe it either but I've been to the FIFA hotel with him and saw the people he got them from. Believe me, this is really happening!' It was at this point that it seemed to dawn on Gina that I was in fact telling the truth and she burst into tears. That set Charlie off snivelling and I wasn't far from crying myself.

Andrew took his decision and said, 'OK, let's go for it.'

All we needed to do now was get rid of his ticket. It was just over an hour before kick-off, but the touts' lowest price was holding firm at £300. It was rumoured that in order to protect future sales, if they had any tickets over just before kick-off the touts were tearing them up rather than sell them for face value or below. Eventually we found a bunch of Geordie lads, five of whom had tickets but one did not and likewise could not afford the touts' prices. 'Would you buy one for face value?' I asked him.

'Why aye, man, you must be joking!' he said. I told him to come with me and introduced him to Andrew who offered him his ticket for £60. The lad, who was about 19 or 20, simply could not believe it. He took out a small roll of £20 notes and peeled them off and passed them to Andrew in exchange for his ticket. The Geordie was so excited that he tried to give him more money. I put my hand across his and stopped him peeling off more notes. 'No. £60 face value and that's all he'll take.' He was grinning from ear to ear, shaking his head and staring reverentially and unbelievingly at his ticket as he disappeared into the crowd with his mates.

As we set off for the turnstiles I could feel the anxiety in the others as we headed for the first security checkpoint. I handed over my ticket for scrutiny by one of the gatekeepers. 'Ohhhh, VIP, VIP,' he muttered, 'you must come with me.' With that we were escorted into the no man's land between the outer walls and the seating areas. It was teeming with English fans buying food and drinks and singing loudly. We were taken to another entrance and once more our tickets were scrutinised. Mobile-phone calls were made and we were given a new escort to take us further into the bowels of the Sapporo Dome. At one point we found ourselves in the kitchens walking past chefs in tall white hats stirring pots of boiling, savoury-smelling liquid. By now I was certain that Andrew, Gina, and even Charlie thought that we were going to be arrested at any moment. I was even beginning to have a few doubts myself when suddenly a door opened and we were ushered outside once more. I could see a look of dread on my new friends' faces, but I smiled reassuringly. 'Look over there,' I said pointing to where a red carpet extended out into an enclosed car park, 'this is the VIP entrance and that's where we go in.'

We were shown inside and had our tickets inspected one last time. 'One moment please,' said one of the attendants walking off with our tickets. Another wave of blind panic for my guests, but I saw what the attendant was doing. He was putting our tickets into the special pouches that allow entry into the FIFA VIP lounge.

'Charlie,' I said, 'just when you think things can't get any better, they just did.'

'What d'you mean?' he replied.

'Just follow me,' I said laughing. Without Charlie Dempsey as a mentor I had not expected to be given access to the VIP lounge. Instead I thought that we would be shown directly to our seats. Now that we had VIP lounge passes I realised that we were for the Full Monty.

I will never forget the look on Charlie's, Andrew's and Gina's faces as we entered the blue-carpeted lounge and took our places among the who's who of the power brokers of international football. By chance the first person I bumped into was the UEFA president, Lennart Johansson. I had been trying to make an appointment to interview him for more than a week about FIFA stuff, but kept missing his secretary, Mea. He strode up to me and shook my hand. 'Wait here,' he told me, 'I'll go and get Mea and we'll make that appointment now.' When he returned he told me that unfortunately Mea had already gone into the stadium and that we would have to make our arrangement at half-time. I then spotted David Davis of the English FA and needed to talk to him about the FA's view of the corruption charges against Blatter who had just swept regally into the lounge. Blatter knows me because of my critical work on FIFA with Alan Tomlinson, which is why he does not care for either of the 'English Professors' as he famously once called us. 'Evening, Mr President,' I said as he marched past. He gave me a sideways glance but kept walking, no doubt making a note to himself to have the head of the person who had let me in. I turned and saw that my guests were virtually paralysed with shock and had not moved since we entered the room. I laughed and went up to them. 'Listen,' I said, 'this is never going to happen to you ever again in your lives, so lighten up, relax and enjoy yourselves. What do you want, wine – white, red – or beer?' I left them with their drinks, told them to help themselves to food and went off once more to work the room.

As we took our halfway-line seats just before kick-off in the Tribune d'Honneur, all Charlie could say was: 'I can't wait to tell Cully, I can't wait to tell him, he's not going to believe it!' Then he spotted Cully's huge Basingstoke St George Cross in the right-hand corner of the England end. 'There he is, there he is, look – in the QPR shirt!' Sure enough, through a borrowed pair of binoculars we could make out Charlie's mate in the crowd. I was having such a fantastic day that I managed to convince myself that England were sure to spoil it by losing to Argentina. Famously, of course, they did not. Owen fell, Beckham stepped up and nightmare memories of St-Étienne 1998 ended as his penalty went straight past the keeper and struck the back of the Argentine net like a thunderbolt. Led by the colossal Rio Ferdinand, the English defence played faultlessly and when the final whistle went, Charlie, Andrew, Gina and I danced and hugged along with Adam Crozier, David Davis and what seemed to be the whole of the stadium. The only way to finish such a perfect day is to take the FIFA VIP coach back to town and celebrate until dawn, which is precisely what we did, my guests not allowing me to pay for a thing.

In my short time in Japan I had met so many colourful characters and had gathered so many improbable tales of derring-do that I felt that I had been away for months. I was sure I had more than enough material to finish this book and despite having a wonderful trip was ready to come home. I was scheduled to fly back from Tokyo on the Monday following the England game and I flew back from Sapporo on Sunday determined to have a quiet final evening. It was not to be. Sat directly behind me on the Sapporo–Tokyo flight was Huw, a man that I had met very briefly in a bar called the Havana Café in Roppongi. He was an Englishman who lived in Roppongi and was just having a few beers on the way home from work. We had chatted for no more than five minutes, during which time he had told me that he had bought a ticket for the England–Argentina match from a tout for £450. Naturally I was interested in this story and I asked him if I could see his ticket, which he kindly produced. It had 'FIFA Guest' printed on it. I thanked him, made a note in my note pad and thought not much more of it until Huw recognised me and said 'hello' on the plane. When we landed at Heneda Airport, we agreed to travel together into the city on the Tokyo monorail. I had one bit of unfinished business to take care of. I still had a ticket for England versus Nigeria left over from those that I had brought over for Big Tommy. Nobody had told me what to do with it so I decided to sell it to somebody at face value. It gave me a certain perverse pleasure to be selling a tout's ticket at face value. Huw seemed like a nice enough guy so I asked him if he wanted to buy it. He said he might, but needed to check out a few work things before he committed himself. We agreed to meet for a few beers and watch the Japan versus Russia game in a sports bar called Bar Tokyo six floors above Roppongi crossing.

When I arrived Bar Tokyo was a heaving mass of sweltering, mainly Japanese bodies who had already packed the place out three hours before the scheduled kick-off. 'House Full' read a sign above the door. I headed back downstairs and waited outside for a while to see if Huw would show. I had just about given up and was walking away when I heard 'John!' shouted above the din of the traffic. It was Huw still dressed in his T-shirt and shorts. He had a woman with him, a pretty Australian girl called Celia. I assumed that Celia was Huw's girlfriend, but later over drinks and tapas, once more in the Havana Café, he explained that she was just a friend, a hostess who was having a night off. This was a side of Roppongi that I had watched from a distance but had no real sense of. Some of the prettiest women I had seen for a long time were in Roppongi. Certainly there were many beautiful Japanese girls, but it was the significant number of drop-dead-gorgeous Westerners that caught my attention. Huw explained that virtually all of them worked full or part time as hostesses in one or more of Roppongi's many nightclubs.

I felt a bit embarrassed with Celia sitting there as Huw explained the subtle distinctions between hostesses, escort girls, call girls and in-your-face whores. Most hostesses like Celia do exactly what it says on the tin: they are hostesses. Their job is to entertain the mainly Japanese businessmen who frequent the district's VIP clubs, encouraging them to buy wildly expensive food and drink for which they are paid a percentage. Celia admitted that some hostesses will sleep with their clients, but not many, which was perhaps surprising given the scale of reward that she claimed was on offer: anything from thousands of dollars to an apartment in the South of France. Huw seemed to know everybody in and everything about Roppongi. This was the neighbourhood from where the English hostess Lucy Blackman had been abducted in July 2000; she was found murdered and mutilated in a cave south west of Tokyo the following year. I learned later that Huw was the 'anonymous' British businessman who had freely given Lucy's parents the use of his Roppongi office as they relentlessly pursued their investigations into their daughter's disappearance. 'Yeah, everybody knows Huw around here,' Celia told me. 'They call him Sir Huw of Roppongi.'

It was no surprise later when Huw took out his mobile and phoned Rick – the owner of Bar Tokyo – and told him to create a space for us as we were coming over. By the time we got there Sir Huw had gathered an entourage of about eight people. Even though the place was more jammed than ever, with three or four times as many people packed in as it could safely hold, with Rick leading the way we fought our way to the bar where we formed a bridgehead for the duration of Japan's game with Russia. I may have been hotter, but I cannot remember when. Cheekily, Celia kept lifting bags of ice from behind the bar and passing them around for us to cool ourselves. At the same time Sir Huw was buying beer and passing it around to anybody that wanted it. When Japan scored the place went absolutely wild and when the referee blew the final whistle to record Japan's first ever World Cup victory all hell broke loose. As the bar staff started to throw gallons of water over the steaming crowd Huw suggest that he and I go out into the street to watch the locals celebrating their country's famous win.

It was madness. Thousands of Japanese, English, Swedes, Belgians, Australians and who knows who else had spilled out of the bars and clubs to share in a spontaneous expression of raw unconfined joy on a scale hitherto unknown in Japanese society. The massed ranks of the police looked bewildered as this friendly riot unfolded. The high point for me came when Japanese youth culture decided to take on the police in a bizarre game of British Bulldog. One thing you never do in Japan is cross the road until the little green man says you can. On this night hundreds of Japanese youths waited at the side of Roppongi's main drag waiting for the little red man to come up on the light that regulated the six-lane crossing. As soon as it did they would swarm across, dodging past the police who waited in the middle clumsily failing to catch any of them. Once on the other side these dangerous subversives turned round, waited for the little red man and charged again. Huw laughed and tugged my shirt. 'Come on,' he said, 'I'll give you a glimpse of the other side of Roppongi.'

We crossed the road – after waiting for the little green man of course – and walked towards Tokyo tower before Huw stopped outside a place called Bar 911. Like many of these joints Bar 911 had a couple of black American bouncers standing at the doorway. Huw took out his wallet and flashed a silver VIP member's card and we were ushered into another heaving celebration. I followed Huw as we marched toward the back of the club and through into the quieter VIP lounge where Huw was greeted by Irena, the Club's Russian materfamilias. He ordered a couple of champagne cocktails and asked if Valentina was around. When Irena left to find out, Huw explained that Valentina was another Russian and a hostess with whom he used to have a relationship. 'Problem is they're all mercenary bitches,' he told me. 'In the end they're only with you when you're spending money.' And Huw was spending money – lots of it. I was getting a bit embarrassed. I always like to stand my corner and wanted to make at least a gesture towards a round. 'Forget it,' Huw told me. 'My living expenses for one week alone in Roppongi can be as much as $35,000.' My jaw slackened, but before I could speak Valentina and her friend called Julia came and joined us. 'Julia's an ex-whore from Russia,' he whispered to me. 'She's now a madam, but she's hard as nails, so be careful of her.' Beautiful though she was, I had no intention of 'being' anything with her.

As if to prove a point about his profligacy Huw proceeded to order two bottles of Dom Pérignon Moet champagne at $500 a pop.

How to conclude this book was something that had been exercising my mind for a few weeks. As I sat there sipping the most expensive drink that I had ever tasted in the company of outrageous Sir Huw and a pair of beautiful Russian hookers, I thought to myself, what an entirely appropriate way to end *Scum Airways.* I had been halfway around the world following football and Big Tommy and his chums. En route I had met a cast of characters that would provide material for a dozen books. Some were bad, some were good, some were very, very ugly and some were all of these things. Above all else, I had learned that life was a matter of definition and that grafters come in all shapes and sizes. Some are not much more than small-time market traders and petty thieves eking out a living against considerable odds, others are more serious career villains who use football as a vehicle and network for their violence and villainy; then there are those like Big Tommy himself, who start out on the dark side of the tracks and who, while still dabbling in the affairs of Lads, work hard to change their label from grafter to businessman. Then there are the Sir Huws of this world who make and lose millions playing with other people's money and lives on the global stock market. If they are successful, if it pleases Her Majesty, they may indeed be knighted. Fail and, like Nick Leeson, they may end up on Her Majesty's pleasure. However, the master grafters of my story must surely be Sepp Blatter and his cronies: the people who have found in football a staircase to power without accountability and with it the licence to exploit football for their own vainglorious interests while plundering millions from the people's game. As one book finishes another begins: *Badfellas*, available soon in all good bookshops.

# Postscript

## Berlin, April 2003

The lads, aged between 25 and 50, tumbled out of their hotel at around midnight and headed past the remnants of the old wall into the eastern heart of the city. This was their first night out in Germany's reinstated capital and it would be after sun-up, with the dawn chorus for company, before they would trudge in ones and twos beerily and wearily home. Between times there were gallons of strong German lager and wheat beer to be drunk, jokes to be told, songs to be sung, drinking games to play, and fools to be made. One idiot, Jake, had picked up his son's passport by mistake and it was only through Kissenger-like negotiation skills that he had been able to get into the country on a temporary passport. As a forfeit he was required to wear all night the full Vegas Elvis regalia that one of the lads had brought with him, complete with white sequinned suit, shades, mask and wig.

Led by Elvis, they made their way to Potsdamer Platz, a square ringed with cafes, bars and clubs, many of which stayed open all night. Outside, in ones and twos, flaxen-haired working girls plied their trade. 'Hey big boy, blow job and massage only fifty Euros. Only one hundred and fifty Euros for good time with two of us!' The lads shuffled past cracking lurid jokes and cackling nervously. A bit early in the tour to take the plunge, but by tomorrow German lager and Dutch courage would have more than one digging deep into his pockets. Once inside the nearest Bierkeller, talk turned towards tomorrow's game in Potsdam about 20 miles away. It was their team's first game in Europe and they looked forward to the encounter with excitement and apprehension in equal measure. Would they win, could they get an invaluable away goal?

Same old, same old? Yes and no. Yes, it was another case of middle-aged men behaving badly in another European city. Wine, women and song, away from home, family and work, out of structure, and determined to have a good time. No, it wasn't one of big Tommy's tours and these weren't Lads from Leeds or Manchester. They were in fact the staff and graduate football team from the University of Brighton in Berlin to play a friendly with their counterparts from the University of Potsdam. We (yes, I still turn out now and again!) had just won the Sussex Junior County Cup and were on tour by way of celebration. We were set to return the compliment and host a German team later in the year. For fun we fantasised that we were now representing Sussex in the European Junior Cup and that this was out first away leg.

What set this visit apart from most of the trips recounted in the preceding chapters in this book was the total lack of any sense of menace. Admittedly, whether it was Manchester United in Amsterdam, or Leeds and England in Munich, there was always an element of carnival in the Lads' behaviour, but there was always also a strong undercurrent of menace. The Lads occupied foreign space whereas in Berlin we shared it with our German hosts, playing together, partying together and crawling home together. Bleary-eyed the following day we exchanged stories about the night's adventures, but none of them included punch-ups and baton charges.

If the Laddish element could be stripped away from English football's travelling support, leaving only the passion for the game and the accompanying cosmopolitan carnival, what a difference it would make, particularly at an international level. We had a glimpse of what this might be like during Japan 2002, but those who saw the English fans' full participation in this transnational football love-in as portend to a bright new-England future had the rudest of awakenings when England played Turkey in Sunderland in April 2003. The night of the match there were more than 100 arrests as highly organised rival firms fought with each other and hundreds of police in the city centre and outside the Stadium of Light. Inside, the Turkish national anthem was drowned by wolf-whistles and boos while as an accompaniment to the game we had significant sections of the crowd chanting 'I'd rather be a Paki than a Turk' and 'die Turkey die', the odd 'sieg heil' thrown in for good measure.

For those of us who had been on the inside this came as no surprise. Turkey is the gateway to the East and the Arab world. Ever since the Ottoman Empire Western European folklore has demonised the Turk and Turkish migrant workers have been persecuted across the continent. Set against the backdrop of the war against terrorism – for this read Arab terrorism – and Gulf War II, England versus Turkey was always going to be a tense fixture. Add to this the murder in Istanbul of the two Leeds United supporters, Kevin Speight and Christopher Loftus, featured in Chapter 3, then the game was sure to be a prime target for Ingerland's foulest.

Worried by the prospect of being punished by UEFA and having to play their next home game behind closed doors, the English FA 'volunteered' not to take up their official allocation of tickets for the away fixture in Istanbul. In return UEFA stung the FA with a big fine. This will not necessarily prevent some of the Lads travelling. Most of them do not source their tickets through the FA anyway and there are always tickets available on the black market in Turkey. Whether they will travel or not is a different question. Close up they are a scary, ugly bunch and mob-handed they are violent and dangerous. But there are limits to their appetite for risk taking. Through Leeds United's fatal Galatasaray expedition and Manchester United's 'Welcome to Hell' experience, the word is out that Turkey takes no prisoners. It's one thing to face a fine, a couple of nights in a Dutch or Belgian police cell and deportation, it's quite something else to be chased through the streets by an angry mob brandishing kebab knives! Most, I believe, would not have the bottle. This, sadly, will not be the case should England qualify for Euro 2004 in Portugal.

How then do you take the Scum out of Scum Airways and leave behind the football carnival? Part of the answer is to reduce their critical mass. As revealed in Chapter 9 some of the hard core made it to Japan but not in sufficient numbers to spoil the party. Try as they might, the relative few Category C types who got through the net were unable to spark and ignite the appetite for riot among the throngs of decent England fans who had made the trip. On the contrary, when they tried to start something with the Irish, these thugs were booed and jeered by other England fans.

There were many reasons why many of the hard core Lads didn't make it to Japan, including cost, distance and the hardening of legal restrictions on travel. There are those who like to characterise England's troublemakers as angels with dirty faces. Not me. A hard core of them are devils without make-up and they need to be taken out of circulation. Despite my own reservations about the civil liberties implications of the enhanced football disorder legislation (discussed in Chapter 4), the increase in the numbers of banning orders, the increase in the severity of fines, and the increase in the number and duration of prison sentences meted out in the courts, are undoubtedly having an impact on the number of people involved in hard-core hooliganism.

But the use of the iron heel alone will not be enough. There is a parallel need to educate and empower the large numbers of fans who are forced to share the same physical and cultural space as the hard-core hooligan gangs by the football establishment, aided and abetted by the police and the press. What became obvious to me as I researched this book is that most of the people who travelled with the independents did so to avoid official travel schemes of any kind. They did this not because they were hooligans, but because official travel clubs were too expensive; their trips too short; they were over-organised and regimented; the fans had political bones to pick with those who ran their clubs/national team; or combinations thereof. The alienation of these large numbers of fans created a thriving market that Big Tommy and his likes have been only too pleased to exploit.

Tommy may have started out with the firms and the Lads as his core customers, but it soon became obvious to him that his future rested not crookedly with the hoods but legitimately with the nonconformist football anoraks. This trend should be encouraged. With nobody to plan their trips for them the hooligans' numbers will be further eroded. In this regard the Big Tommys of the football world could be key mediators between the football authorities and the independent travelling support. To do this they need to be brought on-side, given an integrated and open role in the planning and execution of club and country trips abroad. Not as in-and-out military operations, but as popular cultural visits and festivals with a football focus. Of course, to do this the clubs and the FA will have to stop viewing their non-aligned travelling support as the enemy and start to treat them with a little more respect. They will also have to give up some of their power and privileges and even some of their tickets. This is something that the suits will be very reluctant to do as rarely do the elite give up power without a struggle.

Then there's the media. No wonder many football fans, good and bad, hate the sports media. As the big tournament approaches, they spend weeks selling papers and screening documentaries and news items with jingoistic headlines and bylines, building up nationalistic fervour. Always siding with the authorities, when it kicks off, they sell even more papers and programmes condemning the behaviour of the fans, which they partly incited. With nothing other than football and festival to train their cameras on, in Japan the media circus was unable to perform its traditional 'shock, horror' hooligan amplification role. Instead they joined the party and added to the feel-good factor. We can learn from this.

The media need to be much more discriminating in the way that they cover the fans that watch the sports that sell their newspapers. They should stop making celebrities of the hooligan fringe and give up their practice of lurking in the shadows, ready for a charge of the 'lights, camera, action!' brigade whenever they spot a gathering of likely lads at a pavement cafe. This as much as anything else can act as a catalyst for trouble. And when they witness the many innocent supporters who get unjustly swept and beaten up as a result of indiscriminate policing, the media should report this with the same power and venom that they usually reserve for the thug minority.

Post-Thatcherism may have given way to Blair's new Labour, but 'get rich quick' remains as a dominant business ethic. In such circumstances it is hard to envisage football's black economy withering away. Football clubs could help to remove the popular legitimacy of this through abandoning their monopolistic market position and introducing more reasonable pricing structures for their replica kits and related merchandise. Likewise, while the touts are equally unlikely to disappear, the introduction of more community sensitive distribution and pricing systems for tickets would reduce the scalpers' impact. To its credit the FA has endeavoured to get its act together on ticketing with an overhaul of the England members scheme. On the other hand, if the World Cups in France and Japan are anything to go by, FIFA's leaky system of ticket distribution could not have been more tout-friendly had it been designed by the late Stan Flashman himself. Football's world governing body needs to introduce a ticketing policy that recognises that the global game belongs to the peoples of the world and not to the FIFA fiefdom and their media and marketing allies. The policy for filling up World Cup stadia should not be driven by corporate favours and camera angles, but by the legitimate needs and deserts of loyal fans.

Taking the Scum out of Scum Airways will also need the independent operators to turn their backs on the Lads. Big Tommy's well on his way to doing this anyway. In a roundabout way the publication of the first edition of this book may have made an unintended contribution to his conversion from small-time Grafter to legitimate businessman. When it was first published in October 2002 all hell broke loose in Manchester's football-related underworld. I had anticipated that I would not be very popular among the Lads once the book hit the high street, but thought that their venom might be mostly directed towards me. I was naively mistaken. For those in the know, the aliases that are used in the book are easy to see through and the cognoscenti soon identified all of the key characters. It was, of course, Big Tommy who became the focus their wrath. He had let me into their world and I had exposed it for what it was. The black market around football is a competitive one and the book was seized upon as ammunition in a turf war among rival groups of Grafters.

Not long after the book came out I had a series of calls from an extremely angry and agitated Big Tommy who felt betrayed by what I had written. Firstly, while he had known from day one that I was writing a book, he did not expect to see it in Waterstone's window in Manchester's Oxford Street. He told me that he thought that it was going to be an academic project that would end up gathering dust on some obscure university library shelf. I must confess, on reflection, I did little to discourage this view as I knew that if he thought I was writing for a popular market he would be far less willing to let me inside. He did not challenge the truth of the narrative. On the contrary, he was shocked at how much I had managed to pick up during my days in the field. I had neglected to tell him that, with more than 20 years of participatory social-anthropological work under my belt, in the field I was like a highly tuned radio telescope. During my time in the field I had got to like the Big

Man and I felt bad about his feeling of betrayal. This goes with the turf, however. If the telling of the tale can be deemed to be in the public interest, as I believe this story is, then sometimes you have to hurt people's feelings to get to the truth.

Hurting people's feelings is one thing, but causing their lives and livelihoods to be threatened is a different matter altogether. Tommy told me that as a consequence of the book some serious villains were on his case. They believed, wrongly as it happens, that he had given me detailed advice and inside information about the activities of his rivals and sent me out to places like Spain and Thailand enabling me to expose their violent behaviour and illegal trafficking. At one stage he had thought that there might be a bullet with his name on it and that the least he could expect was to have his legs broken. He went on to say that his business was in ruins and that he would never be able to work with the Lads again. While in a perverse way it was a powerful testimony of the book's impact, I still felt mortified. All I could do was to make it clear in radio interviews and newspaper articles about the book that Big Tommy had not been a collaborator and that I had duped him into letting me into the Manchester Grafters' world – which I guess is the truth.

In truth, when I reflect back on this book, I'm not sure what all of the fuss is about. Part travelogue, part autobiography, part sitcom, it does little more than weave together a story about colourful characters ducking and diving to eke out a living around football. For the most part I don't condemn this, neither do I dig too deep. I just tell it the way it appeared to me. There is nothing in these pages that anybody should get too upset about, let alone arrested or hurt for. My own assessment is born out by a couple of book reviews which, while broadly applauding the book, chided me for not following up some of the more pernicious aspects of the Grafters' game and sitting on the fence when it came to any moral judgements.

True to form, Big Tommy bounced back. No longer able to operate easily on the Grafters' turf in Manchester, he moved premises and turned increasingly towards the more legitimate end of the independent travel business and is all the better for it.

I hope that by the time this second edition is published some of the Lads will be upset not because their caricatures are in the book but because they are absent. Another unanticipated consequence of the book's publication is the number of enquiries that I have had from friends and acquaintances about getting tickets for matches! 'I can't,' I tell them, 'but I know a man who can.' By the way, for those interested, the University of Brighton's staff and alumni team beat the University of Potsdam 3–2. With three precious away goals surely the tie's in the bag.

*John Sugden*
*Eastbourne*
*May 2003*

# BHOYS, BEARS AND BIGOTRY
## *Rangers, Celtic and the Old Firm in the New Age of Globalised Sport*

### Bill Murray

ISBN 1 84018 810 3
£7.99 (pb)
September 2003
198 x 129mm
240pp
Mainstream Sport

Rangers entered the new world of sport and big business in April 1986 when they signed Graeme Souness and shortly afterwards he was joined by new owner, millionaire businessman David Murray. After years of squabbling at Celtic, Rangers' great Glasgow rivals, Celtic's saviour arrived in the form of expatriate millionaire Fergus McCann.

Celtic's origins as an Irish Catholic club set up the rivalry with Rangers that became known as the Old Firm, once said to be 'a business based on bigotry'.

But under McCann and Murray, the Old Firm rivalry took on a different image as the new owners sought to expunge the worst elements of sectarianism. In the new world of globalised sport, bigotry was a barrier to the riches awaiting the top clubs in Europe. Celtic with their 'Bhoys Against Bigotry' and Rangers with their 'Pride and Prejudice' tried to present a new image of the Old Firm that emphasised the best aspects of their long history. Getting rid of this old image, however, has often seemed as difficult as winning the big prizes in Europe.

# BADFELLAS
## *FIFA Family at War*
### John Sugden and Alan Tomlinson

ISBN 1 84018 684 4
£7.99 (pb)
Now available
198 x 129mm
288pp
Mainstream Sport

World football's governing body FIFA has claimed credit for the success of the football World Cup and the expansion of the world game generally, but behind the scenes the administration of the world game is in a shambles. *Badfellas* catalogues FIFA's expanding fortunes, recurrent crises and internal rivalries and traces the growth of the World Cup from its politically driven origins in Uruguay in 1930 to one of the world's most lucrative media spectacles. It shows how Dr João Havelange and Sepp Blatter have carved up the riches of the football bonanza over the last 25 years and details why the good guys in football's corridors of power find it so hard to mount any successful challenge to the badfellas and their legacy.

# HOOLIGAN

### Eddy Brimson

ISBN 1 84018 083 8
£7.99 (pb)
Now available
198 x 129mm
196pp
Mainstream Sport

The highly acclaimed co-author of *Everywhere We Go* makes his fiction debut with this hard-hitting, no-holds-barred account of football violence. Hooligan shoots down the myths behind those involved and exposed the lengths they will go to to achieve their ambitions . . .

Steven Morris and his firm of football thugs are the most feared in the country. For them the days of fighting on the terrace are long gone, a mug's game for the juniors and wannabes, a place wghere innocent people can get hurt and that's not what Mozzer's firm are about. They only want to take on those who wish to take their 'title' away, and somehow Mozzer always knows who, where and when to hit hard.

Up until now, his network of scouts and spotters has always kept the firm one step ahead of the opposition, but there is someone trying to set him up for a bloody ending, and are the police finally closing in?

# GOING ORIENTAL
*Football after World Cup 2002*

Edited by Mark Perryman

ISBN 1 84018 677 1
£7.99 (pb)
Now available
198 x 129mm
208pp
Mainstream Sport

World Cup 2002: there has never been a tournament like it. With an upset arising almost every day, *Going Oriental* explores the event's substantial impact on the world. Has the football world order been changed for good? How will the power struggle in FIFA unfold? And what does the way the English follow their team say about the state of the nation? All of this and more is extensively analysed in a gripping new collection of essays.

Contributors include Simon Kuper, Pete Davis, Jim White, John Williams, Philip Cornwall and Japanese writer Hiroyuki Morita.

# HOMELAND
## *Into a World of Hate*
### Nick Ryan

ISBN 1 84018 465 5
£15.99 (hb)
Now available
234 x 156mm
320pp
Social History

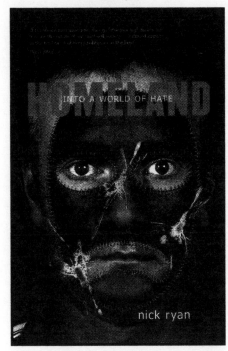

You're alone. Trapped in a pub with soccer hooligans, as their gang leader is sentenced for murder. Or unmasked in a hotel in North Carolina, by henchmen of the world's most infamous neo-nazi. You're invited to a gathering of Holocaust deniers in Beirut. You meet a US Presidential candidate, once revered by the white supremacists you've befriended. You encounter the political zealots rising within the heart of Europe.

These are just some of the events that award-winning writer Nick Ryan recounts in his ground-breaking narrative, Homeland, a six-year journey into the terrifying heart of white nationalism, already being hailed as a classic.

**Fascinating material . . . great stuff**
*Hari Kunzru, bestselling author, The Impressionist*

**As relevent to our time as Orwell's *Homage to Catalonia***
*Ethan Casey, editor-in-chief, BlueEar.com*

# HOOLIFAN
## *30 Years of Hurt*
### Martin King and Martin Knight

ISBN 1 84018 174 5
£7.99 (pb)
Now available
198 x 129mm
224pp
Mainstream Sport

Martin King has long been a key player in the Chelsea Headhunters – the most feared football gang of the 1980s and 1990s. At times funny, sad and shocking, Hoolifan describes the leading characters of the hooligan phenomenon, not just from Chelsea but from across the country. King grabs the reader by the collar and drags us through the confrontations that the Chelsea boys craved. Famous fights, frightenening chases, meticulously planned ambushes and dark acts of revenge are all recorded here in vivid detail, as is the cameraderie amongst the gang members. This is not just another book on football violence; unlike previous authors on the subject, King makes no attempt to distance himself from the violence and leaves the reader to draw his own conclusions, but his observations are likely to do more to place football hooliganism in its true social context than any previous work.

# WHO WANTS IT?

### Colin Ward and 'Chubby' Chris Henderson

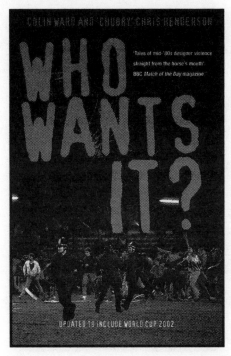

ISBN 1 84018 325 X
£9.99 (pb)
Now available
234 x 156mm
208pp
Mainstream Sport

Chris Henderson formed the Chelsea Headhunters as well as the band Combat 84, the antithesis of middle-class England with it's raw, uncut lyrics of punk and the thoughts of George Orwell. Chelsea fans later earned the reputation as the most dangerous in Britain.

After Stephen "Hickey" Hickmott's jailing, Henderson organised a gang of Chelsea fans who travelled to matches by luxury coach and were arrested. Their subsequent trial was meant to be the crowning glory of Thatcher's squashing of football hooligans. But it was the dramatic collapse of this trial which signed the death warrant for the undercover police operations and mass indiscriminate arrests and jailings.

Told in Henderson's exact words, this is the dramatic story of that era of music and football, when how you looked counted as much as how you performed.

# HOOLIGAN WARS
## *Causes and Effects of Football Violence*
### Edited by Mark Perryman

ISBN 1 84018 670 4
£7.99 (pb)
Now available
198 x 129mm
256pp
Mainstream Sport

What lies behind the scourge of football violence? *Hooligan Wars* looks behind the easy answers and all those quick-fix solutions and investigates the real causes and effects, analysing concepts of race and fan culture throughout Europe and the influence of media coverage of violence. Asking awkward questions and drawing on a diverse list of esteemed contributors, this book is a timely analysis of the ugly underbelly of the 'beautiful game'.

Contributors include Vivek Chaudhary, Nick Lowles, Simon Inglis, Patrick Barclay, Alan Tomlinson and David Shayler.

Mark Perryman, a writer and journalist, edited *The Ingerland Factor: Home Truths from Football* and has been described as 'an intelligence rare in football writing' by *Total Football.*